A Pilgrim's Companion

A Pilgrim's Companion

Readings from Buddhist Texts
to Enhance a Pilgrimage
to the Sacred Sites

Edited by
Ken and Visakha Kawasaki

Russa Road Young Buddhist Student Literacy Mission
in Collaboration with
MAHA BODHI BOOK AGENCY
4-A, Bankim Chatterjee Street, College Square
Kolkata-700 073, India

A Pilgrim's Companion:

Readings from Buddhist Texts to Enhance a Pilgrimage to the Sacred Sites, edited by Ken and Visakha Kawasaki

Second Edition - 2020

Published By
Russa Road Young Buddhist Student Literacy Mission
in Collaboration with
MAHA BODHI BOOK AGENCY
4A, Bankim Chatterjee Street, College Square
Kolkata 700 073, India
Phone : +91 9831077368, 9831529452
Email : mahabodhibookagency@hotmail.com

ISBN : 978-93-84721-59-6 Price -Rs. 400/-

Table of Contents

Part 1, The Sacred Sites

Part 2, Daily Meditation

Foreward

Literature to assist and enrich pilgrimage is as old as the endeavor of pilgrimage itself. The encouragement to visit places connected with the Buddha's life goes back to the Buddha himself, and the first person we know to have gone to the sacred places was King Ashoka, who went to BuddhaGaya in 256 BCE and to Lumbini a few years later. According to the *Asokavadana*, this pious king was guided to and around the sacred places by his preceptor Upagupta, and, if this story is true, he would not have needed a guide book. However, we know that later pilgrims to the holy places did take such books with them and, sometimes, other literature, too.

The recently rediscovered *The Flower Ornament Guide to the Diamond Throne* (*Vajrasanavidesa Amalakapuspanama*) by Bcom-ldan Rigs-pa'i-ral-gri (1250-1311) is a practical and detailed guide book to BuddhaGaya. It tells the reader what to see and the significance of each place. In 1202, the Japanese monk Myoe Shonin (1173-1232) decided to make a pilgrimage to India, and, as part of his preparations for this heroic undertaking, he actually tried to compile a route map by calculating the distances involved and the time it would take if he set out from Châng-an, the Chinese capital. His calculations are to be found in the *Dainihon shiryo*. He wrote; "I am unable to contain my affection and longing for India, the land where the Buddha was born, so I have drawn up plans for the journey thither. Oh, how I wish I were there! If I walked seven long ri a day, I could reach India in 1130 days, arriving on the twentieth day of the second month of the fourth year of my travels. If I walked five ri a day, I could at long last arrive on the tenth day of the sixth month of the fifth year, a total of 1600 days." Myoe was not making a complete stab in the dark; he had carefully studied Faxian's and Xuanzang's accounts of their pilgrimages to India and had, at least, some idea of what was involved. Unfortunately, he was never able to embark on his pilgrimage, but, in trying to draw a map, he was following the example of earlier devout Buddhists. During the Song Dynasty (960-1279), hundreds of monks made the long and perilous journey from China to India, taking route guides with them. The most well-known of these is *The Way to India (Xitian lujing)*, which gives the distance and direction of all the towns and landmarks from Wu Tai Shan in China to Nalanda in India. Sources tell us that, in 966, the Chinese monk, Xingqin, and his companions were guided during their pilgrimage to India by a map. Unfortunately, this map has not survived to the present.

Ken and Visakha Kawasaki's *A Pilgrim's Companion* is only the most recent of an ancient literary genus meant for Buddhist pilgrims. It is not a guide book, there are already several of these. Rather, it resembles the *muttipotthaka* that Sri Lankan pilgrims used to carry in ancient times. These little books listed the virtues of the Buddha so that pilgrims could read and contemplate them while on the road or at the sacred places. A pilgrimage should be more than just sightseeing, photo ops, and buying souvenirs for friends back home. It should also be seen as a unique opportunity to contemplate Buddha's Dhamma in the actual places where the Buddha delivered it. The Kawasakis' useful and inspiring book has been written with this understanding in mind.

Venerable S. Dhammika

Introduction

As we were planning our pilgrimage in 2001, we relied on Venerable S. Dhammika's excellent *Middle Land, Middle Way* to learn about the sites we would be visiting, but we thought, "Wouldn't it be good to read some suttas the Buddha taught in the places we visit?" We soon realized that no one had compiled such a collection, and finding suitable readings for each site was not easy. We satisfied ourselves with several obvious selections and made photocopies from various anthologies to carry with us. On that pilgrimage, we had the great privilege of traveling with Venerable Pannasila from Maharashtra and Venerable Nandobatha from Burma, so, at some sites, they recited the suttas in Pali, and we read the English aloud, which greatly enhanced our pilgrimage. We will never forget the joy of sitting in front of the Dhammarajika Stupa in Sarnath reading "Setting in Motion the Wheel of the Dhamma." By the end of the pilgrimage, however, our loose pages were dog-eared and disorganized.

We repeated the exercise for our pilgrimage in 2007, including more suttas, and our friends appreciated them. Again, however, the stapled pages were once more filed and forgotten. A few years later, we started developing a Buddhist ESL textbook, Merit, based on a pilgrimage to the sacred sites, and, in one of the early lessons, the pilgrims received a book of readings titled *A Pilgrim's Companion*, but it was still not much more than an idea and a cover.

For our pilgrimage in 2012, we collected more readings, edited them, arranged them according to the places we would visit, and printed a copy for each pilgrim in our small group. This became the prototype of *A Pilgrim's Companio*n, which, to our knowledge, is unique, with readings arranged for a pilgrimage. Our group meditated together at each site, including the Mahabodhi Vihara, Veluvana, Jivaka's Mango Grove, the ruins of Nalanda University, Jetavana, and the Mahaparinibbana Stupa.

For the present volume, we have added many more readings, deleted a few, and refined the writing. Some are teachings which the

Buddha gave at the site, while others tell stories related to that place. The one exception is Lauriya Nandangar, where there is an Ashokan pillar but no incidents whatsoever connected to the life of the Buddha. For that site, we chose a Jataka which occurs in an unidentified forest. For the city of Baranasi, we have included a Jataka which begins, as many do, "Long, long ago, when Brahmadatta, was reigning in Baranasi ..." and relates a tale about the king of a previous eon.

The daily meditations are based on a format we have used since the founding of "Students of the Lotus" in Japan in 1983. Each session begins with taking refuge and the five precepts and reciting homage to the Triple Gem. In a group sitting, a leader might read the longer reading aloud, and the group recite the reflection. After silent meditation, either sitting or walking, the session closes with the dedication of merit.

The selections in this collection are almost all excerpts, which have been edited for ease of reading. The Buddha's teachings, preserved in the Pali, were originally transmitted orally, and contain a great deal of repetition to serve as an aid to memorization. Also, the Buddha often used a number of terms differing only slightly so that all nuances were included. The style of some translations can be dauntingly dry and ponderous, which is not in keeping with the inspiration and joy of a pilgrimage. We recall a comment we overheard in a traditionally Buddhist country. When a local devotee was asked whether she had enjoyed the Dhamma lesson, she sternly replied, "We just listen to the Dhamma. We don't enjoy it!" We, however, feel that, especially when visiting these sacred places, the Dhamma is to be savored. Pilgrims should not be troubled by technical footnotes and labored expressions.

This selection of suttas, stories, and verses includes some of our personal favorites. We have tried to put all of them into language that is smooth and accessible, without altering the essential meaning of the original Teaching. We have read, compared, and drawn from a number of translations. Almost all of the readings are excerpts–adapted, abridged, condensed, rephrased, and retold. We encourage readers to refer to the texts in the List of Original Sources for complete and scholarly translations.

We hope that our modest efforts will help to gladden the hearts of all pilgrims, both those who are able to walk where the Buddha walked and those who imagine listening to his Teaching in the places where he taught.

Ken and Visakha Kawasaki
Kandy, Sri Lanka, September 2012

Part 1

The Sacred Sites

Four Places

"Ananda, there are four places which, when visited, should arouse emotion in the faithful. What are they? First, where the Tathagata was born; second, where the Tathagata attained supreme enlightenment; third, where the Tathagata set in motion the Wheel of the Dhamma; and fourth, where the Tathagata attained Parinibbana. Faithful monks, nuns, male lay-followers, and female lay-followers will visit those places. Anyone who dies while making a pilgrimage to these sacred places with a devout heart will, at the breaking up of the body after death, be reborn in a heavenly realm."

–Digha Nikaya 16

The Ancient Path

The Buddha said, "Suppose that a man, wandering through a forest, saw an ancient path, traveled upon by people in the past. He followed it and saw an ancient city, a delightful ancient capital that had been inhabited by people in the past, with parks, groves, ponds, and ramparts. If the man were to tell the king, 'Sire, while wandering through the forest I saw an ancient path. I followed it and saw a delightful ancient capital. Renovate that city, Sire!' The king would restore the city, and it would become successful, prosperous, and well-populated.

"So, too, I saw the ancient path, traveled by the Perfectly Enlightened Ones of the past. What is that ancient path? It is the Noble Eightfold Path —Right view, Right intention, Right speech, Right action, Right livelihood, Right effort, Right mindfulness, and Right concentration. I followed that path, and, by doing so, I have directly known aging-and-death, its origin, its cessation, and the way leading to its cessation. I have directly known birth, existence, clinging, craving, feeling, contact, the six sense bases, name-and-form, consciousness, and volitional formations, as well as the origin, the cessation, and the way leading to their cessation of each. Having directly known them, I have explained them to the bhikkhus, the bhikkhunis, the male lay followers, and the female lay followers. This spiritual life has become successful, prosperous, widespread, and well-proclaimed among devas and humans."

—Samyutta Nikaya 12, 65

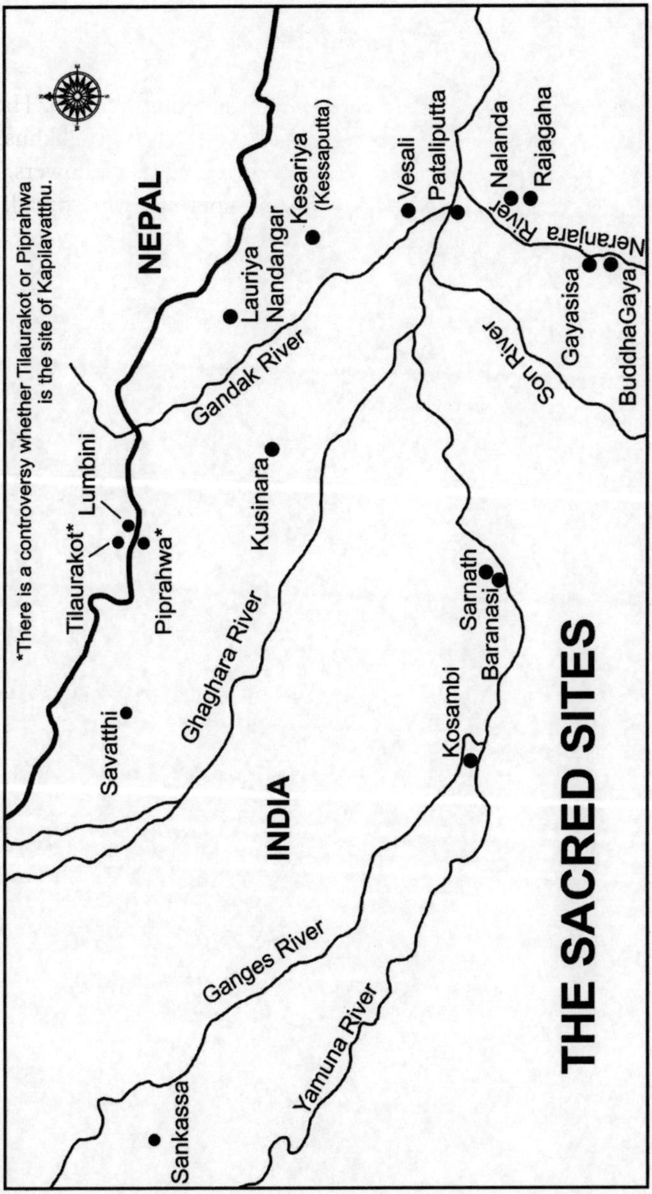
THE SACRED SITES
*There is a controversy whether Tilaurakot or Piprahwa
is the site of Kapilavatthu.
NEPAL
INDIA
Sankassa
Savatthi
Tilaurakot*
Lumbini
Piprahwa*
Kusinara
Lauriya
Nandangar
Kesariya
(Kessaputta)
Vesali
Pataliputta
Nalanda
Rajagaha
Gayasisa
BuddhaGaya
Kosambi
Baranasi
Sarnath
Ganges River
Yamuna River
Ghaghara River
Gandak River
Son River
Neranjara River

Lumbini

Asita Meets the Bodhisatta

One afternoon, the accomplished sage, Asita, used his supernatural powers to go to Tavatimsa. There he found the celestial city beautifully decorated and the thirty-three gods gathered in happy celebration, with banners flying and music playing. Seeing the gods' excitement, Asita respectfully asked why they were so joyful.

"In a village called Lumbini, in the Sakyan kingdom," answered one of the devas, "a Bodhisatta has been born! A being intent on Buddhahood has been born, a being without comparison, a precious pearl of goodness in the human world. That's why we're so glad! Of all beings, this one is the hero! This is the one who will set in motion the Wheel of the Dhamma!"

When he heard this news, Asita left Tavatimsa and went directly to the palace of the Sakyans, where, long before, he had been spiritual advisor to the present king's father. As soon as he met King Suddhodana, he asked to see the prince.

The baby was beautiful; his body glowed like molten gold just poured from a crucible. To see the prince was to see brightness, and the sage was thrilled. The king lifted his son to have him pay respects to the sage, but, as he did so, the baby's feet turned up and touched the sage's head. Asita understood that that meant that there was no one deserving the infant's reverence. Recognizing all the signs of greatness in the baby, Asita proclaimed, "There is nothing to compare with this! Here is the ultimate! This is the perfect man!"

Suddenly, he began weeping. This so alarmed the king and queen that they asked, "Is the prince in danger?"

"No," Asita reassured them, with a smile. "There is no threat to the prince's life. In fact, for him, there won't be any obstacles at all. There cannot be any danger to him; he is not an ordinary being. This prince will reach the fulfilment of perfect Enlightenment."

"Then why did you shed tears just now, great sage?" the king asked.

"I do not have much longer to live. I will die too soon to see this man of unparalleled greatness teach the truth of how things are. Because I will be reborn in the formless realm, I will be unable to benefit from his liberating teaching. That's why I wept."

The Sakyans were relieved that the baby faced no danger and thrilled to hear Asita's predictions of the infant's future greatness.

As Asita was leaving the palace, he stopped to see his nephew, Nalaka, and, full of compassion, he told him about the baby. "For your own benefit," he urged Nalaka, "give up your fortune immediately, become an ascetic, and keep yourself in readiness. One day, you will hear talk about a Buddha, a man who has attained supreme Enlightenment. When you hear this, don't hesitate. Go and learn the details of his teaching. Find this Master, live with him, and follow his discipline."

Nalaka did as his uncle advised, and, helped by the merit he had accumulated by performing wholesome deeds, he remained alert and restrained, waiting to hear of the appearance of a Buddha in the world. In time, the news did come, and Nalaka set out to find the Enlightened One He arrived in Isipatana seven days after the Buddha had delivered the First Sermon in the deer park. After taking refuge in the Buddha, Nalaka was ordained and returned to the Himavat, where he stayed alone in the forest and, in no long time, attained arahatship. After his death, the Buddha visited that place with a group of bhikkhus, cremated Nalaka's body, and had a stupa built over the remains.

—Sutta Nipata 3, 11, and Vessantara Jataka

A Quarrel Between Neighbors

Once, when the Buddha was staying at Kapilavatthu with his relatives, the rains failed. The Rohini River, which formed the border between the Sakyan and Koliyan kingdoms, had been dammed, and farmers from both sides of the river were taking water to irrigate their crops. As the drought intensified, farmers on each side saw their crops wither and demanded more water. Each side claimed the right to the lion's share of the water, and laborers began building channels to divert the scarce water to their fields.

Discussions between the farmers failed, insults were exchanged, threats were made, and the laborers and farmers continued quarreling. Soon, the two groups resorted to violence and appealed to the officials. Armies were mobilized, and the two kingdoms were on the verge of war.

That morning, as the Buddha surveyed the world at dawn, he saw the armies moving into place. "If I fail to go to them," he thought, "these men will destroy each other. I must intervene!"

The Buddha traveled quickly to that spot and appeared seated, poised in the air in the middle of the river.

As soon as they saw the Teacher, the soldiers on both sides of the river put down their weapons, and everyone paid obeisance to him.

In a clear voice, the Buddha asked, "Great kings, what is all this quarrel about?"

"Venerable Sir, we do not know," replied the Sakyan king.

Venerable Sir, we have not been told," replied the Koliyan king.

"Who would be likely to know?"

"The commander-in-chief of the army should know, Venerable Sir," both kings replied.

The commanders-in-chief were likewise unable to answer and suggested that their subordinates would know.

The generals referred him to the lower officers, who referred him to the soldiers, and they referred him to the farmers and the laborers.

Finally, the laborers admitted, "The quarrel is about water, Venerable Sir."

Turning back to the two kings, the Buddha asked, "Great kings, what is the value of water?"

"Very little, Venerable Sir," the kings answered.

"Great kings," the Buddha asked, "how much is a warrior worth?"

"Venerable Sir," the kings answered in unison, "a warrior is beyond price."

"Great kings," the Buddha intoned solemnly, "it is not fitting that, for water of little value, you would destroy warriors who are beyond price!"

Both sides were perfectly silent.

"Great kings," the Buddha continued, "why are you acting in this manner? If I had not come here today, you would have caused rivers of blood to flow. You have behaved in a most unseemly manner. You live in strife, indulging in every kind of hatred, afflicted by evil passions, and in constant pursuit of sensual pleasures. I live free from those evils."

Then the Buddha recited these verses:

Happily we live without hating amid those full of hate.
Among those who hate, let us live free from hatred.
Happily we live free from passions amid the passionate.
Among those who are afflicted with passions, let us live
unafflicted.
Happily we live free from longing amid the discontented.
Among those who are obsessed by longing, let us live
contented.

—Dhammapada Commentary on Verses 197-199

Kapilavatthu

Mahanama

On one occasion, the Buddha was staying at Nigrodha Monastery in Kapilavatthu, the Sakyan capital.

At that time, Mahanama approached, paid homage to the Buddha, sat down to one side, and said, "Venerable Sir, this Kapilavatthu is rich and prosperous, populous, crowded, with congested thoroughfares. In the evening, when I am entering Kapilavatthu after visiting the Blessed One or the bhikkhus worthy of esteem, I sometimes come across a stray elephant, a stray horse, a stray chariot, a stray cart, or a stray man. On that occasion, Lord, my mindfulness regarding the Buddha, the Dhamma, the Sangha becomes muddled. At such a time, I wonder, 'If I should die at this moment, what would be my destination, where would I be reborn?'"

"Don't be afraid, Mahanama! Your death will not be a bad one; your demise will not be a bad one. A noble disciple who possesses four things slants, slopes, and inclines toward Nibbana. What four? First, a noble disciple possesses confirmed confidence in the Buddha thus: 'The Blessed One is an arahat, perfectly enlightened, accomplished in true knowledge and conduct, well-gone, a knower of worlds, the unsurpassed trainer of people to be tamed, a teacher of devas and humans, Enlightened, and exalted.' Second, he possesses confirmed confidence in the Dhamma thus: 'The Dhamma is well-expounded by the Blessed One, directly visible, immediately effective, inviting one to come and see, leading onwards, to be realized personally by the wise.' Third, he possesses confirmed confidence in the Sangha thus: 'The Order of the Blessed One's disciples is practicing the good way. The Order of the Blessed One's disciples is practicing the straight way. The Order of the Blessed One's disciples is practicing the true way. The Order of the Blessed One's disciples is practicing the proper way. That is, the four pairs of persons, the eight types of individuals—this Order of the Blessed

One's disciples is worthy of gifts, worthy of hospitality, worthy of offerings, and worthy of reverential salutation. It is the unsurpassed field of merit for the world.' Fourth, he possesses the virtues dear to the noble ones—unbroken, unblemished, freeing, praised by the wise, ungrasped, leading to concentration.

"Suppose, Mahanama, that a tree was slanting, sloping, and inclining toward the east. If it was cut down at its foot, in what direction would it fall?"

"To the east, in the direction in which it was leaning, Venerable Sir."

"So, too, Mahanama, a noble disciple who possesses these four things slants, slopes, and inclines toward Nibbana."

—Samyutta Nikaya 55, 22

Prince Vessantara

It was while staying at Nigrodha Monastery in Kapilavatthu that the Buddha told this story about an extraordinary shower of rain.

After spending a winter in Rajagaha, the Buddha proceeded to Kapilavatthu, capital city of his father's kingdom, attended by twenty thousand bhikkhus. The Sakyan princes were very eager to see the chief of their clan. They went to inspect the residence where he would be staying and declared, "This Banyan Grove is a delightful place, worthy of Sakka himself." Then they went with flowers to greet the Buddha, accompanied by all the young princes and princesses and many children.

The Sakyans were a notoriously proud people. The older princes thought to themselves, "Suddhodana's boy is younger than we are. He is merely our little cousin, our nephew, our grandson!" After the Buddha was seated in the appointed place, surrounded by all the bhikkhus, they sent the younger princes to pay obeisance to him, while they, in their pride and stubbornness, sat toward the back without bowing.

The Buddha realized their intention and thought, "My relatives do not pay me proper respect as a Buddha, but I will make them do so." He concentrated his mind, rose into the air, and, as though shaking the dust from his feet on to their heads, caused fire and water alternately to stream from his body, which is called the Twin Miracle.

When King Suddhodana saw that wonder, he exclaimed to his son, "Soon after your birth, when I saw your feet placed on the head of the brahmin Asita, I bowed to you for the first time. On the day of the Plowing Festival, as you sat on the royal seat in the shade of a jambu tree whose shadow had not moved, I bowed to you for the second time. Now I see this glorious miracle, and I bow to you for the third time."

As soon as the Sakyan princes saw the king paying reverence, they were compelled to do likewise. Satisfied, the Buddha came down and sat again on the appointed seat. All who were there became calm with peace in their hearts. Suddenly, the skies opened and released a refreshing shower of rain. However, the rain fell on only those who wanted to get wet. Not a single drop fell on those who wished to remain dry.

"Look at this miracle!" everyone cried. "What power the Buddha has to make such a rain fall on his kinsmen!"

The Buddha said to them, "This is not the first time that such a great shower of rain has fallen upon my relatives because of me." At their request, he told this story of the past.

Long, long ago, a king named Sivi reigned in his capital city of Jetuttara in the kingdom of Sivi. King Sivi had a son named Sanjaya. When Prince Sanjaya came of age, the king chose for his bride the daughter of King Madda, Princess Phusati, who, by the time she was sixteen, had become the most beautiful woman in the world.

In her preceding life, Phusati had been born in Tavatimsa. When her time there was nearly over, because of innumerable merits she had accumulated in previous lives, Sakka granted her ten boons. After careful consideration, she chose: to live in Sivi's realm, to be chief queen, to have dark eyes and dark eyebrows, to be named Phusati, to have a son who loved giving, to keep her figure, to remain youthful so as to keep the king's affection, to have soft skin, not to become gray, and to be able to save those who had been condemned.

As soon as Sanjaya and Phusati were married, King Sivi abdicated and handed the kingdom over to his son. King Sanjaya loved his wife dearly.

Sakka remembered the boons he had granted Phusati and noted that one remained unfulfilled. "She asked for a good and generous son," he thought. "I will send him to her."

At that time, the Bodhisatta was in Tavatimsa, and his time there was ending. Sakka approached him and said, "Venerable Sir, you must be reborn in the realm of men. Now is the time for you to be conceived by Queen Phusati, consort of the king of Sivi." The Bodhisatta agreed and descended to earth. At the same time, sixty thousand other devas from that heaven were conceived by the wives of the king's courtiers.

As soon as Queen Phusati had conceived, she expressed the desire to have six almshalls built, one at each city gate, one in the city center, and one at her own door so that every day she could distribute six hundred thousand coins in alms.

When the king learned that his queen was expecting, he consulted his fortune tellers, who said, "Your Majesty, your wife is pregnant with one who will be so devoted to generosity that he will never be satisfied with giving." The king was pleased with their prediction, and he, too, made a practice of generosity. Because of the king's goodness, other rulers from all over Jambudipa sent him presents. There seemed to be no limit to the king's revenue.

After ten months, the queen informed the king that she wished to tour the capital. He ordered the city decorated, seated his queen in a royal chariot, and made a procession around the city. When they reached Vessa Street, the merchant quarters, the queen went into labor. The king had a lying-in chamber prepared, and she gave birth to a son right there.

The Bodhisatta was born free from impurity, with his eyes wide open. Immediately after he was born, he held out his hand to his mother and said, "Mother, I wish to make some gifts. Is there anything for me to give?"

She dropped a purse with one thousand coins into his outstretched hands and said, "Yes, my son. Give as you wish!"

Because he was born on Vessa Street, he was called Vessantara. On the same day, in the royal stables, a beautiful white elephant was born. This was regarded as an auspicious omen, and, because the elephant would be essential to the prince when he grew up, it was named Paccaya, which means "support."

The king appointed nurses for Vessantara and for the sixty thousand boys born at the same time. Vessantara grew up surrounded by these companions.

When the prince was four years old, the king ordered jewelers to make a precious necklace for him at a cost of one hundred thousand coins. He presented it to his son, but Vessantara immediately gave it to his nurses. They tried to return it to him, but he refused to take it back. When the nurses reported this, the king answered, "What my son has given is well given." He then had another necklace made, but the prince gave that away too. This happened nine times in all.

When Vessantara was eight years old, he thought to himself, "Everything that I give comes from outside. This does not satisfy me. I wish to give something of my very own. If someone should ask for my heart, I would tear it out and give it. If someone asked me for my eyes, I would pluck them out and give them. If someone asked for my flesh, I would cut off every bit from my bones and give it." As he pondered these thoughts in the depths of his heart, the great earth shook like a mad elephant. Mount Sineru, the highest of mountains, bowed like a sapling in the direction of the city of Jetuttara. Thunder rumbled, lightning flashed across the sky, and the seas churned as in a storm. Sakka clapped his hands, and Maha-Brahma signaled his approval. The entire universe was in an uproar.

By the age of sixteen, Vessantara had mastered all the arts and sciences. His parents chose his first cousin, Maddi, as his bride. On the appointed day, the young girl arrived from her father's palace with a full retinue of attendants. The grand ceremony was both their wedding and the investiture of Vessantara as crown prince.

In time, Maddi gave birth to a son who was named Jali because he was first placed in a golden hammock. Later she had a baby girl, who was named Kanhajina because, right after birth, she was placed on a black skin.

From the time Vessantara became heir apparent, he gave away six hundred thousand coins every day. Six times each month, mounted upon his magnificent white elephant, Paccaya, the prince visited his six almshalls to supervise donations and to make offerings with his own hand.

It so happened that there was a severe drought in the kingdom of Kalinga. When the crops failed, there was a terrible famine. Many people were reduced to begging to escape outright starvation. In desperation, the people crowded into the king's courtyard. They cried out for help and blamed him for their troubles. "What is it, my children?" the king asked. When the people told him about conditions in the kingdom, he promised that he would bring rain. For the next seven days the king strictly observed the precepts, but no rain fell.

On the eighth day, King Kalinga appeared before the people and announced, "My loyal subjects, although I have strictly kept the precepts for seven days, I have not been able to bring any rain. What more can I do?"

One citizen spoke up, saying, "Sire, if you yourself cannot bring rain, King Sanjaya's son, Vessantara, in the city of Jetuttara, has a glorious white elephant, and, wherever that elephant goes, rain falls. We have heard reports that the prince is devoted to generosity. Send brahmins to ask for that elephant and to bring it back here to Kalinga."

Accepting that suggestion, the king promptly selected eight brahmins, gave them provisions for the journey, and sent them to fetch Vessantara's elephant.

When the eight brahmins reached Jetuttara, they were given hospitality in an almshall. On the full-moon day they went to the eastern gate to wait for a chance to ask for the elephant.

Early that morning, Vessantara bathed with perfumed water and ate breakfast. Mounting his noble, richly adorned elephant, he proceeded to the almshall at the eastern gate. From the knoll where they were standing, the brahmins could see the prince giving alms, but they had no chance to speak to him. They hurried to the southern gate.

When the prince reached the southern gate, the brahmins stretched out their hands and cried, "Victory to the noble Vessantara!"

"Brahmins, what is it that you desire?" Vessantara asked.

The brahmins replied, "We crave a precious thing, great prince. We ask for your marvelous elephant with tusks like poles."

When Vessantara heard this, he thought, "Here am I, willing to give anything that is asked for, including my head, my flesh, and my heart, but all they want is a mere possession. Of course, I'll give it to them." In a loud voice he declared, "I give and never shrink from giving. This noble beast, this mighty tusked elephant, is given freely to these brahmins who have asked for it." He climbed down from the elephant's back and presented the magnificent animal to the brahmins. The noble elephant Paccaya was fully adorned with precious ornaments. The gold and jewels decorating his tusks alone were worth hundreds of thousands of coins, and the magnificent howdah on his back was beyond price. When the prince relinquished this incomparable elephant and its priceless accessories, along with the grooms and stablemen to attend the great beast, the earth shook.

The brahmins immediately climbed on the elephant's back and rode down the main street of the city. When the crowd saw them, they shouted, "Hey, Brahmins, why are you mounted on our elephant? Where are you taking our elephant?"

The brahmins shouted back, "The great prince Vessantara has given the elephant to us. What's it to you?" Then, with derogatory gestures to the crowd, they continued riding through the city and out the northern gate.

The people were outraged.

"When the great elephant was given away," one man cried out, "I'm sure I felt an earthquake!"

"Yes," shouted another, "and I heard a horrible noise!"

A raging mob rushed to the palace in protest. "The kingdom is ruined!" someone shouted to the king. "Why did Vessantara give away our elephant!" another asked. Others cried out, "How dare he make a present of our precious elephant!" "Let him be satisfied by giving food, clothing, jewelry, or horses to those rude brahmins." "Why did the prince do this?" "Explain your son's actions or we'll deal with him ourselves!"

The people sounded so angry that the king was afraid they wanted to kill Vessantara. "Let me be king no more," he shouted over the din. "I will not harm an innocent prince. No matter what you say, I could never kill him. He is my true-born son."

A spokesman from the crowd shouted in reply, "Sire, we are not demanding that Prince Vessantara be killed or even that he be imprisoned. Still, when he gave away our elephant he went too far! He must be banished from the kingdom. Send him into exile on Mount Vamka !"

Unable to appease the crowd in any other way, the beleaguered king capitulated to the people's will, but he asked that his son be allowed one happy night before he had to leave the capital. The people accepted that condition, and the king sent a message to his son, informing him of the people's anger and of his banishment. Unaware of any offense he might have committed, Vessantara asked the messenger why the people were so angry. The messenger told him that the people of Sivi were outraged at his gift-giving and were demanding that he be banished to Mount Vamka, the traditional place of exile.

"My good man," the prince replied, "since I would willingly give away my own eyes and my own heart, there should be no question of my giving mere gold and treasure. If anyone asked me, I would give away my own right hand without hesitation. My delight is in gifts! Even if the people banish me or kill me, I will never stop giving! I have committed no crime, but I will leave the city by the criminals' gate. Even though I am being banished for the gift of the white elephant, I am not through with giving. Please ask the citizens to grant me a reprieve of an additional day. Before I go, I want to make one more offering. Tomorrow I would like to give the great Gift of the Seven Hundreds, and the following day I will leave."

The messenger returned and reported everything to the people. As soon as the man had left, Vessantara summoned his servants and ordered them to arrange everything so that he could give away seven hundred of each of the following: elephants, horses, chariots, cows, male servants, and female servants. Leaving all the preparations to them, he went to see Maddi.

He sat on a couch and spoke gently to his wife, "You must find a safe place for the wealth and presents that I have given you in the past and for your father's dowry, too. Hide all this treasure well."

"Where should I find a place to hide these things, my husband?"

"Give your wealth in gifts to those who are deserving. I know of no better or safer place than that, my dear."

"Of course, that is true, My Lord, but …"

"Take good care of your children and your husband's parents," the prince continued. "Take good care of him who will be your new husband. If no one comes forward to marry you when I'm gone, seek a husband for yourself. Don't languish all alone."

"My Lord," Maddi cried, not understanding at all, "why are you saying these things that make no sense to me?"

Vessantara answered, "Lady, the people of Sivi are angry with me for the gift of the white elephant. They are banishing me from the kingdom. Tomorrow I will give the Gift of the Seven Hundreds, and the next day I will leave. I will go to the dark and dangerous forest, full of fierce beasts of prey. Who can predict whether or not I will be able to survive there? Nevertheless, the day after tomorrow, I must go."

Understanding at last Vessantara's meaning, Maddi cried with all earnestness: "No, My Lord, I will not let you go alone! Wherever you go, I will go. Given the choice to die with you or to live apart from you, death will be my choice. I'll follow wherever you lead. The children and I will stay with you. I promise that you will never find me a burden. When you see your darling children playing and hear them prattling in our new forest home, you will forget that you were born to be king. When you hear the trumpeting of the elephants, the crying of the screech owls, and the roaring of the rivers, you will forget that you were born to be king."

Neither Vessantara nor Maddi knew that Queen Phusati was overhearing their conversation. Distraught at the news of the banishment, she had gone to visit her son, but, finding him alone with Maddi, she hesitated to interrupt. "Better I should drink poison or leap off a cliff and die," she moaned to herself. "Why are they banishing my unoffending son, Vessantara, who is so respected, so free from greed, so generous to all who ask, so beloved by family, by friends, and by everyone in the kingdom! Why banish my innocent son, Vessantara?"

The queen hurried to the king and pleaded, "Please, Sire! Do not banish Vessantara just because some people are shouting! If this blameless boy is banished," she warned the king, "your kingdom will fall like an overripe mango. You will be like the crippled wild goose when the pond is dry—deserted by your courtiers and living alone."

"My dear," the king replied, "by sending your son into exile, I fulfill my royal duty, which is dearer than life itself."

"My son! My son!" the queen cried in despair. "Once hosts of men escorted him with banners as he rode in a chariot, but soon he'll trudge unattended on foot. And Maddi—she is used to being carried in a palanquin. How can she, with her delicate hands and feet, go into the rough forest?

"I am like an eagle that finds its nest empty, its young chicks all slain. I cannot bear the emptiness they will leave behind. How I shall endure the pain of never seeing my son again? If my innocent son is banished, my life will be over!"

Alerted by the devas, people from all over Jambudipa flooded into Jetuttara and, as dawn was breaking, Vessantara began giving his gifts. In addition to the Gifts of the Seven Hundreds, he gave freely of every other imaginable thing; everyone received what he desired. He gave food to the hungry and even strong drink to those who required it. He was still distributing his gifts when evening fell. Banishing Vessantara from the kingdom was like cutting down a veritable wishing tree!

Having finished his great donation, the prince returned to his apartments to prepare for his departure. Then he and Maddi went to bid farewell to his parents.

Bowing to his father, he announced, "I go now to Mount Vamka. Having wronged my people by giving bounty from my hand, I accept this sentence of exile. I will atone for my mistake, but I will continue to do good."

Turning to the queen, he said, "Mother, I take leave of you as an outcast."

"I give you permission to go," Queen Phusati replied, "and I give you my blessing, but, please, I beg you to leave Maddi and the children behind. She is unsuited for the forest. Why should she go with you?"

The prince replied, "I wouldn't even take a slave away against his will. If Maddi wishes, let her come. If not, let her stay."

"Princess," the king urged his daughter-in-law, "please stay with us. Rough bark cloth does not suit you. You are suited for fine Baranasi silk. Your nature is very delicate. Forest life is too hard for you."

"Without Vessantara," Maddi answered calmly, "I have no desire to go on living."

The king persisted by explaining the hardships of forest life, with all its biting and stinging insects, frightening noises, deadly snakes, and fierce beasts. Maddi listened and replied, "I willingly accept all the terrible things you describe. I am resolved to go. I will forge my way through the thickest forest without complaining. Any wife who loves her husband must do her duty. The wife who shares her husband's lot, whether it is rich or poor, is praised even by the devas. Your Majesty, I will go into exile with your son. He is my joy and my very life."

"Go if you will," the king relented, "but leave your two little ones behind. What can they do in the forest? Let us keep them here with us where they will be well cared for."

"My Jali and Kanhajina are dearest to my heart," Maddi answered. "They will live with us in the forest and ease the pain of exile."

"These children have always eaten the finest rice and meat," the king insisted. "How can they survive if they are forced to eat wild fruit and berries? They have lived in beautifully painted rooms, safely guarded at night. How can they sleep at the roots of trees, on a bed of grass, bothered by mosquitoes and flies? It will be more than they can bear."

Even as they talked, dawn came. An elaborate carriage with a team of four Sindh horses was brought. Maddi paid her respects to her husband's parents and entered the carriage with her two children. "Do not worry," she said to the king. "Wherever we go, we will care for the children."

Vessantara also bowed to his parents and climbed into the carriage. As they drove in the direction of Mount Vamka, he shouted, "A blessing on my relatives. Farewell!"

"If my son desires to give," the queen announced as they drove away, "let him give." She sent two carts with him, each loaded with all sorts of precious things, but, in a short time, he had distributed everything to beggars he met on the road. Before they left the city, he had given away even all the jewelry he was wearing. Vessantara turned around to take one last look at his ancestral home in all its loveliness and ordered the people who had followed them to turn around and to return to the city. Then the carriage continued on its journey.

As soon as the prince had left the city, four brahmins arrived, asking about the Gift of the Seven Hundreds. When they were told that the ceremony was over and that the prince had left, they asked if he had taken anything with him. Learning that he had a coach and horses, they rushed after him.

Vessantara had asked Maddi to watch for other beggars, and, when she saw the four, she said, "Mendicants, My Lord." The prince immediately stopped the carriage. When the brahmins asked for the horses, he gave one horse to each.

Instantly, four devas, disguised as red deer, appeared and yoked themselves to the carriage. Vessantara, realizing who they were, smiled and said, "Look, Maddi! It's a miracle!" Before they had gone very far, a fifth brahmin approached and asked Vessantara for his carriage, which he gave willingly.

"Maddi," Vessantara instructed, "you take Kanhajina for she is light. Jali is a heavy boy, so I'll carry him myself." With the two children on their hips, they proceeded on foot, talking together happily and asking the way of people they met. Other travelers, touched by the sight of the little family, told them that Mount Vamka was a long way off and that they still had a hard task ahead.

The children became hungry and cried when they saw all the different kinds of fruit on the tall trees beside the road. Because of Vessantara's virtue, the trees bowed down so that the parents could reach the ripe fruit. Maddi marveled at this wondrous event.

Out of pity for the children, the devas shortened the way. That evening, the family arrived in the kingdom of Ceta, which was ruled by one of Vessantara's uncles. The prince chose to rest in a hall outside the city gate, without entering the city itself. Maddi brushed the dust off his feet and rubbed them. Then she went toward the gate, intending to announce her husband's arrival. Some local women recognized her and wondered why this princess, who should have been riding in a palanquin, appeared on foot. Realizing that Vessantara, Maddi, and the children had all come in this unbecoming manner, they hurried to inform the king.

As soon as the princes of Ceta heard of the royal family's peculiar arrival, they went to meet Vessantara. "What has happened to your kingdom, mighty prince?" they asked. "Where is your army? Where is your royal carriage? Why are you without a chariot or even a horse? You've come a long way. Were you defeated by an enemy? Is that why you are here without an entourage?"

"Thank you, sirs," Vessantara answered. "My father is well, but misfortune has befallen me. The other day, some brahmins came and asked for my great elephant because their kingdom was having a drought, so I gave them the elephant and all his trappings. This made the people of Sivi so angry that they called for my banishment, and my father was forced to accept their demands. Now I am on my way to Mount Vamka. Though I am only an exile, please show me a place to stay in the meantime."

The royal cousins welcomed Vessantara warmly, gave him many presents, and prepared a delicious feast for the family. They even offered Vessantara their own kingdom, and asked him to stay.

Vessantara accepted their gifts but insisted that he had to continue on to Mount Vamka to live in exile. "You must not even inform my father that I was here," he told the princes. "I must go away a banished man. If the people of Sivi knew that you had asked me to become your king, they would be furious. I would hate to start a quarrel."

Vessantara refused even to enter the city, so the princes furnished and decorated the hall where he was going to sleep and made it comfortable. Vessantara, Maddi, and the children stayed two nights in Ceta. When they left early the next morning, the princes accompanied them for fifteen yojanas.

"You must continue for another fifteen yojanas," they told Vessantara. "That rocky mountain in the distance is Mount Gandhamadana. You, your wife, and your children may safely pass that way. From there, go straight northward, and you will see Mount Vepulla, a pleasant place with many shady trees. When you get there, you will find the Ketumati River, whose fresh, sweet water is full of fish. Bathe and rest there, and let the children play. After that, you will see Mount Nalika, which is full of songbirds and kinnaras. Continuing north, you will find Lake Mucalinda with blue and white water lilies. A little further along, you will come to a thick forest with lots of fruit trees and flowers. Follow the mountain cataracts to their spring, and you will see a lotus-covered lake. Build yourself a hut a little to the north. There is plenty of food nearby. It should be a safe haven for you." Not satisfied with just giving directions, however, before returning to their capital, the princes assigned a trustworthy forester from that region to watch over Vessantara and his family.

When the family reached the Ketumati River, they took the princes' advice and stopped to bathe and to rest. The forester prepared a delicious lunch for them and Vessantara gave him a golden hairpin. As they crossed the river, Vessantara's mind became very calm. The family rested under a banyan tree and ate some of its fruit. Then they proceeded to Mount Nalika and to Lake Mucalinda. They walked along the northeast shore of the lake and entered the thick forest by a narrow footpath.

Sakka looked down and saw that Vessantara had entered the Himavat. He immediately called Vissakamma, chief architect among the devas, and ordered him to build a suitable place for Vessantara to stay. Vissakamma built two lovely hermitages, with sleeping rooms and day rooms, connected with covered walks, lined by banana plants and flowering shrubs. Then he drove away all unfriendly devas and all harsh-voiced animals and birds. At the entrance to the settlement he posted a sign saying, "All of this is for anyone who wishes to become an ascetic."

When Vessantara saw the path, he felt sure it would lead to a settlement of ascetics. As soon as he saw the empty hermitage and the sign, he knew that Sakka had provided it for him. Accepting the gift of the hermitage, Vessantara took off his royal robe and put on the rough garb of an ascetic. When Maddi saw him dressed like that, she could not keep herself from crying, but, following his example, she also changed her clothes and the children's. At that moment, because of Vessantara's compassion, all beings within a radius of three yojanas, even the fiercest carnivores, stopped their violence and began treating each other gently. None even thought of hunting or hurting another.

Maddi suggested that Vessantara stay with the children during the day so that she could gather food, and he agreed. Vessantara told his wife that he also had a request. He asked her to stay apart from him so that they might maintain the modesty appropriate to their new ascetic life.

Every morning, Maddi arranged drinking water, food, and toothsticks. After sweeping out the hermitage, she left the children with their father and went to the forest with a basket, a pruning hook, and a trowel to find fruit, roots, berries, and flowers. She returned in the evening and bathed the children. Then the four of them sat at the door of the hermitage to eat their meal. At night, Maddi took the children to her own cell to sleep. For seven months, they lived peacefully in this way deep in the mountains.

At that time, in the kingdom of Kalinga, in the village of Dunnivittha, there was a brahmin by the name of Jujaka. In the past, Jujaka had collected one hundred coins in donations. He had left this fortune in the safekeeping of a family in the village and had gone off in search of more. He stayed away such a long time, however, that the family assumed that he would never come back, and they spent the money. When Jujaka finally returned, he was furious to discover that his savings were gone. Too poor to replace the money, the couple gave Jujaka their daughter, Amittatapana, instead.

Amittatapana took very good care of Jujaka. In fact, some young men said to their wives, "Look at Amittatapana. See how well she cares for that old man while you are careless of your young husband!" Naturally, this infuriated the other women, and they decided to drive Amittatapana out of the village.

At every opportunity, the women mocked her and made her life miserable. When they went to the river with their pots to get water, they teased her: "How your parents must have hated you to give you to an ugly, decrepit old man like that! How can you bear to look at that hideous old man? You are a young girl! How could that old dotard give you any happiness? Why don't you go back where you came from?"

This abuse upset Amittatapana very much, and she usually returned home in tears.

One day, Jujaka saw her crying and asked, "What is wrong, my dear?"

"I can't fetch water anymore. Whenever I go out, the other women make fun of me."

"Don't worry. You don't have to carry water. From now on I'll fetch it myself."

"That is impossible. That would just make things worse! If you did that, I would be ashamed to stay with you. You must get a slave to do the work."

"My dear, how can I get a slave? I have no money. Don't be angry; I'll do your work myself."

"Now, listen to me! I've heard that Prince Vessantara is staying on Mount Vamka. People say he is devoted to giving. Go and ask him for a slave. He will certainly give you what you want."

"I'm an old man, and Mount Vamka is far away. The road there is rough. Please don't be unreasonable; I'll do the work myself."

"So! You're going to give up without even trying! I'll say it once more: if you don't get a slave to do the work for me, I'll leave you. You'll soon see me in someone else's arms," she taunted him, "and then you'll be sorry! You'll miss me so much, your gray hairs will multiply, and you will be miserable and lonely in your old age."

Terrified that his young wife would carry out her threat and leave him, Jujaka gave in. "All right! All right!" he cried, "I'll go and return with a pair of slaves who will wait on you hand and foot."

While his wife prepared the provisions for his journey, Jujaka laid in a supply of wood and water so that she would be safe and comfortable until he returned. "Don't go out after dark," he warned her. "Be careful until I return. I promise not to be gone long." Then, with tears in his eyes, he set out.

As soon as he reached the capital city of Sivi, he asked where he could find Prince Vessantara. He was shocked that his question provoked such anger. Everyone he asked shouted at him and pushed him away. "It's people like you," they said, "who ruined our prince. Because of giving to you beggars, he has been banished from the kingdom. It's your fault that he had to leave with his wife and children to live on Mount Vamka." Some people were so angry that they threw sticks and stones at Jujaka to chase him away.

The devas, however, guided the brahmin and set him on the right road to Mount Vamka. He soon reached the forest, but then he got hopelessly lost and whined loudly, "Does anyone know where Vessantara, the great and generous prince, is staying? Won't someone tell me how to find Prince Vessantara?"

When the forester who had been assigned to look after Vessantara heard Jujaka, he thought, "This man is up to no good. I'll bet he wants to ask for Maddi or the children. I cannot let that happen. I will kill him!"

The forester drew his bow and approached Jujaka. "Because of men like you," he shouted at the brahmin, "Prince Vessantara has been exiled. You worthless fool! Rather than let you harm his wife and children, I'll kill you myself!"

Shaking with fear, Jujaka quickly devised a bold lie. "My friend," he said as sweetly as he could, "you cannot kill a messenger. That's an ancient rule! I am an ambassador from the king of Sivi. The people have come to repent their hasty anger with Prince Vessantara. The king misses his son, and the queen is pining away. I have come to escort Vessantara back to the capital. If you know where I can find him, it is your duty to help me."

The forester was delighted to hear this wonderful news. He quickly put down his bow, called off his hunting dogs, and invited Jujaka to a feast of roast leg of deer and a pot of honey. Completely taken in by Jujaka's deceit, the forester described Vessantara's peaceful hermitage and gave detailed directions to get there.

Jujaka was so pleased that he offered the forester a piece of his homemade barley bread, but the forester refused, insisting that he was fully provisioned. To make sure Jujaka would not make a mistake, the forester explained the path once more.

Further along, Jujaka came upon an ascetic by the name of Accuta. "Holy man," the brahmin greeted the ascetic, "I trust that you are prosperous and well, with plenty of roots and fruit, that you are not bothered by flies or gnats or creeping things, and that wild beasts leave you alone."

"Thank you, Brahmin," the ascetic replied. "Yes, I am quite well, and there is plenty of fruit here. I am not troubled by insects or animals. As a matter of fact, in all the years I've lived here, I have never been bothered by any sickness whatsoever. Please wash up, and rest from your journey. Have some tender leaves and ripe fruit. This water is from a cave up the hill. It is very cool and refreshing."

Jujaka wasted no time in explaining his errand. "I am looking for Vessantara, King Sanjaya's son, who was banished by the people of Sivi. If you know where he is, please tell me."

"I'm afraid your intentions are not good," the ascetic replied suspiciously. "No doubt, you have come to ask for his wife or to take his children as your servants. The prince has no wealth or property here."

Jujaka quickly protested. "No, no, you misunderstand me! I have only the best of intentions. It is a joy to be able to visit a good man. I have never met this prince before. I have just come here to see him; that's all. If you know where he is, please tell me."

"All right then," Accuta answered, also taken in by the brahmin's honeyed words. "Stay with me tonight, and tomorrow I'll tell you how to get there."

The next morning, the ascetic pointed out the route to Vessantara's hermitage, and Jujaka set out. By evening, he had reached the lake. He thought to himself, "Vessantara's wife will be returning from the forest. Women are always in the way, so, tomorrow, after she has gone out to gather fruit, I will approach Vessantara and ask him for the children. I'll get them and be on my way before she comes back." Satisfied with his plan, he climbed a small hill and lay down to sleep in a pleasant spot.

Just before dawn, Maddi dreamed that a black man, wearing yellow robes and with red flowers in his ears, came into the leaf hut. He grabbed her by the hair, dragged her out, and threw her down. As she lay shrieking on the ground, he gouged out her eyes, lopped off her arms, cut open her breast, and tore out her heart, which he carried off, dripping with blood. She awoke in terror. "What an unspeakably evil dream!" she cried. "I must ask Vessantara to tell me what it means. Surely he will understand it."

Although it was still dark, she hurried to Vessantara's hut and knocked at the door. "Who is it?" Vessantara asked.

"It is I, My Lord," Maddi answered.

"Why have you come at this hour?" Vessantara asked, without opening the door. "Are you not breaking our agreement?"

"I am very sorry, but I am not coming out of desire. I have had an evil dream, and only you can explain it."

"I see," Vessantara replied, opening the door. "Please tell me what you saw."

As soon as Maddi had explained the nightmare, Vessantara understood its meaning. "My generosity will soon be perfected," he thought. "Today someone will come and ask for the children. I must comfort Maddi and let her go back to bed."

Aloud he said, "Your mind must have been disturbed by indigestion. Don't worry."

Reassured by his words, Maddi returned to her own hut, but the dream continued to haunt her so much that she could not get back to sleep. When it finally became light, she emerged and prepared things as she did every day. As she hugged and kissed the children, she told them that she had had a bad dream and warned them to be careful. She asked Vessantara to look after the children with extra care. Then, wiping away her tears, she picked up her basket and tools and went to the forest to gather food.

Jujaka waited until he was sure that Maddi would be out of the way. In joyful anticipation, Vessantara had come out of his hut and was sitting on a stone slab. "Now the supplicant will come!" he thought. As the children played at his feet, he eagerly watched the road. As soon as Vessantara saw the brahmin approaching the hermitage, he sensed that his seven idle months were at an end. He once again took up the burden of generosity and called out happily, "Welcome, Brahmin! Come here!"

"Jali," he called to his son, "stand up! Here comes a brahmin! Isn't it wonderful? It's just like old times!"

"Yes, Father," the boy answered. "I see him too. It looks like he wants to ask a favor. Let's welcome him." Jali quickly ran to meet the brahmin and offered to carry his bag.

"This must be Jali, the prince's son," Jujaka thought. "I must start out by treating him roughly." He snapped his fingers at the lad and snarled under his breath, "Get back! Get away!"

"What a harsh man this is!" thought the boy.

To Vessantara, however, Jujaka was extremely polite. He greeted him warmly, inquired after his health, and asked about the family's welfare.

"We are all faring quite well, thank you," Vessantara replied. "We have plenty of food and good water, the surroundings are comfortable, and no wild animals annoy us. Please have some of our fruit, and drink some of the delicious cold water from a cave on the hill."

As soon as Jujaka was seated comfortably, Vessantara addressed him directly, "Tell me, good sir, why you have come to this deep forest. What business do you have here?"

"You are like a great flood which never fails," Jujaka replied, praising Vessantara's virtues. Then just as directly as the question had been posed, he answered, "I have come to ask for your children. Please give them to me."

Vessantara was delighted. "I give them to you without hesitation," he announced. "You will be their master. But, sir, my wife went a little while ago to collect food. She'll be back this evening. Please stay here tonight. My wife will wash the children and garland them with flowers. Tomorrow morning, we will send you on your way with them."

"No, great prince," Jujaka answered, "I must go. I do not want to stay. I'll leave right away to make sure that nothing happens to delay me. Women are not generous givers. Give me your children now. There is no need for them to see their mother's face. No need at all!"

"If you don't want to meet my wife—and a faithful wife she is, indeed," Vessantara said, "take Jali and Kanhajina to their grandfather. As soon as my father sees them, he will give you a fortune."

"Oh no, my friend," Jujaka answered quickly. "I'm sure your father, the king, would punish me, perhaps even kill me. I want the children to serve my wife, and I'll take them away right now."

When the children heard this, they ran to hide in the bushes behind the hut, but they were so frightened that they couldn't keep still. They scampered here and there, looking for a safer place. Finally, in desperation, they jumped into the lake and hid among the lotus leaves.

Jujaka looked for the children but could not find them.

"Vessantara!" he cried. "You're nothing but a liar and a fraud! You said that you would give me the children, but as soon as I told you that, instead of taking them to the capital, I was going to take them home and make them my wife's servants, you signaled to them to hide. And now you just sit there, looking so innocent!"

"Don't worry," Vessantara said calmly to Jujaka. "They have probably just run away. I'll get them." Seeing their footprints behind the hut, he started walking toward the lake, calling, "Jali, my beloved son! Please come and fulfill my perfection now by following my will. You will be the ship to carry me across the sea of existence beyond the realms of devas and men. Through you, I will be free."

When the boy heard his father, he pushed aside the lotus leaves and came out. "Let that old brahmin do what he wants with me," he sobbed as he embraced his father's feet. "I will never disobey my father."

"My boy, where is your sister?" Vessantara asked.

"Father," Jali answered, "in times of danger, all creatures take care of themselves."

Realizing that the children had made a pact, Vessantara called again, "Kanha, my beloved daughter! Please come and fulfill my perfection now by following my will. You will be the ship to carry me across the sea of existence beyond the realms of devas and men. Through you, I will be free."

"I will not quarrel with my father," Kanhajina resolved as she too emerged from the water. Falling beside her brother at her father's feet, she grasped Vessantara's left ankle and wept. As Vessantara stood looking down at his two young children, his own tears fell upon their backs. "My dear, dear children," he said, lifting them up and comforting them, "don't you know that I have gladly given you away so that my desire may attain fulfillment? Now you must go with this brahmin.

"Jali, my son, if you wish to become free, you must pay him one thousand coins, but your sister is very beautiful. Should a person of low birth give the brahmin money to free her, it would break her noble birthright. No one but a king can pay the price of the one hundreds. Therefore, for your sister to be free, the brahmin must be paid one hundred elephants, one hundred horses, one hundred bulls, one hundred coins, one hundred male servants, and one hundred female servants."

Then he led the children back to the hermitage and called the brahmin. Vessantara took his water pot and poured water, signifying that his gift was freely given. "Dearer than my son one-hundredfold, one-thousandfold, one-hundred-thousandfold," he declared, "is omniscience!"

As he handed the brahmin the precious gift of his beloved children, his mind was filled with joy, and the earth trembled at the greatness of his gift.

Impatient to be off, Jujaka tied the boy's right hand to the girl's left hand with a vine and dragged them away. As the children staggered forward, he beat them until they bled. When they came to a very rough place in the road, the old man stumbled and fell. Instantly the children slipped off their bonds and ran back to Vessantara.

"Father! Father!" they cried, "please let us wait until Mother returns! Don't send us away before she comes back. Let the brahmin sell us or kill us, but please let us see our mother again. His hands are rough; his nails are torn; he's covered with spots and wrinkles; and he has squinty eyes. He's cruel and inhuman; maybe he's even a cannibal."

"Father!" Jali cried. "I appeal to you on behalf of my dear sister. Let her stay! She has never known such harshness before."

When Vessantara did not answer, Jali continued, lamenting, "I'm not afraid of death; I know that we all must die. What I regret is that I will never see my mother's face again. Never again will I see my beloved father. I know how much they, too, will grieve. How they will weep after my sister and I have gone! Now we must leave our playground and our toys. No more will we wear these lovely flowers, nor eat this delicious fruit. Farewell to all the animals that we have loved in this forest home!"

Jujaka roughly retrieved the children, tied their wrists together again, and drove them away even more roughly.

"Father!" Jali cried. "Give Mother all our toys. They will ease her grief."

Seeing the children treated like this and hearing their plaintive cries, Vessantara trembled violently. When he thought of never seeing his son and daughter again, he began to weep uncontrollably. "Who will feed my children when they are hungry?" he cried, as he entered the hut alone. "How could that brahmin strike my defenseless, innocent children in front of me? Has he no shame? No man with any decency would treat even the lowliest slave like that! Though I can no longer see them, I know that he is scolding and whipping my darlings while I am here, helpless and unable to protect them."

As he stood alone in the hut, his love for the children welled up in his mind. The vision of the brahmin beating them was more than he could bear. He felt an urge to follow Jujaka, to kill him, and to bring the children back. He even picked up his bow and started for the door.

"No!" he thought, restraining himself with great effort. "To give a gift and then to regret it would be a great sin. That is not the way of righteousness. Although the children are suffering, I cannot ask for them back. It's wrong to rescind a gift once given. I must not even allow myself to feel any pain."

Jujaka hurried the children along, beating them the whole while.

"Now I understand," Jali cried, "what people mean when they say that a child who has no mother is fatherless, as well. Without mother and father, life is nothing to us. We might as well be dead, Kanha. We are nothing more than the chattel of this horrible, greedy man. Farewell, beautiful forest! Good-bye, lovely home! Oh, Kanha, everything is lost!"

Once again, the clumsy old brahmin fell and dropped the cord. As fast as they could, the children ran back to their father.

Jujaka became very angry. He got up quickly and followed them back to the hut. "You two are clever at running away, but I'll fix that!" he shouted. He tied the cord even tighter than before and led them away a third time.

Kanhajina turned back and called, "Father, this man beats me as if I were a slave. Brahmins are said to be upright men. He cannot be a brahmin. He must be a yakkha, taking us away to eat us. How can you just stand there and watch us being dragged away to be a yakkha's meal?"

This plaintive cry from his beloved daughter was like a flame burning Vessantara's heart. Tears welled up in his eyes and rolled down his cheeks like drops of blood. Then he thought, "All this pain comes from affection and not from any other cause. I must quiet this affection and become calm." By the power of this insight, he overcame his sorrow and was able to sit perfectly still.

"My feet are very sore and the road is very hard," Kanhajina continued lamenting. "It's already evening, but still this hateful brahmin drives us on. To devas that dwell in these hills and forests, we bow in greeting. Devas of this lake, keep our mother well. She's been gone a long time. She must have gathered a lot of wild fruit and roots by now. When she sees our empty hut, she'll cry! Perhaps she will follow us. If she does, I hope she hurries. If she had met this cruel man and given him fruit and honey, he never would have treated us so cruelly."

When Vessantara gave his dearly beloved children to the brahmin, the earth resounded so loudly that the sound reached the Brahma heavens and touched the hearts of all the deities dwelling there. When those devas heard the sobs of the children being beaten by the brahmin, they thought, "When Maddi returns to the hermitage, she will ask Vessantara about the children. As soon as she learns that they have been given away, if it is still daylight, she will run after them. This would not be right." They assigned three devas to assume the shapes of a lion, a tiger, and a leopard. They were told to keep Maddi from returning before sunset, to guard her from other wild animals, and to allow her to come back only by moonlight.

All day, Maddi had been thinking about the evil dream she had had. She wanted to gather food very quickly and to return early to the hermitage. She tried to hurry, but, as she became more flustered and worried, her hand trembled, she dropped her trowel, and the basket slipped from her shoulder. She could no longer tell the barren trees from those laden with fruit. Her head began throbbing, and the whole world felt upside down. "Why do I feel so strange?" she asked herself. "What can be the meaning of this? Look!" She cried. "It's time for dinner. My children are waiting for me. They are hungry and thirsty." She turned to go, but she found the three wild animals standing in front of her. "What is this? The only path blocked! Oh, mighty beasts, mighty monarchs of the wood," she pleaded, "please let me pass. I am royal, too! A banished prince's wife. When you return home this evening, you can see your children. Let me return to my Jali and Kanhajina. My father is a king; my mother, a queen. Be brothers now in righteousness, and let me pass."

Although she continued pleading, the three great beasts refused to move. They remained there, watching her until the moon was shining overhead. Then they got up and silently moved away, finally allowing Maddi to return to the hermitage.

By the time she reached the end of the covered walk, it was dark, except for the light of the full moon. When she reached the entrance to the hermitage, she cried out, "My children, all dusty from their play, like little fawns with their ears pricked up, always wait for me here. Today I cannot see Jali and Kanhajina. My head is spinning. My children must be dead! Why is the hermitage so quiet? Even the crows and songbirds are silent!"

Confused and frightened, she approached Vessantara and set down the basket of fruit. "Why are you so quiet?" she asked, trembling. "Where are the children? That nightmare comes back to me! Have my children been carried off by some beast of prey? Have they wandered off to play? Are they asleep?"

Vessantara said nothing.

"My husband, why don't you speak to me? What have I done wrong? That I cannot find my children is pain enough, but, if you do not speak to me, I will die from grief!"

"Maddi, royal princess whose glory is great," Vessantara said slowly, "you went for food early in the morning. Why are you so late?"

"Didn't you hear the lion, the tiger, and the leopard roaring? I had so much trouble in the forest. I kept dropping my spade, and my basket kept slipping off my shoulder. My head was spinning, and the dream haunted me all day. I bowed to all four quarters, praying that no harm should come to my daughter or my son. Then, when I tried to come home, those three fierce animals blocked my path. That is why I am late."

Vessantara did not answer.

"I have tended my husband and my children night and day," Maddi cried, becoming more and more distracted. "I have brought wild fruit and roots from the forest. Here is a lily for our daughter, and here is one for Jali. Let's give them these flowers and see them dance. Call them, Sivi, call them! Oh, mighty monarch, since we were banished, we have shared all our joy and sorrow. Please tell me now where my beloved Kanhajina and my Jali are. What have I done to offend the devas so that I cannot see my darlings?"

Vessantara remained perfectly still and silent.

Trembling, Maddi ran from the hut to look for the children. By the light of the full moon she could see the jambu trees, the great banyan, and all the other places where they played. She found some fruit half-eaten, flowers they had cast off, and toys they had been playing with, but there was no trace of the children. After searching all through the hermitage again, she returned to where Vessantara was sitting. He had not moved since she arrived.

"You haven't split the kindling or lit the fire," she said to him. "You haven't even carried water. Why are you sitting here idly? When I return at the end of the day, I would like to rest, but, today, I cannot find Jali and Kanhajina!"

Vessantara neither moved nor spoke.

Maddi ran back to search again in every corner of the hermitage, fearing that she might have overlooked some hiding place.

"Husband!" she wept. "I cannot find my children, nor can I see how they have died!"

Still Vessantara said nothing.

Unable to accept the possibility that the children were not there, Maddi frantically searched a third time in all the same places.

"I have searched everywhere for them or for a sign of what has happened to them, but I can find nothing! Silence hangs over this hermitage like a great black cloud. I can endure no more!" she cried, as she stretched out her arms and fell in a swoon.

"Oh no! She's dead!" thought Vessantara, becoming agitated. "This is not a fit place for Maddi to die. If she had died in Jetuttara, there would have been great splendor. Two entire kingdoms would have mourned. Here in the forest, I am alone. What should I do? What can I do?"

Recovering his presence of mind, he knelt beside her and felt her pulse. Her heart was still beating, and her body was still warm. Although they had lived as ascetics for seven months, Vessantara tenderly laid her head upon his lap, sprinkled her with water, and, with tears in his eyes, rubbed her face and her bosom, trying to revive her. After a few minutes, Maddi opened her eyes. As soon as she had regained her senses, she asked, "My husband, where have the children gone?"

"I have given them to a brahmin," he answered softly.

"My dear, if you gave the children to a brahmin, why didn't you tell me? Why did you let me weep and carry on?"

"I didn't want to cause you pain," Vessantara answered. "This morning, a poor old brahmin came begging for the children. I gave them to him." Before Maddi had a chance to say anything, he continued, "Don't worry, Maddi. Please don't grieve too much. Look at me. Breathe again. We'll get them back, and we'll be happy again. When asked, good men should give whatever they can—grain, cattle, wealth, and even sons. Maddi, rejoice with me! There is no greater gift than one's children."

"I do rejoice!" Maddi reassured him. "I know that there is no greater gift than one's children. Set your mind at ease. My dear husband, in a world of selfish men, you give gifts with a lavish hand. Your generosity does you credit. I pray that you may always give like that!"

"Maddi," he said, greatly relieved and overjoyed that she agreed with him, "if I had not been able to give away my children and, thus, to gain this sublime peace of mind, these great miracles would not have happened." He told her that, when he gave the children to

Jujaka, he had felt a great earthquake, the sky was filled with thunder and lightning, and a great cry arose from the devas.

"Yes," Maddi cried, "I, too, felt the earthquake. I saw the lightning and heard the thunder. Of course, both the Brahmas in the highest heavens and the devas in Tavatimsa rejoiced. There is no greater gift than one's children."

From their arrival in the forest, Sakka had been watching over Vessantara and the hermitage. While Vessantara and Maddi were talking, Sakka thought, "Vessantara willingly gave his children to Jujaka. It is very possible now that some vile creature will come and ask him for the incomparable and virtuous Maddi. It would not do for an undeserving beggar to take her away, leaving the prince alone, helpless and destitute. I must prevent that. I will prevent it, and in so doing, I will enable Vessantara to attain the supreme height of perfection!"

At dawn the next morning, another brahmin appeared at the hermitage and politely greeted Vessantara, inquiring as to his health and well-being.

"Thank you, Brahmin," Vessantara replied. "I am prosperous and well. There are abundant roots and wild fruit here. There are neither annoying insects nor wild beasts of prey to trouble me. I've lived here seven months, and you are the second brahmin to visit. Welcome. Please make yourself at home. Wash your feet, and enjoy the simple hospitality I can offer. Taste this sweet fruit, and drink some of this cool water which comes from a cave hidden high on a hill."

After they had spoken pleasantly for a few minutes, Vessantara asked the brahmin why he had come to the remote forest.

"Mighty prince," the brahmin answered, "you are like a great flood which never fails. I am old, but I have come here to ask for your wife Maddi. Please give her to me."

Vessantara thought, "Yesterday, I let another take both Jali and Kanhajina. Now it is Maddi, my dear devoted wife. I cannot say that I do not love my children or that I do not treasure my faithful wife, but dearer than these is wisdom. Above all, I love perfect knowledge."

He answered the brahmin without hesitation, "I will not hide that I am weary, but gifts delight my heart. Good sir, of my own free will, and with an open hand, I offer you my wife." As he poured water from a pitcher to consecrate the gift, the earth again shook and lightning flashed.

As Maddi listened to this conversation, she neither frowned nor showed surprise. Holding her head erect, she thought, "Vessantara knows best what he is doing." When Vessantara looked at her to see her reaction, she said, as clearly as if a lion were roaring, "From childhood, I have been his wife, and he is my husband still. Prince Vessantara is free to give me to whomever he wishes."

Delighted with her composure and her resolution, the brahmin praised Maddi for her fortitude. He affirmed that the earthquakes and the lightning had been the result of Vessantara's mighty gifts and of his overcoming obstacles, both human and divine. "It is hard to do as good men do," he proclaimed, "and to give as they can give. Virtuous and generous men like you go to heaven, while the evil and stingy fall into hell."

"Now, good prince," he continued, "I give Maddi, your good and lovely wife, back to you. The two of you are perfectly matched to live together harmoniously. Since both of you are of one mind in all things, it is fitting that you stay on here in this forest hermitage and continue doing good."

Then, rising into the air like the morning sun, the brahmin identified himself. "I am Sakka!" he declared. "I have come to test you, and I am satisfied. Eight boons I grant to you. Choose what you will."

"First," Vessantara began, "I wish to be reconciled with my father. Let him call me back and set me on the throne.

"My second wish is that I may never condemn any man to death, even the guiltiest. Instead, let me be able to release from death those who have been condemned.

"May all people—young, middle-aged, and elderly—feel free to look to me for help. This is my third wish.

"Fourth, may I always be contented with my own wife, never straying, never unfaithful.

"My fifth wish, Sakka, is that you grant long life to my beloved son, that he may conquer the world with righteousness.

"Every morning may I receive celestial food. This is my sixth wish.

"My seventh wish is that the means of giving may never fail me and that I may always give wholeheartedly and gladly.

"Finally, may I, at the end of my life, be reborn straightway in heaven."

"These eight boons I grant," Sakka declared. "Very soon, your beloved father will long to see you and will send for you." Then the king of the gods disappeared and returned to his heaven. Confident after having received Sakka's blessing, Maddi and Vessantara resumed their ascetic life.

Meanwhile, Jujaka and the children were trudging through the forest. Every night, Jujaka tied the children with vines and left them lying on the ground. He himself was so terrified of wild beasts that he climbed a tree to sleep safely in the branches. Devas, however, were constantly watching over the children. As soon as Jujaka was gone, they appeared, disguised as the children's parents, and released the bonds. The devas gently massaged the children's hands and feet, washed and fed them, and placed them on a heavenly couch. At dawn, when Jujaka came down from his tree, he would find the children just as he had left them. He never knew that anything had happened. In this way, the children journeyed onward unharmed.

The devas were also guiding Jujaka. He thought he was headed for his home in Kalinga, but, after fifteen days of walking, he had walked sixty yojanas and arrived, instead, in Jetuttara.

The night before they arrived, King Sanjaya had a dream. He dreamed he was sitting on his throne when a man came and handed him two beautiful flowers. He hung the blossoms over his ears, and pollen fell from them, covering his chest. When he awoke, he asked his advisors what the dream meant. "Some noble warriors, Sire, who have been absent for a long time, will return to your kingdom."

After breakfast, the king went to the audience hall, sat on his throne, and waited. The devas guided Jujaka to the courtyard of the palace. As soon as the king saw the children, he asked, "Whose faces are those, shining like gold? Who can those children be? The boy looks like Jali, and the girl very much resembles Kanhajina! They are as beautiful and as golden as two little lion cubs." Excitedly, he sent a courtier to bring them to him.

"Good sir," he said to the brahmin, "tell me where you have brought these children from?"

Jujaka replied, "Two weeks ago they were given to me by one who was quite pleased with his gift."

"By what sort of speech did you manage to get them?" the king asked. "From whom did you receive these children, greatest of all gifts?"

Jujaka replied, "From Prince Vessantara, who, like the great earth, gives without discrimination. He gave me his own children as slaves."

When they heard this, the courtiers heaped scorn upon Vessantara. "That is outrageous!" they cried. "We banished him for giving away his elephant, but now he goes beyond all decency and gives away his children! A man might well give servants, a horse, a mule, a cart, or even an elephant; but how could anyone give away his own children to become slaves? It certainly is good that we got rid of him; he is not fit to be king!"

"Grandfather!" Jali cried, when he heard his father thus wrongly criticized. "What they are saying is not fair! How could my father have given slaves, a horse, a mule, a cart, or an elephant? He has nothing at all!"

"Children, I praise your father's gift," the king quickly reassured them. "I have no words of blame for him. But, tell me, how did he feel? What was in his heart when he gave you to this brahmin?"

Jali replied, "His heart was burning, and it seemed that it would break. His eyes were red, and tears rolled down his cheeks."

"Grandfather," Kanhajina said, speaking out for the first time since they arrived, "this brahmin enjoys beating us with creepers as if we were slaves. He is not really a brahmin, but a yakkha pretending to be a man!"

"My dears," the king said gently, "you used to climb up on my lap. Why are you standing over there so far away?"

Jali answered, "We may be children of a king and queen, but now we are this brahmin's slaves, so we must stay where we are."

King Sanjaya was greatly shaken by their answer. "My dearest children, don't say that. You will break my heart. Come, let me buy you back, and you'll be slaves no more! Tell me what price your father set when he gave you away."

Jali replied, "My price was set at one thousand coins, but, to free my sister, you will have to pay the price of the one hundreds, that is, one hundred each of elephants, horses, bulls, coins, male servants, and female servants."

The king immediately ordered his steward to pay Jujaka the one thousand coins for Jali as well as the full price of the one hundreds for Kanhajina. He also had them prepare a seven-story mansion in which Jujaka could keep all his newly-acquired treasure.

Thoroughly gratified by this unexpected outcome, the old brahmin retired to his new residence to enjoy his wealth. He reclined on a luxurious couch and let himself be served plate after plate of rice, with servings of succulent meat and spicy curries. He indulged his appetite without restraint.

Servants took the children, bathed them, and provided them with fine clothes. After Jali and Kanhajina had been properly fed, they returned to their grandparents. The king took one in his lap, and the queen held the other.

"My dear boy," the king said to Jali, "tell me how your parents are doing. We trust they are both well. Do they have enough to eat? Are they bothered by insects and wild beasts in the forest?"

"Thank you, Sire, for your concern," Jali answered. "Our parents are both well. They are not troubled by insects, nor do wild beasts disturb them. Every day, Mother finds plenty of herbs, nuts, and fruit for us, but she has grown very thin. The exposure to the sun, the heat, and the wind has aged her and darkened her skin. Every night, she sleeps on animal skins spread on the ground."

He paused for just a moment, but, before his grandfather could ask more questions, he continued, "It is customary in the world for a man to love his son, but it seems that you have failed at this. You have not loved my father adequately."

"Yes, my boy. You are right," the king admitted reflectively. "It was wrong of me to drive your father away. I knew that he was innocent. I should not have listened to the people's angry cries. Seeing the error of my decision, I am now ready to bestow upon him my title, all my wealth, and all my power. Let Vessantara, your noble father, come and rule the kingdom of Sivi."

"But, Grandfather," Jali quickly replied, "he will not return at my word. You yourself must go and personally give him your blessing."

"Again you are right, dear boy!" Turning to his commander-in-chief, King Sanjaya ordered, "Prepare my elephants, my horses, and my chariots! Mobilize the entire army! Prepare armor, shields, and banners! Summon all my brahmins and advisors! Invite all my loyal subjects! Let us proceed to Mount Vamka to find Prince Vessantara and to invite him back to the capital!"

The king commanded that the road from Jetuttara all the way to Mount Vamka be leveled and widened to accommodate the procession. He instructed the people to decorate the roadside and to prepare music, entertainment, and refreshments along the entire length of the thoroughfare by which his son would return.

Caught up in the festive atmosphere of these preparations, Jujaka ate so much rich food that his stomach burst, and he died. Although his death was proclaimed throughout the city, no relative could be found, so all his newly acquired property reverted to the king, who arranged a funeral for the brahmin.

In seven days, everything was ready. The king seated himself upon Paccaya, the great white elephant, which had been returned by the grateful king of Kalinga after rains ended their kingdom's drought. The elephant trumpeted loudly with joy at the prospect of being reunited with his master, Vessantara, once more, and the grand procession set out from Jetuttara with Jali as a guide. The chariot wheels and the horses created a thundering din as the army marched in a cloud of dust toward Mount Vamka. They entered the forest and continued marching for one more day and one more night. On the shore of Lake Mucalinda, Prince Jali suggested that a camp be built.

From the hermitage, Vessantara heard the noise of horses and elephants and wondered what it was. "Have they killed my father and come here after me?" he asked Maddi. The two of them climbed the hill to see what was going on.

"Can they be hunters looking for wild animals?" Vessantara wondered. "Are they enemies who have come to kill us?" Maddi looked more carefully and saw that it was the army of Sivi. "Do not worry," she said to her husband. "All will be well. Your enemies could no more hurt you than fire could overcome the sea."

Reassured by these words, Vessantara returned with her to the hermitage.

King Sanjaya called Queen Phusati and said, "My dear, if we all go together, it will be a great shock for the prince. I will go first, alone. Give me time to greet him. After a few minutes, when you are sure that Vessantara and Maddi are calm and reassured, please bring the children, and come with the rest of the company."

Accordingly, the king posted guards at each entrance to the camp, mounted his royal elephant, and set out for the hermitage. His heart filled with delight when he beheld his handsome son sitting fearless and self-composed in front of the hut of leaves. As soon as the prince and Maddi saw the king, they went forward to greet him. Maddi knelt and embraced the king's feet, weeping with joy to see him again.

"I trust, my son, that you are prosperous and well, with plenty of food," the king greeted Vessantara. "Have you been bothered by insects and wild beasts?"

"Sire," Vessantara answered, "it is a wretched life that my wife and I lead here, eating what can be gleaned from the forest. Adversity breaks in a man just as a charioteer breaks in a horse. Adversity has tamed us, and the separation from our parents has made us thin and gaunt, as you can see. Our greatest hardship, however, is that Jali and Kanhajina, your hapless heirs, are no longer here. Even now, I fear, they are being goaded and abused by a merciless brahmin. If you know anything of our royal children, please tell me. If you can, please ease my mind."

"Both Jali and Kanhajina, your lovely children, have been released. I myself paid the brahmin the price you set. Let your heart rest easy, my son, for all is well."

"Father," Vessantara said, greatly relieved to hear this wonderful news, "I hope that you are also well. I would like to hear that my mother has recovered from her sorrow and that she no longer weeps for us."

"Thank you, my son," the king replied. "Both your mother and I are well."

"Is the kingdom peaceful and prosperous?" Vessantara continued.

As the king was about to answer, Queen Phusati appeared with a great company. Vessantara and Maddi went to greet her, and Maddi embraced her mother-in-law's feet. As soon as Jali and Kanhajina saw their mother, they raced forward. The instant Maddi saw the children, she, likewise, ran to meet them. As they threw their arms around each other, laughing and crying, a great quake shook the earth, and lightning flashed across the sky. The entire party swooned, overwhelmed by great emotions of love and joy.

When Sakka saw these six royal personages and their attendants lying senseless on the ground, he sent a gentle shower of rain to revive them. This was, however, a miraculous rain which wetted only those who desired to be wet. When the rain fell on those who wished to remain dry, it rolled off as water rolls off a lotus leaf.

When the courtiers and citizens realized all that had happened, they clamored for Vessantara and Maddi to become their king and queen.

Vessantara turned and faced the king. "Your Majesty," he said, addressing his father, "when I was a royal prince, even though I was behaving righteously, you and the people banished me from the kingdom."

"I was wrong to condemn an innocent man!" the king proclaimed. "I made a grievous mistake in heeding the heated and ill-considered opinion of the populace. I erred in driving my virtuous son into exile."

In a contrite voice, the king spoke pleadingly to his son, "To relieve the suffering of his father and mother, a son should not hesitate to give even his very life, let alone forgiveness of their faults."

Having heard himself exonerated and having regained the respect of the people and of his father, Vessantara agreed to accept the throne his father sought to abdicate.

"Come, Your Majesty!" the people cried to their new king. "It is time to bathe and to wash off the dirt of the forest."

"Wait a moment," Vessantara answered. He went into the hut, took off his ascetic's clothes, and put them away. When he came out, wearing his royal robes, he announced, "This is the place where I have spent nine and a half months in ascetic practices. It was here that I attained the summit of the Perfection of Generosity. Here the perfection of my giving caused the earth to quake."

He silently circumambulated the hut clockwise three times and performed the five-point prostration in front of it, touching the earth with knees, forearms, and forehead. At last, he allowed the courtiers to wash and trim his hair and beard and to pour lustral water over him. As the newly-consecrated king, Vessantara shone in all his glory. When he mounted his richly caparisoned white elephant, surrounded by his sixty thousand courtiers in gorgeous array, joyous music filled the air.

Meanwhile, women attendants bathed Maddi and dressed her in fine robes. As lustral water was sprinkled on her head, the people shouted, "May Vessantara protect our queen!"

Maddi stood beside the children, beaming with joy. "While you were gone, I ate only one meal a day," she told them, "and I slept upon the bare ground. That was the vow of love I made for you. Now that you are safely back, I pray that you may always be protected by whatever good your father and I have done!"

"Let my daughter-in-law wear these robes and jewels," Queen Phusati proclaimed as she presented innumerable boxes to Maddi. So magnificent were these adornments that, when Maddi was dressed, she was as beautiful as a nymph from Tavatimsa. Maddi mounted another noble elephant and rode beside Vessantara back to the camp.

The royal party and all the courtiers stayed in the forest for a month, enjoying various games and sports, but, by the glorious virtue of Vessantara, no animal or bird suffered any injury during that time, and no creature harmed another. When it was time for Vessantara to leave the forest, all the birds and beasts came together to pay their respects. When he finally left the woods, it seemed that all the sounds of joy were gone, and only silence remained.

The return journey of sixty yojanas took two months. All along the way, the royal road was adorned with flowers and bunting. When they arrived in Jetuttara, they found the city richly decorated, and all the citizens came out to welcome the new king and queen.

King Vessantara commanded that all creatures in the realm be set free, even the cats, dogs, birds, and fish. Soon after entering the city, he thought, "Tomorrow morning, supplicants who have heard of my return will come to ask me for gifts. What can I give them?" As a result of this noble thought, Sakka's throne grew hot. As soon as the king of the devas understood the reason, he caused a shower of the seven precious things to fall upon the city, filling the palace grounds waist-high and the city streets knee-deep in precious gems. Vessantara allotted certain areas to various families, but most of the jewels were collected and deposited in a vault in the palace so that he would always have enough to distribute in the future. For the rest of his life, King Vessantara continued giving unstintingly, and, when he died, he was reborn in Tusita heaven.

Having concluded his story, the Buddha identified the birth: "At that time, Devadatta was Jujaka, Cinca-Manavika was Amittatapana, Channa was the forester, Sariputta was the ascetic Accuta, Anuruddha was Sakka, King Suddhodana was King Sanjaya, Queen Maha-Maya was Phusati, Rahula's mother was Queen Maddi, Rahula was Prince Jali, Uppalavanna was Princess Kanhajina, my followers were the rest of the people, and I was King Vessantara."

—Vessantara Jataka

BuddhaGaya

The Search for Enlightenment

"Bhikkhus, before my enlightenment, while I was still only an unenlightened Bodhisatta, I, too, being myself subject to birth, sought what was also subject to birth; being myself subject to aging, sickness, death, sorrow, and defilement, I sought what was also subject to aging, sickness, death, sorrow, and defilement. Then I thought, 'Why, being myself subject to these forms of suffering, do I seek what is also subject to them? Being myself subject to these forms of suffering but having understood the danger in what is subject to them, let me seek the unborn supreme security from bondage, Nibbana.'

"Later, while still young, a black-haired young man in the prime of life, though my mother and father wished otherwise, I shaved off my hair and beard, put on the yellow robe, and went forth from the home life into homelessness.

"Having gone forth in search of the supreme state of sublime peace, I went to Alara Kalama and said to him: 'Friend Kalama, I want to lead the holy life in this doctrine and discipline.'

"Alara Kalama replied: 'You may stay here. This doctrine is such that a wise man can soon realize it for himself through direct knowledge.'

"I soon learned that doctrine. As far as mere reciting went, I could speak with knowledge and assurance, and I claimed, 'I know and see,'' and there were others who did likewise.

"Realizing that it was not through mere faith alone that Alara Kalama realized this doctrine, I went to Alara Kalama and asked him: 'Friend Kalama, in what way do you declare that you realize this doctrine?' In reply, he declared the base of nothingness.

"Making use of faith, energy, mindfulness, concentration, and wisdom, I, too, realized that doctrine and abided in that sphere of nothingness, which is the seventh jhana.'

"Then I went to Alara Kalama and asked him: 'Friend Kalama, is it in this way that you declare that you realize this doctrine?'

"'That is the way, Friend,' he replied.

"I said, 'In the same way, Friend, I also realize this doctrine.'

"'It is a gain for us, Friend,' Alara Kalama replied, 'that we have such a venerable one for our companion in the holy life. The doctrine that I realize is the doctrine that you realize, each for himself with direct knowledge. We are the same. Come, Friend, let us now lead this community together.'

"Thus, Alara Kalama, my teacher, placed me, his pupil, on an equal footing with himself and awarded me the highest honor. It occurred to me, however: 'This doctrine does not lead to dispassion, to peace, to Nibbana, but only to reappearance in the formless plane of nothingness. Not being satisfied with that doctrine, I left.

"Still in search of what is wholesome and of the supreme state of sublime peace, I went to Uddaka Ramaputta and said to him: 'Friend, I want to lead the holy life in this doctrine and discipline.'

"Uddaka Ramaputta replied in the same way that Alara Kalama had. I quickly learned that doctrine, as well. I went to Uddaka Ramaputta and asked him the same question I had asked Alara Kalama. In reply Uddaka Ramaputta declared the base of neither-perception-nor-nonperception.

"Making use of faith, energy, mindfulness, concentration, and wisdom, I, too, realized that doctrine and abided in that sphere of neither-perception-nor-nonperception, which is the eighth jhana.' Then I went to Uddaka Ramaputta and asked him: 'Friend, is it in this way that you declare that you realize this doctrine?'

"'That is the way, Friend,' he replied.

"I said, 'In the same way, Friend, I also realize this doctrine.'

"Uddaka Ramaputta replied in the same way that Alara Kalama had done, and he invited me to lead his community.

"Thus, Uddaka Ramaputta, my companion in the holy life, placed me in the position of a teacher and accorded me the highest honor. It occurred to me, however: 'This doctrine does not lead to dispassion, to peace, to Nibbana, but only to reappearance in the formless plane of neither-perception-nor-nonperception.' Not being satisfied with that doctrine, I left.

"Still in search of what is wholesome and of the supreme state of sublime peace, I wandered by stages through the Magadhan country until, eventually, I arrived at Uruvela. There I saw an agreeable piece of ground, a delightful grove with a clear-flowing river with pleasant, smooth banks, and nearby a village for alms. I thought, 'This will serve for the striving,' and I sat down there.

"Three similes occurred to me spontaneously, never heard before.

"This is the first simile. Suppose there were a wet sappy piece of wood lying in water. Should a man try to light a fire by rubbing a fire-stick against that wet sappy piece of wood lying in the water, he would reap only weariness and disappointment.

"In the same way, those recluses and brahmins who have not renounced sensual pleasures, and whose desire for sensual pleasures has not been fully abandoned, whether or not they experience painful feelings due to exertion, they are incapable of supreme enlightenment.

"This is the second simile. Suppose there were a wet sappy piece of wood lying on dry land far from water. Should a man try to light a fire by rubbing a fire-stick against that wet sappy piece of wood lying on dry land far from water, he would reap only weariness and disappointment.

"In the same way, those recluses and brahmins who have renounced sensual pleasures, but whose desire for sensual pleasures has not been fully abandoned, whether or not they experience painful feelings due to exertion, they are incapable of supreme enlightenment.

"This is the third simile. Suppose there were a dry sapless piece of wood lying on dry land far from water. Should a man try to light a fire by rubbing a fire-stick against that dry sapless piece of wood lying on dry land far from water, he would succeed.

"In the same way, those recluses and brahmins who have renounced sensual pleasures, and whose desire for sensual pleasures has been fully abandoned, whether or not they experience painful feelings due to exertion, they are capable of supreme enlightenment.

"Then, with my teeth clenched and my tongue pressed against the roof of my mouth, I beat down, constrained, and crushed mind with mind. While I did so, sweat ran from my armpits. It was as if a strong man had seized me by the head or shoulders and beat me down, constrained me, and crushed me, but, although tireless energy was aroused in me and unremitting mindfulness was established, my body was overwrought and uncalm because I was exhausted by the painful striving. Such painful feelings that arose in me did not, however, invade my mind.

"Next, I practiced breathingless meditation by stopping the in-breaths and out-breaths through my mouth and nose. While I was doing this, there was a loud sound of wind coming out from my ears like the loud sound from a blacksmith's bellows, but although tireless energy was aroused in me and unremitting mindfulness was established, my body was overwrought and uncalm because I was exhausted by the painful striving. Such painful feelings those arose in me did not, however, invade my mind.

"As I continued practicing this breathingless meditation, violent winds cut through my head as if a strong man had pierced my head with the tip of a sharp sword, but, although tireless energy was aroused in me and unremitting mindfulness was established, my body was overwrought and uncalm because I was exhausted by the painful striving. Such painful feelings that arose in me did not, however, invade my mind.

"As I continued practicing this breathingless meditation, there were violent pains in my head as if a strong man were tightening a tough leather strap around my head, but, although tireless energy was aroused in me and unremitting mindfulness was established, my body was overwrought and uncalm because I was exhausted by the painful striving. Such painful feelings that arose in me did not, however, invade my mind.

"As I continued practicing this breathingless meditation, violent winds carved up my belly, the same as if a skilled butcher were to carve up an ox's belly with a sharp knife, but, although tireless energy was aroused in me and unremitting mindfulness was established, my body was overwrought and uncalm because I was exhausted by the painful striving. Such painful feelings that arose in me did not, however, invade my mind and remain.

"As I continued practicing this breathingless meditation, there was a violent burning in my body as if two strong men had seized me by both arms and were roasting me over a pit of hot coals, but, although tireless energy was aroused in me and unremitting mindfulness was established, my body was overwrought and uncalm because I was exhausted by the painful striving. Such painful feelings that arose in me did not, however, invade my mind and remain.

"When the devas saw me, some said: 'The recluse Gotama is dead. Others said: 'The recluse Gotama is not dead, but he is dying.' Still others said: 'The recluse Gotama is neither dead nor dying; he is an arahat, for such is the way arahats abide.'

"At first, I considered entirely cutting off food, but devas came to me and said: 'Good sir, do not entirely cutting off food. If you do so, we shall infuse heavenly food through the pores of your skin, and you will live on that.' I realized that, if I claimed to be completely fasting while these devas infused heavenly food through the pores of my skin, I would have been lying.' Therefore, I dismissed those devas, saying: 'There is no need.'

"Then I decided to take very little food, a mouthful of gruel each time. In this way, my body reached a state of extreme emaciation. My limbs became like the jointed segments of vine or bamboo stems. My backside became like a camel's hoof. The projections on my spine stood out like strung beads. My ribs jutted out like the crazy rafters of an old roofless barn. Then my eyes sank far down in their sockets like water in a deep well. My scalp shriveled up like a bitter gourd in the sun. If I touched my belly, I felt my backbone. If I defecated or urinated, I fell over on my face. If I tried to ease my body by rubbing my limbs with my hands, the hair, rotted at its roots, fell from my body as I rubbed. The bright color of my skin deteriorated.

"I knew that, no matter what recluses or brahmins of the past, present, or future had experienced, were experiencing, or would experience, I was experiencing the utmost in painful feelings due to exertion, beyond which there was nothing more. By that racking practice of austerities, however, I had attained neither any superhuman states nor any distinction in knowledge and vision worthy of the noble ones. I wondered whether there was another path to enlightenment.'

"I recalled that once, when my father, the Sakyan king was performing the plowing festival, while I was sitting in the cool shade of a rose-apple tree, quite secluded from sensual pleasures and unwholesome states, I had attained the first jhana, which is accompanied by applied and sustained thought, with rapture and pleasure born of seclusion. I wondered whether that could be the path to enlightenment. Then I realized that, indeed, it was.

"I asked myself why I was afraid of that pleasure that has nothing to do with sensual pleasures and unwholesome states. Then I declared, "I am not afraid of that pleasure."

"I realized that it was not easy to attain that pleasure with a body so excessively emaciated. Thus, I decided to eat some solid food.

"A young woman named Sujata from the nearby village had vowed that if she had a son she would make an offering to the deva of the banyan tree under which I sat. She brought rich milk rice in a golden bowl and offered it to me, as if I were that tree's deva. I took the bowl to the Neranjara bank, bathed at the Suppatitthita Ford, and ate the meal. That portion of milk rice was my only food for forty-nine days, but it was sufficient because devas had infused it with divine sustenance.

"At that time, five ascetics were waiting upon me, thinking, 'If our recluse Gotama achieves some higher state, he will inform us.'

"When they saw that I ate the milk rice, however, those five ascetics were disgusted and left me, thinking, 'The recluse Gotama has given up his striving and reverted to luxury.'

"After I had eaten solid food and regained my strength, quite secluded from sensual pleasures and unwholesome states, I attained that first jhana, but the pleasant feelings that arose in me did not invade my mind.

"With the stilling of applied and sustained thought, I attained the second jhana. With the fading away of rapture, I attained the third jhana. With the abandoning of pleasure and pain, I attained the fourth jhana, but, in each case, the pleasant feelings that arose in me did not invade my mind.

"When my concentrated mind was thus purified, bright, malleable, and steady, I directed it to knowledge of the recollection of past lives. I recollected my manifold past lives with their aspects and particulars.

"This was the first true knowledge, attained by me in the first watch of the night. Ignorance was banished and true knowledge arose, darkness was banished and light arose, but the pleasant feelings that arose in me did not invade my mind and remain.

"Then I directed my mind to knowledge of the passing away and reappearance of beings. With the divine eye, which is purified and surpasses the human, I saw beings passing away and reappearing, inferior and superior, fair and ugly, fortunate and unfortunate, and I understood how beings pass on according to their actions.

"This was the second true knowledge, attained by me in the middle watch of the night.

"Then I directed my mind to knowledge of the destruction of the taints. I directly knew as it actually is: 'This is suffering,' 'This is the origin of suffering,' `This is the cessation of suffering,' and 'This is the way leading to the cessation of suffering.' I directly knew as it actually is: 'These are the taints,' 'This is the origin of the taints,' 'This is the cessation of the taints,' and 'This is the way leading to the cessation of the taints.'

"When I knew and saw all of this, my mind was liberated from the taint of sensual desire, from the taint of being, and from the taint of ignorance. I knew that my mind was liberated, and I directly knew: 'Birth is destroyed, the holy life has been lived, what had to be done has been done, there is no more coming to any state of being.'

"This was the third true knowledge, attained by me in the last watch of the night. Ignorance was banished, and true knowledge arose, darkness was banished and light arose, but the pleasant feelings that arose in me did not invade my mind.

"Then, being myself subject to birth, aging, sickness, death, sorrow, and defilement, having understood the danger in what is subject to them, I attained the supreme security from bondage, Nibbana.

"The knowledge and vision arose in me: 'My deliverance is unshakable; this is my last birth; now there is no renewal of being.'

"I thought: 'This Dhamma that I have attained is profound, hard to see and hard to understand, peaceful and sublime, unattainable by mere reasoning, subtle, and to be experienced by the wise. This generation, however, delights in attachment. Therefore, my mind inclined to inaction rather than to teaching the Dhamma.

"Brahma Sahampati knew what I was thinking and thought: 'The world will be lost, the world will perish, since the mind of the Tathagata, accomplished and fully enlightened, inclines to inaction rather than to teaching the Dhamma.' Just as quickly as a strong man might extend his flexed arm or flex his extended arm, Brahma Sahampati appeared before me. He extended his hands in reverential salutation toward me, and said: 'Let the Blessed One teach the Dhamma, let the Sublime One teach the Dhamma. There are beings with little dust in their eyes who are falling away through not hearing the Dhamma. There will be those who will understand the Dhamma. Open the doors to the Deathless!'

"I listened to the Brahma's pleading, and, out of compassion for beings, I surveyed the world with the eye of a Buddha and saw various kinds of beings. Just as one sees in a pond of lotuses, some lotuses that are born and grow in the water thrive immersed in the water, without rising out of it; some lotuses that are born and grow in the water rest on the water's surface; and some lotuses that are born and grow in the water rise out of the water and stand clear, unwetted by it; in the same way, I saw beings with little dust in their eyes and with much dust in their eyes, with keen and dull faculties, with good and bad qualities, easy to teach and hard to teach.

"Thus, I consented to the request of Brahma Sahampati and determined to teach the Dhamma subtle and sublime. Satisfied, Brahma Sahampati paid homage to me and departed."

—Majjhima Nikaya 26

The Struggle with Mara

"I was staying on the bank of the Neranjara River engaged in deep struggle, practicing meditation with all my strength in the effort to find freedom from bondage. Mara came up to me, stood right next to me, and started talking to me as though he were full of sympathy: 'You're so thin and pale,' he said. 'Why, you're near to death! I'll bet a thousand to one you're going to die; there's only the slightest chance that you'll survive! My dear sir, live! It's far better to live; you could accumulate merit if you stayed alive. You could lead the religious life and perform offerings to the fire god. It's a sure way to get lots of merit. What's the point of all this exertion? The path of exertion and struggle is difficult, hard and strenuous, and full of troubles.'

"I replied, 'Why have you come here, evil one, you friend of negligence? I do not need the least merit you speak of. Mara, you should preach about merits to those who need them. I have confidence, energy, and wisdom, and I have made great effort. Why do you inquire about my living and dying? When the wind blows, even rivers and streams dry up. So why shouldn't my blood dry up in this struggle?

"'As the blood dries up, so, too, will bile and phlegm. The body may waste away, but the mind will become more and more settled, and mindfulness, wisdom and concentration will be established.

"'Experiencing, in this way, the extremes of sensation, my mind no longer aspires for sensuous pleasures.

"'Your first army is desire; the second is discontent; the third is hunger and thirst; the fourth is craving; the fifth is laziness; the sixth is cowardice; the seventh is doubt; the eighth is hypocrisy and obstinacy; the ninth is undeserved praise and gain; and the tenth is praising oneself and disparaging others. These, Mara, are your forces. Anyone less than a hero will not be victorious over them and attain supreme bliss.

"'Look! Do you see this tuft of munja grass I am wearing? It shows that I do not care for life. I would rather die in this conflict than stay alive, defeated.

"'There are ascetics who have drowned in defilements and never see that path which the well-conducted ones tread. I can see the troops all around me, with you, Mara, mounted on your elephant, Girimekhala, and yet I go forward into the struggle.

"'Even though the whole world, inclusive of its gods, cannot defeat your armies, I am going to destroy them with the power of wisdom as an unfired clay pot is smashed with a stone. With disciplined thought and firmly-grounded mindfulness, I shall travel from country to country training numerous disciples. Alert and energetic in the practice of my teaching, contrary to your wish, they will attain that liberation which is the perfect protection from grief.'

"'I've followed the Blessed One for seven years,' said Mara, 'and I've watched every step he's made. Not once have I had access to him, who has always been so alert and mindful. I remember once seeing a crow hovering above what looked like a lump of fat on the ground below. "Ah, food!" it thought. But the lump turned out to be a rock, hard and inedible, and the crow flew away disgusted. I've had enough. I feel like that rock-eating crow. I'm going away. I've finished with Gotama!'

"Mara was so upset by his failure that he dropped the lute he was carrying, and, at the moment it hit the ground, he disappeared."

—Sutta Nipata 3, 2

Mucalinda

Thus have I heard. During the third week after his enlightenment, the Buddha was meditating beside a pond in Uruvela not far from the Neranjara River.

At that time, a tremendous, unseasonable thunderstorm arose, with much rain and strong cold wind.

The naga king, Mucalinda, left his pond, encircled the Buddha's body seven times with his coils, and lifted him above the flood water. Spreading his great hood over the Buddha's head, the naga protected the Buddha from the storm.

After seven days, when the Buddha emerged from his meditation, Mucalinda uncoiled himself, assumed the appearance of a handsome youth, and paid his respects to the Buddha with folded hands.

The Buddha spoke this inspired utterance:

For one who is content, who has learned Dhamma, and
who sees,
Blissful is solitude, non-affliction in the world, and
restraint toward living beings.

Blissful is dispassion and the overcoming of sensual
desires
Blissful is the realization of nonself, which is, indeed, the
highest bliss.

—Udana 2,1

Dependent Origination

For seven days, after the Buddha attained Enlightenment at the foot of the Bodhi Tree beside the Neranjara River in Uruvela, he remained there, sitting cross-legged and experiencing the bliss of liberation. At the end of those seven days, he emerged from that concentration and, during the first watch of the night, directed his full attention to dependent arising in forward order, thus: "This being, that is; from the arising of this, that arises.

That is:

with ignorance as condition, volitional activities come to be;
with volitional activities as condition, consciousness comes
to be;
with consciousness as condition, name-and-form comes to be;
with name-and-form as condition, the six sense bases
come to be;
with the sense bases as condition, contact comes to be;
with contact as condition, feeling comes to be;
with feeling as condition, craving comes to be;
with craving as condition, grasping comes to be;
with grasping as condition, becoming comes to be;
with becoming as condition, birth comes to be;
with birth as condition, aging-and-death, sorrow,
lamentation, pain, grief, and despair come to be.
This is the origin of this whole mass of suffering."

During the middle watch of the night, he directed his full attention to dependent arising in reverse order, thus: "This not being, that is not; from the cessation of this, that ceases.

That is:

from the cessation of ignorance, volitional activities cease;
from the cessation of volitional activities, consciousness ceases;
from the cessation of consciousness, name-and-form ceases;
from the cessation of name-and-form, the six sense bases cease;
from the cessation of the six sense bases, contact ceases;
from the cessation of contact, feeling ceases;
from the cessation of feeling, craving ceases;
from the cessation of craving, grasping ceases;
from the cessation of grasping, becoming ceases;
from the cessation of becoming, birth ceases;
from the cessation of birth, aging-and-death, sorrow, lamentation, pain, grief, and despair cease.
This is the ceasing of this whole mass of suffering."

During the last watch of the night, he directed his full attention to dependent arising in both forward and reverse order, thus: "This being, that is; from the arising of this, that arises; this not being, that is not; from the cessation of this, that ceases.

That is:

with ignorance as condition, volitional activities come to be; ...
with birth as condition, aging-and-death, sorrow, lamentation, pain, grief, and despair come to be.
This is the origin of this whole mass of suffering.

From the complete disappearance and cessation of
ignorance, volitional activities cease; …
from the complete disappearance and cessation of birth,
aging-and-death, sorrow, lamentation, pain, grief, and
despair cease.
This is the ceasing of this whole mass of suffering."

—Udana 1,1~3

The Four Foundations of Mindfulness

After Enlightenment, while still in Uruvela, the Buddha had misgivings about preaching the Dhamma which he had realized to a world blinded by passions and prejudices. Brahma Sahampati, noticing his hesitation, appeared before the Buddha and urged him to teach out of compassion for gods and men. As the Buddha continued pondering this question, he realized that the sole method of winning Nibbana was to cultivate the four foundations of mindfulness. This is the formulation he expounded.

The one-way path for the purification of beings, for the elimination of suffering, and for the realization of Nibbana is the four foundations of mindfulness-contemplation of the body, contemplation of feelings, contemplation of the mind, and contemplation of phenomena.

How does one dwell contemplating the body in the body?

Having gone to the forest, to the foot of a tree, or to an empty hut, one sits down, folds his legs crosswise, straightens his body, and establishes mindfulness in front of him. Mindfully one breathes in and out. Breathing in long, one understands: "I breathe in long"; or, breathing out long, one understands: "I breathe out long." Breathing in short, one understands: "I breathe in short"; or breathing out short, one understands: "I breathe out short." One trains oneself thus: "I will breathe in experiencing the whole body"; "I will breathe out experiencing the whole body"; "I will breathe in calming the activity of the body"; and "I will breathe out calming the activity of the body." Just as a skilled lathe-worker understands, "I make a long turn" or "I make a short turn," one understands his breathing.

When walking, one understands: "I am walking"; when standing, one understands: "I am standing"; when sitting, one understands: "I am sitting"; when lying down, one understands: "I am lying down"; or one understands, accordingly, however his body is disposed.

One acts with clear comprehension when going forward and returning; when looking ahead and looking away; when bending and stretching his limbs; when eating, drinking, chewing, and tasting; when defecating and urinating; and when walking, standing, sitting, falling asleep, waking up, talking, and keeping silent.

One reviews this same body up from the soles of the feet and down from the top of the head, bounded by skin, as full of many kinds of impurity thus: "In this body there are head-hairs, body-hairs, nails, teeth, skin, flesh, sinews, bones, marrow, kidneys, heart, liver, diaphragm, spleen, lungs, intestines, mesentery, stomach, excrement, brain, bile, phlegm, pus, blood, sweat, lymph, tears, serum, saliva, nasal mucous, synovial fluid, and urine." Just as though there were a bag full of many sorts of grain, such as hill rice, red rice, beans, peas, millet, and white rice, and a man with good eyes were to open it and review it thus: "This is hill rice, this is red rice, these are beans, these are peas, this is millet, this is white rice"; so, too, one reviews this body.

One reviews this same body as consisting of elements thus: "In this body there are the earth element, the water element, the fire element, and the air element." Just as though a skilled butcher had killed a cow and were seated at the crossroads with it cut up into pieces; so, too, one reviews this same body as consisting of elements.

As though one were to see a corpse thrown aside in a charnel ground, one, two, or three days dead, bloated, and oozing matter, one compares this same body with it thus: 'This body, too, is of the same nature, it will be like that, it is not exempt from that fate.'

As though one were to see a corpse thrown aside in a charnel ground, being devoured by crows, vultures, dogs, jackals, or worms, one compares this same body with it thus: 'This body, too, is of the same nature, it will be like that, it is not exempt from that fate.'

As though one were to see a corpse thrown aside in a charnel ground—a skeleton with flesh and blood, held together with sinews; a fleshless skeleton smeared with blood, held together with sinews; a skeleton without flesh and blood, held together with sinews; or disconnected bones scattered in all directions—here a hand-bone, there a foot-bone, here a shin-bone, there a thigh-bone, here a hip-bone, there a back-bone, here the skull—one compares this same body with it thus: "This body, too, is of the same nature, it will be like that, it is not exempt from that fate."

As though one were to see a corpse thrown aside in a charnel ground—bones bleached white, the color of shells; bones heaped up; or bones more than a year old, rotted and crumbled to dust—one compares this same body with it thus: "This body, too, is of the same nature, it will be like that, it is not exempt from that fate."

In any of these ways, one may dwell contemplating the body in the body internally, externally, or both internally and externally. One may contemplate in the body its nature of arising, its nature of vanishing, or its nature of both arising and vanishing. Mindfulness that "there is a body" may simply be established to the extent necessary for bare knowledge and repeated mindfulness. In this way, one dwells independent, not clinging to anything in the world. Thus, does one dwell contemplating the body in the body.

How does one dwell contemplating feelings in feelings?

Here, when experiencing a pleasant feeling, one understands: "I experience a pleasant feeling"; when experiencing a painful feeling, one understands: "I experience a painful feeling"; when experiencing a neutral feeling, one understands: "I experience a neutral feeling." It is the same for every carnal feeling and for every spiritual feeling.

In this way, one may contemplate feelings in feelings internally, externally, or both internally and externally. One may contemplate in feelings their nature of arising, their nature of vanishing, or their nature of both arising and vanishing. Mindfulness that "there is feeling" may simply be established to the extent necessary for bare knowledge and repeated mindfulness. In this way, one dwells independent, not clinging to anything in the world. Thus, does one dwell contemplating feelings in feelings.

How does one dwell contemplating mind in mind.

Here one understands a mind with lust as a mind with lust and a mind without lust as a mind without lust. It is the same for a mind with or without hatred, with or without delusion, contracted or distracted, exalted or unexalted, surpassable or unsurpassable, concentrated or unconcentrated, and liberated or unliberated.

In this way, one may contemplate mind in mind internally, externally, or both internally and externally. One may contemplate in mind its nature of arising, its nature of vanishing, or its nature of both arising and vanishing. Mindfulness that "there is mind" may simply be established to the extent necessary for bare knowledge and repeated mindfulness. In this way, one dwells independent, not clinging to anything in the world. Thus, does one dwell contemplating mind as mind.

How does one dwell contemplating phenomena in phenomena?

One contemplates phenomena in phenomena in terms of the five hindrances. When sensual desire is present, one understands: "There is sensual desire in me"; or, when no sensual desire is present, one understands: "There is no sensual desire in me." One also understands how unarisen sensual desire arises, how arisen sensual desire is abandoned, and how abandoned sensual desire does not arise again in the future.

In the same way, one understands ill-will, sloth and torpor, restlessness and worry, and doubt.

One dwells contemplating phenomena in phenomena in terms of the five aggregates subject to clinging. One understands: "Such is form, such its origin, such its passing away; such is feeling, such its origin, such its passing away; such is perception, such its origin, such its passing away; such are the volitional formations, such their origin, such their passing away; such is consciousness, such its origin, such its passing away." Thus does one dwell contemplating phenomena in phenomena in terms of the five aggregates subject to clinging.

One dwells contemplating phenomena in phenomena in terms of the six internal and external sense bases. One understands the eye, forms, and the fetter that arises dependent on both. One also understands how the unarisen fetter arises, how the arisen fetter is abandoned, and how the abandoned fetter does not arise again in the future.

In the same way, one understands the ear and sounds, the nose and odors, the tongue and flavors, and the body and tactile objects.

One dwells contemplating phenomena in phenomena in terms of the seven enlightenment factors. When the mindfulness enlightenment factor is present, one understands: "There is the mindfulness enlightenment factor in me"; or, when no mindfulness enlightenment factor is present, one understands: "There is no mindfulness enlightenment factor in me." One also understands how the unarisen mindfulness enlightenment factor arises and how the arisen mindfulness enlightenment factor comes to fulfillment by development.

In the same way, one understands the discrimination of phenomena enlightenment factor, the energy enlightenment factor, the rapture enlightenment factor, the tranquillity enlightenment factor, the concentration enlightenment factor and the equanimity enlightenment factor.

One dwells contemplating phenomena in phenomena in terms of the Four Noble Truths. One understands as it really is: "This is suffering, this is the origin of suffering, this is the cessation of suffering, and this is the way leading to the cessation of suffering."

In this way, one may contemplate phenomena in phenomena internally, externally, or both internally and externally. One may contemplate in phenomena their nature of arising, their nature of vanishing, or their nature of both arising and vanishing. Mindfulness that "there are phenomena" may simply be established to the extent necessary for bare knowledge and repeated mindfulness. In this way, one dwells independent, not clinging to anything in the world.

If anyone develops these four foundations of mindfulness in such a way for seven years, one of two fruits can be expected for him: either final knowledge here and now, or, if there is a trace of clinging left, non-returning.

Let alone seven years, one year, one month, and even two weeks. If anyone develops these four foundations of mindfulness in such a way for seven days, one of two fruits can be expected for him: either final knowledge here and now, or, if there is a trace of clinging left, non-returning.

This is the direct path for the purification of beings, for the surmounting of sorrow and lamentation, for the passing away of pain and dejection, for the attainment of the true way, for the realization of Nibbana—namely, the four foundations of mindfulness.

—Majjhima Nikaya 10, Satipatthana Sutta

Sarnath

Setting in Motion the Wheel of the Dhamma

Thus have I heard. On one occasion the Buddha was staying at the Deer Park in Isipatana in Baranasi. There he addressed the group of five thus:

"There are two extremes which should not be followed. What two? The pursuit of sensual happiness in sensual pleasures, which is low, vulgar, ignoble, and unbeneficial; and the pursuit of self-mortification, which is painful, ignoble, and unbeneficial. Without veering toward either of these extremes, the Tathagata has awakened to the middle way, which gives rise to vision and knowledge, and which leads to peace, to direct knowledge, to enlightenment, and to Nibbana.

"And what, Bhikkhus, is that middle way which leads to Nibbana? It is the Noble Eightfold Path: that is, Right view, Right thought, Right speech, Right action, Right livelihood, Right effort, Right mindfulness, and Right concentration.

"Here is the noble truth of suffering. Birth is suffering, aging is suffering, illness is suffering, death is suffering, union with what is displeasing is suffering, separation from what is pleasing is suffering, and not to get what one wants is suffering. In brief, the five aggregates of clinging are suffering.

"Here is the noble truth of the origin of suffering. It is craving which leads to renewed existence, along with delight and lust and seeking delight here and there. It is the craving for sensual pleasures, the craving for existence, and the craving for extermination.

"Here is the noble truth of the cessation of suffering. It is the complete fading away and cessation of that craving, the giving up and relinquishing of it, freedom from it, and non-reliance on it.

"Here is the noble truth of the way leading to the cessation of suffering. It is the Noble Eightfold Path, mentioned before: Right view, Right thought, Right speech, Right action, Right livelihood, Right effort, Right mindfulness, and Right concentration.

"In regard to things unheard before, there arose in me vision, knowledge, wisdom, true knowledge, and light: namely,

"'This is the noble truth of suffering';

"'This noble truth of suffering is to be fully understood';

"'This noble truth of suffering has been fully understood';

"'This is the noble truth of the origin of suffering';

"'This noble truth of the origin of suffering is to be abandoned';

"'This noble truth of the origin of suffering has been abandoned';

"'This is the noble truth of the cessation of suffering';

"'This noble truth of the cessation of suffering is to be realized';

"'This noble truth of the cessation of suffering has been realized';

"'This is the noble truth of the way leading to the cessation of suffering';

"'This noble truth of the way leading to the cessation of suffering is to be developed';

"'This noble truth of the way leading to the cessation of suffering has been developed.'

"As long as my knowledge and vision of these Four Noble Truths as they really are in these three phases and twelve aspects was not thoroughly purified in this way, I did not claim to have awakened to the unsurpassed perfect enlightenment in this world with its devas, Maras, and Brahmas, in this generation with its ascetics and brahmins and with its devas and humans. When my knowledge and vision of these Four Noble Truths as they really are in these three phases and twelve aspects was thoroughly purified in this way, however, then I claimed to have awakened to that unsurpassed perfect enlightenment. The knowledge and vision arose in me: 'Unshakable is the liberation of my mind. This is my last birth. Now there is no more renewed existence.'"

The group of five were elated and delighted in the Buddha's words. During this discourse, there arose in Venerable Kondañña the dust-free, stainless vision of the Dhamma: "Whatever is subject to origination is subject to cessation."

The earth-dwelling devas raised a cry: "In the Deer Park in Isipatana, this unsurpassed Wheel of the Dhamma has been set in motion by the Blessed One! It cannot be stopped by any ascetic, brahmin, deva, Mara, or Brahma, nor by anyone in the world!" Having heard this, the devas of the realm of the Four Great Kings raised the same cry. Having heard their cry, the Tavatimsa devas raised the same cry. Thus, it continued through the Yama devas, the Tusita devas, the Nimmanarati devas, the Paranimmitavasavatti devas, and the devas of Brahma's company.

Thus, at that very moment, the cry spread as far as the Brahma world, this ten-thousandfold world system shook, and an immeasurable glorious radiance, surpassing the majesty of the devas, appeared in the world.

Then the Buddha declared: "Kondañña has indeed understood!" Thereafter, Venerable Kondañña was known as "Añña Kondañña—Kondañña Who Has Understood."

—Samyutta Nikaya 56, 11

The Characteristic of Nonself

Thus have I heard. On one occasion, the Blessed One was staying at the Deer Park of Isipatana in Baranasi. There the Blessed One addressed the bhikkhus of the group of five thus:

"Form is nonself. For, if form were self, this form would not lead to affliction, and it would be possible to have it of form: 'Let my form be thus; let my form not be thus.' But, because form is nonself, form leads to affliction, and it is not possible to have it of form: 'Let my form be thus; let my form not be thus.'

"Feeling is nonself....

"Perception is nonself....

"Volitional formations are nonself....

"Consciousness is nonself. For, if consciousness were self, this consciousness would not lead to affliction, and it would be possible to have it of consciousness: 'Let my consciousness be thus; let my consciousness not be thus.' But, because consciousness is nonself, consciousness leads to affliction, and it is not possible to have it of consciousness: 'Let my consciousness be thus; let my consciousness not be thus.'

"What do you think, is form permanent or impermanent?"

"Impermanent, Venerable Sir."

"Is feeling permanent or impermanent?"

"Impermanent, Venerable Sir."

"Is perception permanent or impermanent?"

"Impermanent, Venerable Sir."

"Are volitional formations permanent or impermanent?"

"Impermanent, Venerable Sir."

"Is consciousness permanent or impermanent?"

"Impermanent, Venerable Sir."

"Is what is impermanent suffering or happiness?"

"Suffering, Venerable Sir."

"Is what is impermanent, suffering, and subject to change fit to be regarded thus: 'This is mine, this I am, this is my self'?"

"No, Venerable Sir."

"Therefore, any kind of form, feeling, perception, volitional formations, and consciousness whatsoever, whether past, future, or present, internal or external, gross or subtle, inferior or superior, far or near, should be seen as it really is with correct wisdom thus: 'This is not mine, this I am not, this is not my self.'

"Seeing thus, the instructed noble disciple experiences revulsion toward form, revulsion toward feeling, revulsion toward perception, revulsion toward volitional formations, revulsion toward consciousness. Experiencing revulsion, he becomes dispassionate.

Through dispassion, his mind is liberated. When it is liberated, there comes the knowledge: 'It's liberated.' He understands: 'Destroyed is birth; the holy life has been lived; what had to be done has been done; there is no more for this state of being.'"

That is what the Blessed One said, and, while this discourse was being spoken, the minds of the bhikkhus of the group of five were liberated from the taints by non-clinging.

—Samyutta Nikaya 22, 59

Gayasisa

All Is Burning

The fire-worshiping ascetic, Uruvela-Kassapa, lived at Gayasisa on the bank of the Neranjara with five hundred followers. His brothers, Nadi-Kassapa and Gaya-Kassapa, lived a little downriver with three hundred and two hundred disciples, respectively.

The Buddha visited Uruvela-Kassapa and stayed overnight where the sacred fire was kept, despite Kassapa's warning of a fierce naga there. Using his supernatural powers, the Buddha subdued two mighty nagas which emitted fire and smoke. Kassapa was pleased with the Buddha's exhibition of supernatural power and invited him to stay longer. The Buddha resided in a nearby grove for the entire rainy season, waiting for the time when Kassapa should be ready for conversion.

Kassapa accepted that the Buddha had great powers, but he persisted in believing, "Gotama is not an arahat like me." At last, the Buddha shocked Kassapa with an announcement that the ascetic was neither an arahat nor on the path leading to arahatship. Kassapa admitted defeat and reverently asked for ordination. Following their teacher, all of Kassapa's students cut off their hair, threw it, along with all their fire-worship paraphernalia into the river, and asked for admission to the Sangha.

Nadi-Kassapa and Gaya-Kassapa were amazed to see all the matted locks and the ritual utensils floating down the river and rushed upstream to find out what had happened to their brother. They, too, along with their pupils, were ordained.

Then the Buddha delivered this discourse to them.

"All is burning. And what is the all that is burning? The eye is burning, forms are burning, eye-consciousness is burning, eye-contact is burning, and whatever feeling arises with eye-contact as condition—whether pleasant, painful, or neutral—that, too, is burning.

Burning with what? Burning with the fire of lust, with the fire of hatred, with the fire of delusion; burning with birth, aging, and death; with sorrow, lamentation, pain, displeasure, and despair.

"The ear, sounds, ear-consciousness, ear-contact, and whatever feeling arises with ear-contact as condition—all that is burning with the fire of lust, hatred, and delusion.

"The nose, odors, nose-consciousness, nose-contact, and whatever feeling arises with nose-contact as condition—all that is burning with the fire of lust, hatred, and delusion.

"The tongue, tastes, tongue-consciousness, tongue-contact, and whatever feeling arises with tongue-contact as condition—all that is burning with the fire of lust, hatred, and delusion.

"The body, tactile objects, body-consciousness, body-contact, and whatever feeling arises with body-contact as condition—all that is burning with the fire of lust, hatred, and delusion.

"The mind is burning, mental objects are burning, mind-consciousness is burning, mind-contact is burning, and whatever feeling arises with mind-contact as condition-whether pleasant, painful, or neutral—that, too, is burning. Burning with the fire of lust, with the fire of hatred, with the fire of delusion; burning with birth, aging, and death; with sorrow, lamentation, pain, displeasure, and despair.

"Seeing thus, the instructed noble disciple experiences revulsion toward the eye, forms, eye-consciousness, eye-contact, and whatever feeling arises with eye-contact as condition—whether pleasant, painful, or neutral.

"In the same way, he experiences revulsion toward the ear, the nose, the tongue, the body, and the mind.

"Experiencing revulsion, he becomes dispassionate. Through dispassion his mind is liberated. When it is liberated, there comes the knowledge: 'It's liberated.' He understands: 'Destroyed is birth, the holy life has been lived, what had to be done has been done, there is no more for this state of being.'"

Elated, those one thousand bhikkhus delighted in the Buddha's words, and their minds were liberated from the taints by non-clinging.

—Samyutta Nikaya 35, 28

Rajagaha

The Road to Rajagaha

Once, a brahmin asked the Buddha, "Master Gotama, why do some of your disciples attain Nibbana and some do not?"

The Buddha replied, "Suppose a man comes to you and says, 'Sir, I want to go to Rajagaha. Please show me the way.' Then you tell him, 'Now, good man, this road goes to Rajagaha. Follow it for awhile, and you will come to a village. Go a little further, and you will come to a town. Go a little further, and you will arrive at Rajagaha with its lovely parks, groves, meadows, and ponds.' Then, having been thus advised and instructed by you, he takes a wrong road and goes to the west. Then a second man comes to you and says, 'Sir, I want to go to Rajagaha. Please show me the way.' You reply in the same way as before. Having been thus advised and instructed by you, he follows the road and arrives safely in Rajagaha. Now, since Rajagaha exists, the path leading to Rajagaha exists, and you are present as the guide, why, when those men have been thus advised and instructed by you, does one man take a wrong road and the other arrive safely in Rajagaha?"

"What can I do about that, Master Gotama? I am only one who shows the way."

"So too, Nibbana exists, the path leading to Nibbana exists, and I am present as the guide. Yet, when my disciples have been thus advised and instructed by me, some of them attain Nibbana, the ultimate goal, and some do not. What can I do about that? The Tathagata is one who shows the way."

—Majjhima Nikaya 107

The Fruits of the Homeless Life

On the full-moon night of the fourth month, King Ajatasattu of Magadha, went up to the roof of his palace and was surrounded by his ministers. "Delightful, friends, is this moonlit night!" he exclaimed. "Charming and auspicious is this moonlit night! Can we not visit some ascetic or brahmin this evening who would bring peace to our heart?"

"Sire," one minister replied, "Purana Kassapa has many followers. He is well-known, renowned, the founder of a sect, highly honored by the multitude, long-since gone forth, aged and venerable. May Your Majesty visit this Purana Kassapa. He may well bring peace to Your Majesty's heart." At these words King Ajatasattu was silent.

Other ministers successively suggested Ajita Kesakambali, Makkhali Gosala, Pakudha Kaccayana, Sanjaya Belatthaputta, Nigantha Nataputta, all of whom were equally famous. At each suggestion, King Ajatasattu remained silent.

All this time, Jivaka was sitting silently near King Ajatasattu. The King said to him: "Friend Jivaka, why are you silent?"

"Sire," Jivaka replied, "the Buddha, the arahat, the fully-enlightened One, is staying in my mango grove with twelve hundred and fifty bhikkhus. It is said: 'The Blessed One is an arahat, perfectly enlightened, accomplished in true knowledge and conduct, well-gone, a knower of worlds, the unsurpassed trainer of people to be tamed, a teacher of devas and humans, Enlightened, and Exalted.' May Your Majesty visit the Buddha. He may well bring peace to Your Majesty's heart."

"Then, Jivaka, have the riding-elephants made ready."

"Very good, Sire," said Jivaka, and he had five hundred she-elephants prepared and, for the king, the royal tusker. Then he reported, "Sire, the riding-elephants are ready. Now is the time to do as Your Majesty wishes." King Ajatasattu placed his wives on the she-elephants, mounted the royal tusker, and proceeded in royal state.

Accompanied by torch-bearers, the procession marched from Rajagaha toward Jivaka's mango grove.

When King Ajatasattu came near the mango grove, he became terrified, and his hair stood on end. "Friend Jivaka," he said, "are you deceiving me? Are you tricking me? Are you delivering me up to an enemy? How is it that from this great number of twelve hundred and fifty bhikkhus not a sneeze, a cough, or a sound is to be heard?"

"Have no fear, Your Majesty, I would not deceive you, trick you, or deliver you up to an enemy. Approach, Sire. There are lights burning in the pavilion."

King Ajatasattu rode on his elephant as far as was appropriate. Then he dismounted and continued on foot to the door of the pavilion. "Jivaka," he asked, "where is the Blessed One?"

"That is the Blessed One sitting against the middle column with his order of bhikkhus in front of him."

King Ajatasattu approached the Buddha and stood to one side. As he was standing there, he observed how the order of bhikkhus remained silent like a clear lake, and he exclaimed: "If only Prince Udayabhadda were possessed of such calm as this order of bhikkhus!"

"Are you thinking of the one you love, Your Majesty?" the Buddha asked.

"Venerable Sir, Prince Udayabhadda is very dear to me. If only he were possessed of the same calm as this order of bhikkhus!"

Then King Ajatasattu, bowed down to the Buddha, paid respect to the order of bhikkhus with joined hands, sat down to one side, and said: "Venerable Sir, I would ask something, if the Blessed One would deign to answer me."

"Ask, Your Majesty, anything you like."

"Venerable Sir, there are many sorts of craftsmen, such as elephant-drivers, chariot-drivers, archers, soldiers, barbers, cooks, garland-makers, weavers, basket-makers, potters, and accountants, who enjoy here and now the visible fruits of their skills. They are delighted and pleased with their work, as are their parents, children, colleagues, and friends. They maintain and support ascetics and brahmins, thus assuring for themselves a happy reward tending toward heaven. Can you, Venerable Sir, point to such a reward visible here and now as a fruit of the homeless life?"

"Your Majesty, have you put this question to other ascetics and brahmins?"

"I have, Venerable Sir."

"Would Your Majesty mind telling me how they replied?"

"I would not mind, Venerable Sir.

"Once, I went to see Purana Kassapa. Having exchanged courtesies, I sat down to one side and asked him exactly the same question.

"Purana Kassapa said: 'Your Majesty, no evil is done by the doer or instigator of a thing. If one kills or causes life to be taken, steals or causes something to be stolen, burns or causes something to be burned, causes grief and weariness, lies in ambush, commits adultery, or tells lies, no evil is done by that one. If with a razor-sharp wheel one were to make of this earth one single great heap of flesh, there would be no evil as a result of that. If one were to go along the south bank of the Ganges, killing and destroying, no evil would accrue. If one were to go along the north bank of the Ganges, giving gifts and causing gifts to be given, no merit would accrue, either. In giving, self-control, abstinence, and telling the truth, there is no merit, and no merit accrues.'

"Thus, did he explain his doctrine of non-action. It was as if, on being asked about a mango, he were to describe a breadfruit, or as if, on being asked about a breadfruit, he were to describe a mango. On being asked about the present fruits of the homeless life, Purana Kassapa explained non-action to me. Thinking, 'How should one like me think disparagingly of any ascetic or brahmin dwelling in my territory?' I neither applauded nor criticized Purana Kassapa's words.

I was displeased, but, rejecting scornful speech, I did not express my displeasure. I got up and left without saying anything.

"Another time, I visited Makkhali Gosala and asked him exactly the same question.

"Makkhali Gosala said: 'Your Majesty, there is no cause or condition for the defilement of beings; they are defiled without cause or condition. There is no cause or condition for the purification of beings; they are purified without cause or condition. There is no self-power or other-power. As for humans, there is no power, no strength, nor any exertion. All living beings are without control, without power, and without strength. They experience the fixed course of pleasure and pain through the six kinds of rebirth. There are one million four hundred six thousand six hundred principal sorts of birth. There may be five hundred kinds of kamma, or five kinds, or three kinds. There is whole-kamma and half-kamma. There are sixty-two paths, sixty-two intermediary aeons, six classes of humans, eight stages of human progress, four thousand nine hundred occupations, four thousand nine hundred wanderers, four thousand nine hundred abodes of nagas, two thousand sentient existences, three thousand hells, thirty-six places of dust, seven classes of rebirth as conscious beings, seven classes of rebirth as unconscious beings, and seven classes of rebirth as beings "freed from bonds." There are seven grades of devas, men, and goblins. There are seven lakes, seven great protuberances and seven small protuberances. There are seven great abysses and seven small abysses, seven great dreams and seven small dreams. There are eight million four hundred thousand eons during which fools and wise run on and circle around until they make an end of suffering.

"'Therefore, it is meaningless to say, "By this discipline, this austerity, or this holy life I will bring my unripened kamma to fruition, or I will gradually make this ripened kamma go away." Neither of these things is possible, because pleasure and pain have been measured out with a measure limited by the round of birth-and-death, and there is neither increase nor decrease, neither excellence nor inferiority. Just as a ball of string, when thrown, runs until it is all unraveled, so fools and wise run on and circle around until they make an end of suffering.'

"Thus, Venerable Sir, Makkhali Gosala, on being asked about the fruits of the homeless life, explained the purification of the round of birth-and-death to me. Feeling the same about his response as I felt about Purana Kassapa's and reacting in the same way, I got up and left without saying anything.

"Another time, I visited Ajita Kesakambali and asked him exactly the same question.

"Ajita Kesakambali said: 'Your Majesty, there is nothing given, bestowed, or offered in sacrifice. There is neither fruit nor result of good or bad deeds. There is neither this world nor the next. There is neither mother nor father. There are no spontaneously arisen beings. There are neither ascetics nor brahmins who have attained anything, who have perfectly practiced, who, having realized this world and the next by their own super-knowledge, proclaim them. This human being is composed of the four great elements, and, when one dies, the earth part reverts to earth, the water part to water, the fire part to fire, the air part to air, and the faculties pass away into space. The corpse is carried by four bearers with the bier as fifth; their footsteps are heard all the way to the cremation site. The bones whiten, and the sacrifice ends in ashes. A fool may think about charity, and some may extol the power of merit, but all these ideas are idle. Both the foolish and the wise, at the breaking up of the body, are destroyed and perish; they do not exist after death.'

"Thus, Venerable Sir, Ajita Kesakambali, on being asked about the fruits of the homeless life, explained the doctrine of annihilation to me. Feeling the same about his response as I felt about Makkhali Gosala's and reacting in the same way, I got up and left without saying anything.

"Another time, I visited Pakudha Kaccayana and asked him exactly the same question.

"Pakudha Kaccayana said: 'Your Majesty, these seven things are neither made nor of a kind to be made. They are uncreated, unproductive, barren, false, and as stable as a column. They neither shake, nor change, nor obstruct one another. They are unable to cause one another pleasure, pain, or both. What are the seven? The earth-body, the water-body, the fire-body, the air-body, pleasure, pain, and the life-principle. Thus, there is neither anyone slain nor a slayer, neither hearer nor proclaimer, neither knower nor causer of knowing. Therefore, one who cuts off a man's head with a sharp sword does not deprive anyone of life; he merely inserts the blade into the space between these seven bodies.'

"Thus, Venerable Sir, Pakudha Kaccayana, on being asked about the fruits of the homeless life, answered with something quite different. Feeling the same about his response as I felt about Ajita Kesakambali's and reacting in the same way, I got up and left without saying anything.

"Another time, I visited Nigantha Nataputta and asked him exactly the same question. Nigantha Nataputta said: 'Your Majesty, here a Nigantha is bound by a fourfold restraint. What four? He is curbed by all curbs, enclosed by all curbs, cleared by all curbs, and claimed by all curbs. In that a Nigantha is bound by this fourfold restraint, he is called self-perfected, self-controlled, and self-established.'

"Thus, Venerable Sir, Nigantha Nataputta, on being asked about the fruits of the homeless life, explained the fourfold restraint to me. Feeling the same about his response as I felt about Pakudha Kaccayana's and reacting in the same way, I got up and left without saying anything.

"Another time, I visited Sanjaya Belatthaputta and asked him exactly the same question.

"Sanjaya Belatthaputta said: 'If you asked me: "Is there another world?" if I thought so, I would say so. But I don't think so. I don't say it is so, and I don't say otherwise. I don't say it is not, and I don't not say it is not. If you asked me: "Isn't there another world?" if I thought so, I would say so. But I don't think so. I don't say it is so, and I don't say otherwise. I don't say it is not, and I don't not say it is not. If you asked me: "Are there both another world and not another world?" or "Is there neither another world nor not another world?" or "Is there fruit and result of good and bad deeds?" or "Is there no fruit and result of good and bad deeds?" or "Are there both fruit and result and no fruit and result of good and bad deeds?" or "Is there neither fruit and result nor no fruit and result of good and bad deeds?" or "Does the Tathagata exist after death?" or "Does the Tathagata not exist after death?" or "Does the Tathagata both exist and not exist after death?" or "Does the Tathagata neither exist nor not exist after death?" if I thought so, I would say so. But I don't think so. I don't say it is so, and I don't say otherwise. I don't say it is not, and I don't not say it is not.

"Thus, Venerable Sir, Sanjaya Belatthaputta, on being asked about the fruits of the homeless life, replied by evasion. Hearing this, I thought: 'Of all these ascetics and brahmins, Sanjaya Belatthaputta is the stupidest and most confused.' Feeling much the same about his response as I felt about the other five and reacting in the same way, I got up and left without saying anything.

"Therefore, Venerable Sir, I now ask the Blessed One the same question. Can you, Venerable Sir, point to a reward visible here and now as a fruit of the homeless life?"

"I can, Your Majesty. I will just ask a few questions in return, and you, Sire, shall answer as you see fit.

"What do you think, Sire? Suppose there were a man, a slave or a laborer. He might think: 'How strange and wonderful are the fruits of meritorious deeds! King Ajatasattu is a man, and I, too, am a man. The king is addicted to and indulges in the fivefold sense-pleasures, just like a god, whereas I am a laborer. I get up before him, go to bed after him, and willingly do whatever has to be done. I am well-mannered, pleasant-spoken, and work in his presence. I ought to do something meritorious. Let me shave off my hair and beard, don yellow robes, and go forth from the household life into homelessness!' Suppose that, before long, he does so. If people were to announce to you: 'Sire, that laborer who worked in your presence and who went forth into homelessness, is now living content in solitude, restrained in body, speech and thought, and satisfied with the minimum of food and clothing,' would you say: 'That man must come back and work for me as before'?

"No indeed, Venerable Sir. We would pay homage to him, rise, invite him, offer him the requisites, and make arrangements for his proper protection."

"Is that one fruit of the homeless life visible here and now?"

"Certainly, Venerable Sir."

"Then that, Sire, is the first such fruit of the homeless life."

"But, Venerable Sir, can you show any other fruit of the homeless life?"

"I can, Sire. I will just ask a few more questions, and you, Sire, shall answer as you see fit. What do you think? Suppose there were a man in your service, a farmer, a householder, or the steward of an estate. He might think: 'It is strange, it is wonderful, the destiny and fruits of meritorious deeds! King Ajatasattu is a man, and I, too, am a man. The king is addicted to and indulges in the fivefold sense-pleasures, just like a god, whereas I am the steward of an estate. I ought to do something meritorious. Let me shave off my hair and beard, don yellow robes, and go forth from the household life into homelessness!' Suppose that, before long, he does so. If people were to announce to you: 'Sire, that steward of an estate who worked in your presence and who went forth into homelessness, is now living content in solitude, restrained in body, speech and thought, and satisfied with the minimum of food and clothing,' would you say: 'That man must come back and work for me as before'?

"No, indeed, Venerable Sir. We would pay homage to him and offer him the requisites."

"Is that one fruit of the homeless life visible here and now?"

"Certainly, Venerable Sir."

"Then that, Sire, is the second such fruit of the homeless life."

"But, Venerable Sir, can you show me any other fruit of the homeless life that is more excellent than these?"

"I can, Your Majesty. It happens that a Tathagata arises in the world, an arahat, perfectly enlightened, accomplished in true knowledge and conduct, well-gone, a knower of worlds, the unsurpassed trainer of people to be tamed, a teacher of devas and humans, Enlightened, and Blessed. Having realized this world with its Maras and Brahmas, with its devas and humans by his own super-knowledge, he proclaims it. He preaches the Dhamma, which is lovely in its beginning, lovely in its middle, lovely in its ending, in the spirit and in the letter, and displays the perfected and purified holy life.

"One who hears this Dhamma gains faith in the Tathagata. Having gained this faith, he reflects: 'The household life is close and dusty, the homeless life is as free as air. Living the household life, it is not easy to live the perfected holy life, which is purified and polished like a conch-shell. Let me shave off my hair and beard, don yellow robes, and go forth from the household life into homelessness!' After some time, he abandons his property, leaves his circle of relatives, shaves off his hair and beard, dons yellow robes, and goes forth into the homeless life.

"Having gone forth, he dwells restrained by the rules, persisting in right behavior, seeing danger in the slightest faults, observing the commitments he has taken on regarding body, deed, and word, devoted to the skilled and purified life, perfected in morality, with the sense-doors guarded, skilled in mindful awareness, and content.

"How is a bhikkhu perfected in morality?

"Abandoning the taking of life, he dwells refraining from taking life and from using weapons. He is scrupulous and compassionate and trembles for the welfare of all living beings.

"Abandoning the taking of what is not given, he dwells refraining from stealing. He lives purely, accepting what is given, and awaiting offerings.

"Abandoning unchastity, he dwells refraining from the village-practice of sex.

"Abandoning false speech, he dwells refraining from false speech. He is trustworthy and dependable. He is a truth-speaker, one to be relied on, and not a deceiver of the world.

"Abandoning malicious speech, he neither gossips nor spreads gossip to the detriment of anyone. Thus, he is both a reconciler of those at variance and an encourager of those in harmony. He delights in peace, rejoices in peace, and speaks up for peace.

"Abandoning harsh speech, he refrains from using harsh speech. His words are altogether blameless, agreeable, and pleasing to everyone.

"Abandoning idle chatter, he speaks only at the appropriate time. His speech is correct and to the point of the Dhamma and the discipline. His words are reasoned, well-defined, and connected with the goal, and to be treasured.

"Refraining from eating at improper times, he eats only once a day.

"He avoids making music, singing, dancing, and watching shows.

"He abstains from using garlands, perfumes, cosmetics, ornaments, and adornments.

"He avoids using high or wide beds and chairs.

"He avoids using or accepting gold and silver.

"He avoids accepting raw grain or flesh.

"He does not accept women, young girls, slaves, live animals or plots of land.

"He refrains from running errands, from buying and selling, from cheating with false weights and measures, from bribery and corruption, from deception and insincerity, and from wounding or imprisoning others.

"Whereas some ascetics and brahmins, feeding on the food of the faithful, are heedless about destroying seeds and plant life, he refrains from such destruction.

"Whereas some ascetics and brahmins, feeding on the food of the faithful, are addicted to storing food, drink, clothing, and other goods, he refrains from storing such things.

"Likewise, he refrains from attending displays, such as dancing, singing, music, recitations, drumming, acrobatics, magic, animal fights, sword fights, sports, parades, maneuvers, and military reviews.

"Likewise, he refrains from idle pursuits, such as chess, hopscotch, dice, playing with toys, turning somersaults, guessing games, and mimicking deformities.

"Likewise, he refrains from fancy couches and luxurious quilts, blankets, and covers.

"Likewise, he refrains from all forms of self-adornment and embellishment, such as perfume, massaging, bathing in scented water, shampooing, using mirrors, garlands,, and cosmetics, and wearing bracelets, headbands, decorated sandals, turbans, and gems.

"Likewise, he refrains from unedifying conversation, such as that about kings, robbers, ministers, armies, dangers, wars, food, drink, clothes, beds, garlands, perfumes, relatives, carriages, villages, towns and cities, countries, women, heroes, gossip, the departed, and the concepts of being and non-being.

"Likewise, he refrains from disputation, such as, 'You don't understand this doctrine and discipline—I do!' 'How could you understand this doctrine and discipline?' 'Your way is all wrong—mine is right!' 'I am consistent—you aren't!' 'You said last what you should have said first, and you said first what you should have said last!' 'What you took so long to think up has been refuted!' 'Your argument has been overthrown—you're defeated!' and 'Go on, save your doctrine—get out of that if you can!'

"Likewise, he refrains from running errands and messages for those, such as kings, ministers, nobles, brahmins, householders, and young men, all of whom say: 'Go here—go there!' and 'Take this there—bring that here!.

"Likewise, he refrains from deception, patter, hinting, belittling, and always seeking further gains.

"Likewise, he refrains from making his living by base arts, such as palmistry, fortune-telling, and reading omens.

"Likewise, he refrains from making his living by base arts, such as predicting the outcome of battles and wars.

"Likewise, he refrains from making his living by base arts, such as predicting the future by means of astrology and heavenly phenomena.

"Likewise, he refrains from making his living by base arts, such as predicting economic success or failure, security, danger, disease, and health; accounting; computing; calculating; poetic composition; and philosophizing.

"Likewise, he refrains from making his living by base arts, such as matchmaking, declaring auspicious days, procuring abortions, using charms and spells, and invoking spirits.

"Likewise, he refrains from making his living by base arts, such as appeasing the devas and redeeming vows to them, casting spells, consecrating building-sites, administering medical procedures, and prescribing medicine.

"In all of these ways, a bhikkhu is perfected in morality.

"Just as a duly-anointed king who has conquered his enemies, sees no danger from any side because he has conquered his enemies, that bhikkhu, who is perfected in morality, sees no danger from any side because he is restrained by morality. He experiences in himself the blameless bliss that comes from maintaining this noble morality. In this way, a bhikkhu is perfected in morality.

"How is he a guardian of the sense-doors? On seeing a visible object with the eye, he does not grasp at its major signs or its secondary characteristics. Because greed and sorrow, which are evil and unskilled states, would overwhelm him if he dwelt leaving this eye-faculty unguarded, he practices guarding it. He protects the eye-faculty and develops restraint of it.

"In the same way, he guards the ear, the nose, the tongue, the body, and the mind. He experiences within himself the blameless bliss that comes from maintaining this noble guarding of the faculties. In this way, a bhikkhu is a guardian of the sense-doors.

"And how is a bhikkhu accomplished in mindfulness? He acts with mindfulness in going forth and coming back, in looking ahead or behind, in bending and stretching, in wearing his outer and inner robe and carrying his bowl, in eating, drinking, chewing, and swallowing, in defecating and urinating, in walking, standing, sitting, and lying down, in waking, in speaking and in keeping silent. In this way, a bhikkhu is accomplished in mindfulness.

"How is a bhikkhu contented? He is satisfied with a robe to protect his body, with alms to satisfy his stomach. After he has accepted enough, he goes on his way. Just as a bird flies hither and thither, burdened by nothing but its wings, in this way, a bhikkhu is contented.

"Equipped with this noble morality, with this noble restraint of the senses, and with this noble contentment, he finds a solitary lodging, at the root of a forest tree, in a mountain cave or gorge, in a charnel ground, in a jungle thicket, or on a heap of straw in the open air. Having eaten after his return from the almsround, he sits down cross-legged, holding his body erect, and concentrates on keeping mindfulness established before him.

"Abandoning worldly desires, he dwells with a mind purified of worldly desires. Abandoning ill-will and hatred, he dwells compassionate for the welfare of all living beings, with a mind purified of ill-will and hatred. Abandoning sloth-and-torpor, he dwells perceiving light, with a mind purified of sloth-and-torpor. Abandoning worry-and-restlessness, he dwells inwardly calm, with a mind purified of worry-and-restlessness. Abandoning doubt, he dwells without uncertainty as to what things are wholesome, with a mind purified of doubt.

"Suppose that a man took a loan to develop his business and, then, his business prospered. He might think: 'Before this, I developed my business by borrowing, but now it has prospered, so that I can pay off my old debts, and with what is left over I can support a wife.' He would rejoice and be glad about that.

"Suppose that a man was ill, suffering, terribly sick, with no appetite and weak in body, but, then, after a time, he recovered. He might think: 'Before this, I was ill, suffering, terribly sick, with no appetite and weak in body, but now I have recovered and regained my appetite and bodily strength.' He would rejoice and be glad about that.

"Suppose that a man was bound in prison, but, after a time, was freed from his bonds without any loss from his possessions. He might think: 'Before this, I was in prison, but now I am freed from my bonds without any loss from my possessions.' He would rejoice and be glad about that.

"Suppose that a man was a slave, not his own master, unable to go where he liked, but, after some time, he was freed. He might think: 'Before this, I was a slave, not my own master, unable to go where I liked, but now I am freed from slavery, able to go where I like.' He would rejoice and be glad about that.

"Suppose that a man who was laden with goods and wealth went on a long journey through the desert where food was scarce and danger abounded, but, after a time, he arrived safe and sound at the edge of a village. He might think: 'Before this, I was in danger in a desert where food was scarce and danger abounded, but now I am safe at the edge of a village.' He would rejoice and be glad about that.

"As long as a bhikkhu does not perceive the disappearance of the five hindrances in himself, he feels as if in debt, in sickness, in bonds, in slavery, or on a desert journey. When he perceives the disappearance of the five hindrances in himself, it is as if he were freed from debt, from sickness, from bonds, from slavery, and from the perils of the desert.

"When he knows that these five hindrances have left him, gladness arises in him. From gladness comes delight. From delight comes tranquility. From tranquillity comes joy. From joy comes concentration. Being thus detached from sense-desires, detached from unwholesome states, he enters and remains in the first jhana, which is with thinking and pondering, born of detachment, and filled with delight and joy. With this delight and joy, he suffuses his body so that there is no spot in his entire body that is untouched by delight and joy.

"Just as a skilled bath attendant, kneading the soap powder which he has sprinkled with water, forms from it, in a metal dish, a soft ball, so that the soap powder becomes one oleaginous mass, bound with oil, so that nothing escapes, a bhikkhu suffuses his body with delight and joy born of detachment so that no spot remains untouched. This is a fruit of the homeless life, visible here and now, that is more excellent than the former ones.

"With the subsiding of thinking and pondering, a bhikkhu gains inner tranquillity and enters and remains in the second jhana, which is without thinking and pondering, born of concentration and filled with delight and joy. With this delight and joy, he suffuses his body so that no spot is untouched by delight and joy.

"Just as in a lake fed by a spring, with no other inflow, the cool water welling up from below mingles and mixes with the lake water, so that no part of the pool is untouched by it, a bhikkhu suffuses his body with delight and joy born of concentration so that no spot remains untouched. This is a fruit of the homeless life, visible here and now, that is more excellent than the former ones.

"With the fading away of delight, a bhikkhu remains imperturbable and mindful and experiences that joy of which the Noble Ones say: 'Happy is he who dwells with equanimity and mindfulness,' and enters and remains in the third jhana. And with this joy devoid of delight he suffuses his body so that no spot remains untouched by it.

"Just as, in a pond, blue, red, or white lotuses, which were born in the water, have grown submerged in the water, and are fed from the water's depths, are suffused with the cool water, a bhikkhu suffuses his body with this joy devoid of delight so that no spot remains untouched. This is a fruit of the homeless life, visible here and now, that is more excellent and perfect than the former ones.

"Abandoning pleasure and pain and with the previous disappearance of joy and sorrow, a bhikkhu enters and remains in the fourth jhana, which has neither pleasure nor pain and is purified by equanimity and mindfulness. He sits, suffusing his body with that mental purity and clarification so that no part of his body is untouched by it.

"Just as if a man were to sit and wrap himself from head to foot in a soft white garment so that no part of him was untouched by that garment, a bhikkhu suffuses his body with that mental purity and clarification so that no part of his body is untouched. This is a fruit of the homeless life, visible here and now, that is more excellent than the former ones.

"With mind thus concentrated and purified, a bhikkhu directs his mind toward knowing and seeing.

"Just as man with good eyesight, taking in his hand an excellent gem, well-cut into eight facets, perfect in every respect, and strung on a cord, inspects it and describes it exactly as it is, a bhikkhu, with mind thus concentrated and purified, directs his mind toward knowing and seeing, and he knows: 'This, my body, is material, made up of the four great elements, born of mother and father, impermanent, liable to be injured and destroyed, and this is my consciousness which is bound to it and dependent on it.' This is a fruit of the homeless life, visible here and now, that is more excellent than the former ones.

"With mind thus concentrated and purified, a bhikkhu directs his mind to the production of a mind-made body. Out of this body, he produces another body, having a form, mind-made, and complete in all its limbs and faculties.

"Just as a man draws a reed from its sheath and thinks: 'This is the reed, and this is the sheath. Reed and sheath are different. Now the reed has been drawn from the sheath'; just as a man draws a sword from the scabbard and thinks: 'This is the sword, and this is the scabbard. Sword and scabbard are different. Now the sword has been drawn from the scabbard'; or just as a man draws a snake from its old skin and thinks: 'This is the snake, and this is the skin. Snake and skin are different. Now the snake has been drawn from its skin'; a bhikkhu, with mind thus concentrated and purified, directs his mind to the production of a mind-made body, and, out of this body, he produces another mind-made and complete body. This is a fruit of the homeless life, visible here and now, that is more excellent than the former ones.

"With mind thus concentrated and purified, a bhikkhu directs his mind to supernatural powers and enjoys various powers. Being one, he becomes many; being many, he becomes one. He appears and disappears. He passes through fences, walls, and mountains as if they were air. He sinks into the ground and emerges from it as if it were water. He walks on the water without breaking the surface as if it were solid ground. He flies cross-legged through the sky like a bird with wings, even touching the sun and the moon with his hand. He travels in the body as far as the Brahma world.

"Just as a skilled potter can make from well-prepared clay whatever kind of bowl he likes, or as a skilled ivory carver can produce from well-prepared ivory any object he likes, or as a skilled goldsmith can make from a lump of pure gold any article he likes, a bhikkhu, with mind thus concentrated and purified directs his mind to supernatural powers and enjoys various powers. This is a fruit of the homeless life, visible here and now, that is more excellent than the former ones.

"With mind thus concentrated and purified, a bhikkhu directs his mind to the divine ear. With the divine ear, which surpasses that of human beings, he hears sounds both divine and human, far or near.

"Just as a man going on a long journey hears a sound and knows at once whether it is a big drum, a small drum, a conch, cymbals, or a kettledrum, a bhikkhu, with the divine ear hears sounds, both divine or human, far or near. This is a fruit of the homeless life, visible here and now, that is more excellent than the former ones.

"With mind thus concentrated and purified, a bhikkhu directs his mind to the knowledge of others' minds. He knows and distinguishes with his mind the minds of other beings or other persons. He knows the mind with passion to be with passion and the mind without passion to be without passion. He knows the mind with hate to be with hate and the mind without hate to be without hate. In the same way, he knows and distinguishes the mind which is deluded or undeluded, narrow or broad, expanded or unexpanded, surpassed or unsurpassed, concentrated or unconcentrated, or liberated or unliberated.

"Just as a woman, fond of her appearance, examines her face in a brightly polished mirror or in water and, by examination, knows whether or not there is a spot there, a bhikkhu, with mind thus concentrated and purified, directs his mind to the knowledge of others' minds and knows the true state of each mind. This is a fruit of the homeless life, visible here and now, that is more excellent than the former ones.

"With mind thus concentrated and purified, a bhikkhu directs his mind to the knowledge of previous existences. He remembers many previous existences: one, two, three, four, five, ten, twenty, thirty, forty, fifty, a hundred, a thousand, a hundred thousand births, and several periods of contraction, of expansion, and of both contraction and expansion. He remembers his name, his clan, his caste, his food, the pleasant and painful conditions he experienced, and his lifespan for each existence. Thus, he remembers various past births, their conditions, and their details.

"Just as a man who has gone from his village to another village, from that to yet another, and from that back to his own village, remembers each village and how he went there, as well as where he stood, where he sat, what he said, and when he remained silent in each, a bhikkhu, with mind thus concentrated and purified, remembers past births, their conditions, and their details. This is a fruit of the homeless life, visible here and now, that is more excellent than the former ones.

"With mind thus concentrated and purified, a bhikkhu directs his mind to the knowledge of the passing away and arising of beings. With the divine eye, he sees beings passing away and arising, and he knows: 'These beings, on account of misconduct of body, speech, or thought, or of disparaging the Noble Ones, have wrong view and will suffer the kammic fate of wrong view. At the breaking up of the body after death they are being reborn in a lower world, in a bad destination, in a state of suffering, in hell. These other beings, on account of good conduct of body, speech, or thought, or of praising the Noble Ones, have right view and will reap the kammic reward of right view. At the breaking up of the body after death, they are being reborn in a good destination, in a heavenly world.' Thus, with the divine eye, he sees beings passing away and re-arising as kamma directs them.

"Just as a man with good eyesight, standing on the top of a lofty building at a crossroads, discerns, 'Those people are entering a house, those others are leaving a house, those others are walking in the street, and those others are sitting in the middle of the crossroads,' a bhikkhu, with the divine eye, sees beings passing away and re-arising as kamma directs them. This is a fruit of the homeless life, visible here and now, that is more excellent and perfect than the former ones.

"With his mind thus concentrated and purified, a bhikkhu directs his mind to the knowledge of the destruction of the taints. He knows as it really is: 'This is suffering,' 'This is the origin of suffering,'

'This is the cessation of suffering,' and 'This is the path leading to the cessation of suffering.' He knows as it really is: 'These are the taints,' 'This is the origin of the taints,' 'This is the cessation of the taints,' and 'This is the path leading to the cessation of the taints.' Through his knowing and seeing, his mind is delivered from the taints of sense-desire, of becoming, and of ignorance, and the knowledge arises in him: 'This is deliverance!' He knows: 'Birth is finished, the holy life has been led, done is what had to be done, and there is nothing further here.'

"Just as a man with good eyesight, standing on the edge of a mountain pond, discerns, 'This pond is as clear as a polished crystal, and there are oyster shells, gravel banks, and shoals of fish, on the move or stationary,' a bhikkhu, with his mind thus concentrated and purified, directs his mind to the knowledge of the destruction of the taints, and he knows: 'Birth is finished, the holy life has been led, done is what had to be done, there is nothing further here.' This is a fruit of the homeless life, visible here and now, which is more excellent than the previous fruits. There is no fruit of the homeless life, visible here and now, that is more excellent than this."

At this, King Ajatasattu exclaimed: "Excellent, Venerable Sir! It is as if someone were to set upright what had been knocked down, to point out the way to one who was lost, or to bring an oil lamp into a dark place, so that those with eyes could see what was there. Just so the Blessed One has expounded the Dhamma in various ways, and I go for refuge to the Buddha, to the Dhamma, and to the Sangha. May the Blessed One accept me from this day forth as a lay follower, as long as life shall last! Transgression overcame me, Venerable Sir, foolish, erring, and wicked as I was, in that, for the sake of the throne, I deprived my father, that good man and just king, of his life. May the Blessed One accept my confession of my evil deed that I may restrain myself in future!"

"Indeed, Sire, transgression overcame you when you deprived your father of his life. Since you have acknowledged the transgression and confessed it, as is right, we will accept it. One who acknowledges his transgression and confesses it for betterment in future, will grow in the noble discipline."

At this, King Ajatasattu said: "Venerable Sir, permit me to depart now. I am busy and have much to do."

"Your Majesty, do as you think fit."

Rejoicing at and delighting in these words, King Ajatasattu rose from his seat, paid respect to the Buddha, and departed with his right side toward the Buddha.

As soon as the king had gone, the Buddha said to the bhikkhus: "The king is done for; his fate is sealed! If the King had not deprived his father of his life, as he sat here, the pure and spotless Dhamma-eye would have arisen in him."

The bhikkhus were delighted and rejoiced at the Buddha's words.

—Digha Nikaya 2

The Heart Sutra

This was taught at Gijjakuta.

While Avalokitesvara, the Bodhisattva of Compassion, was meditating deeply on the Perfection of Wisdom, he clearly saw that the five aggregates are empty, and he crossed beyond all suffering and difficulty.

"Shariputra," he said, "form is empty, and emptiness is form. Form itself is emptiness; emptiness itself is form.

"The same is true of feelings, perception, mental formations, and consciousness.

"Shariputra, all phenomena are void of characteristics. They neither arise nor vanish. They are neither defiled nor pure. They neither increase nor decrease. Therefore, in emptiness, there is no form, no feeling, no perception, no mental formations, and no consciousness. In emptiness, there are no eyes, no ears, no nose, no tongue, no body, and no mind. In emptiness, there is no visual object, no sound, no smell, no taste, no tactile object, and no mental object. In emptiness, there is no seeing, no hearing, no smelling, no tasting, no touching, and no thinking.

"There is no ignorance nor any extinction of ignorance, no volitional activities nor any extinction of volitional activities, no consciousness nor any extinction of consciousness, no name-and-form nor any extinction of name-and-form, no six sense bases nor any extinction of the six sense bases, no contact nor any extinction of contact, no feeling nor any extinction of feeling, no craving nor any extinction of craving, no grasping nor any extinction of grasping, no becoming nor any extinction of becoming, no aging-and-death nor any extinction of aging-and-death.

"There is no suffering, no cause of suffering, no cessation of suffering, and no path leading to the cessation of suffering.

"There is neither attainment nor anything to attain.

"Because nothing is attained, the Bodhisattva relies on the Perfection of Wisdom, and in his mind there is no hindrance. Because there is no hindrance, there is no fear. Leaving all wrong view far behind, he abides in Nirvana.

"All Buddhas—of the past, of the present, and of the future—rely of the Perfection of Wisdom and abide in Supreme Enlightenment.

"The Perfection of Wisdom is the greatest mantra, the clearest and brightest mantra, the highest mantra, and the mantra that removes all suffering. It is genuine and not false. That is why the Mantra of the Perfection of Wisdom was taught. Recite it like this:

'*Gate gate paragate parasamgate bodhi svaha*!'"

('Gone, gone, gone beyond, gone altogether beyond! What an awakening! All hail!')

(This is the shortest and best-known Mahayana sutra.)

Social Stability

At one time, King Ajatasattu of Magadha wanted to attack and destroy the Vajjians of Vesali. He summoned his chief minister, the brahmin Vassakara and said, "Go to the Blessed One, who is staying on Vultures' Peak, pay your respects in my name, ask if he is free from sickness and living comfortably, and say: 'Venerable Sir, King Ajatasattu wishes to attack the Vajjians.' Report back to me exactly what the Blessed One says."

"Very good, Sire," said Vassakara. He went to Vulture's Peak, exchanged courtesies with the Buddha, sat down to one side, and delivered the king's message.

"Ananda," the Buddha asked his attendant, who was standing behind, fanning him, "have you heard that the Vajjians hold regular and frequent assemblies?"

"Yes, Venerable Sir, I have heard that they do."

"Ananda, as long as the Vajjians hold regular and frequent assemblies, they may be expected to prosper and not to decline."

After asking Venerable Ananda for confirmation on the conduct of the Vajjians on each point, the Buddha expounded the following:

"As long as the Vajjians meet in harmony and carry out their business in harmony; as long as they respect their ancient tradition; as long as they respect the elders among them; as long as they pay proper respect to their women; as long as they respect their holy places, both at home and abroad; and as long as they provide for the safety and well-being of arahats; they may be expected to prosper and not to decline."

Then the Buddha said to Vassakara: "Once, when I was at the Sarandada Shrine in Vesali, I taught the Vajjians these seven principles for preventing decline, and, as long as they observe these seven principles, they may be expected to prosper and not to decline."

"Venerable Sir," Vassakara replied, "if the Vajjians keep to even one of these principles, they may be expected to prosper and not to decline—far less all seven. Certainly, the Vajjians will never be conquered by King Ajatasattu by force of arms, but only by means of propaganda and setting them against one another. Now, Venerable Sir, may I depart? I am busy and have much to do."

The Buddha replied, "Brahmin, do as you think fit."

Delighted with the Buddha's words, Vassakara rose from his seat and departed.

Soon after Vassakara had gone, the Buddha said: "Ananda, summon all the bhikkhus in Rajagaha to the assembly hall."

"Very good, Venerable Sir," Ananda replied. After he had done so, he returned and said: "Venerable Sir, the bhikkhus are assembled. Now is the time for the Blessed One to do as he sees fit."

The Buddha went to the assembly hall, sat down on the prepared seat, and said: "Bhikkhus, I will teach you seven things that are conducive to welfare.

"As long as you hold regular and frequent assemblies; as long as you meet in harmony and carry out your business in harmony; as long as you observe the rules of discipline; as long as you honor and respect the elders of the order; as long as you do not fall prey to desires which lead to rebirth; as long as you remain devoted to living in the forest; and as long as you preserve your personal mindfulness, so that you can be good companions to each other; the Sangha may be expected to prosper. As long as bhikkhus maintain these seven principles and are seen to do so, the Sangha may be expected to prosper and not to decline.

"I will tell you another seven things which, if avoided, are conducive to welfare. As long as bhikkhus do not become absorbed in tasks, in chattering, in sleeping, in company, in evil desires, and in associating with evil friends, and as long as they do not rest content with partial achievements, the Sangha may be expected to prosper and not to decline.

"I will tell you another seven things conducive to welfare. As long as bhikkhus continue with faith, with modesty, with fear of doing wrong, with learning, with aroused vigor, with established mindfulness, and with wisdom, the Sangha may be expected to prosper and not to decline.

"Furthermore, as long as bhikkhus develop the seven factors of enlightenment—namely, mindfulness, investigation of phenomena, energy, delight, tranquillity, concentration, and equanimity, the Sangha may be expected to prosper and not to decline.

"I will tell you seven mental qualities which, if developed, are conducive to welfare. As long as bhikkhus develop the perception of impermanence, of nonself, of impurity, of danger, of overcoming, of dispassion, and of cessation, the Sangha may be expected to prosper and not to decline.

—Digha Nikaya 16

Advice to Rahula

One evening, when the Buddha was staying at the Bamboo Grove in Rajagaha, he rose from meditation and went to Nalanda to visit the samanera Venerable Rahula who was staying at Ambalatthika. At that time, Venerable Rahula, the Buddha's son, was only seven years old.

Venerable Rahula saw the Buddha coming in the distance, prepared a seat for him and water to wash his feet. Venerable Rahula washed the Buddha's feet, paid homage, and sat down at one side.

The Buddha picked up the water vessel and dumped out most of the water. "Rahula," he asked, "do you see the little water left in this vessel?"

"Yes, Venerable Sir."

"Even so little is the practice of one who is not ashamed to tell a deliberate lie."

Then the Buddha threw away that little bit of water and asked, "Do you see that little bit of water that was thrown away?"

"Yes, Venerable Sir."

"Even so, one who is not ashamed to tell a deliberate lie has thrown away his practice."

Then the Buddha turned the water vessel upside down and asked, "Do you see this water vessel turned upside down?"

"Yes, Venerable Sir."

"Even so, one who is not ashamed to tell a deliberate lie has turned his practice upside down."

Then the Buddha turned the water vessel right side up again and asked, "Do you see this empty water vessel?"

"Yes, Venerable Sir."

"Even so, empty is the practice of one who is not ashamed to tell a deliberate lie."

"Imagine a royal elephant with tusks as long as chariot poles, full-grown, high-bred, and accustomed to battle. In battle he gallantly uses his body, his feet, his head, his ears, his tusks, and his tail, but he holds back his trunk. His rider will notice this and think, 'This animal holds back his trunk; he has not yet given up his life.' If, however, a royal elephant in battle uses his body, his feet, his head, his ears, his tusks, and his trunk, his rider will think: 'This royal tusker elephant perfectly performs his task in battle. He has given up his life. There is nothing this royal elephant would not do.' So too, Rahula, when one is not ashamed to tell a deliberate lie, there is no evil that one will not do. Therefore, you should train yourself: 'I will not utter a falsehood even as a joke.'

"What is the purpose of a mirror?"

"For reflection, Venerable Sir."

"So too, any action of body, speech, or mind should be done after repeated reflection.

"When you wish to perform an action with the body, you should reflect upon that action in this way. 'Will this action lead to my own affliction, to the affliction of others, or to the affliction of both? Is it an unwholesome action with painful results?' If upon reflection, you know this to be true, you definitely should not perform that action. If, however, upon reflection, you know that that action will not lead to your own affliction, to the affliction of others, nor to the affliction of both, and that it is a wholesome action with pleasant results,' you may perform that action.

"Furthermore, while you are performing an action with the body, you should reflect upon it in the same way. If, upon reflection, you know it to be in the least unwholesome, you should stop doing it. If, however, you know that that action is perfectly wholesome, you may continue doing it.

"Finally, after you have performed an action with the body, you should reflect upon it in the same way with regard to the results. If, upon reflection, you know it to be in the least unwholesome, you should confess and reveal it to your teacher or to your wise companions. If, however, you know that that action was perfectly wholesome, you can be happy about your wholesome practice.

"You should carry out the same practice in regard to actions of speech and mind.

"All those in the past who have purified their actions of body, speech, and mind, did so by repeatedly reflecting in this way. All those in the future who purify their actions of body, speech, and mind, will do so by repeatedly reflecting in this way. All those in the present who are purifying their actions of body, speech, and mind, are doing so by repeatedly reflecting in this way. Therefore, you should train yourself, 'I will purify my actions of body, speech, and mind by repeatedly reflecting upon them.'"

That is what the Buddha said. Venerable Rahula was satisfied and delighted in the Buddha's words.

—Majjhima Nikaya 61

The Death of Venerable Moggallana

One day, ascetics of several different sects gathered in Rajagaha. A leader of the naked ascetics took charge of the meeting and began, "Friends, I'm sure that all of you have noticed that the alms we receive have been steadily decreasing, while Gotama's have greatly increased. The same is true of respect from the people. Do you know why this is?"

None of the others could answer.

"In my opinion," the leader continued, "it is due to the influence of the one called Moggallana. He has great supernatural powers. He travels to the heavens and talks with the devas. He tells people, 'It is because of having performed meritorious deeds, such as generosity, that the devas now enjoy great glory.'

"He also visits hell and relates stories of how those wretches brought suffering upon themselves by performing misdeeds. People are so impressed when they hear him that they lavish alms and attention on him. If we can get rid of Moggallana, our alms and honors will surely increase!"

The other ascetics unanimously agreed that Venerable Moggallana should be killed. After this secret meeting, they stirred up their supporters and collected one thousand coins, with which they hired a group of thugs. They instructed these professional assassins to attack Venerable Moggallana and to kill him.

Those thugs surrounded Venerable Moggallana's kuti at Kalasila, the Black Rock, but he became aware of their plan and used his supernatural power to escape through the keyhole. A few days later, the gang tried again, but Venerable Moggallana again used his supernatural power, escaping through the roof.

After several more attempts, however, Venerable Moggallana realized that, because of previous kamma, he would not be able to escape death that day. He was captured and beaten mercilessly, and his bones were broken into fragments. Believing him to be dead, the thugs threw his shattered and bloody body into a thicket and hurried away unseen.

Venerable Moggallana roused himself and resolved to see the Buddha before entering final Nibbana. Wrapping himself with meditation, as if it were a bandage, he passed through the air, arrived in front of the Teacher, and paid his respects.

"Venerable Sir, I am about to pass into final Nibbana at Kalasila."

"Very well, Moggallana, but before you go, recite the Dhamma for me, for I have no other disciple such as you."

After delivering a discourse, Venerable Moggallana performed several miracles. Then he paid his last obeisance to the Buddha and returned to Kalasila, where he realized parinibbana.

Rumors that the Chief Disciple had been murdered by assassins spread quickly, and King Ajatasattu dispatched spies to hunt them down. One evening, the entire gang was drinking in a tavern when one of bumped another and got him dirty.

"You ill-mannered cur!" the injured party grumbled. "Why did you do that?"

"Well, why did you strike the first blow when we attacked that ascetic, Moggallana?"

"Keep quiet, you fool! How do you know that I hit him?"

"I know what I know, you brute!"

The king's spies overheard their drunken quarreling, arrested all five hundred, and took them before the king.

During interrogation, they admitted killing Venerable Moggallana and testified that they had been paid to do so by the naked ascetics.

King Ajatasattu immediately ordered the arrest of five hundred naked ascetics. In the courtyard of the palace, soldiers buried both the ascetics and the assassins up to their waists, covered them with straw, and burned them alive. Finally, the king ordered his men to break up the blackened bodies with iron plows.

Later, bhikkhus were discussing what had happened. "Venerable Moggallana's death," they agreed, "was unworthy of his life!"

When the Buddha heard what they were discussing, he said, "Bhikkhus, while Moggallana's death was unsuited to his present existence, it was due to kamma from a previous life."

"Venerable Sir, it would be good if you explained this to us."

Then the Buddha told this story of the past.

Long, long ago, when Brahmadatta was reigning in Baranasi, a young man ran the family business and took care of his parents, who were both blind. He even managed the housework himself. Whenever his parents urged him to get married, he replied that he wasn't interested. Furthermore, he pointed out, he was capable of handling everything very well on his own.

His parents prevailed, however, and they arranged for him to marry a woman from a good family. At first, relations were quite smooth, but, in time, the new wife started urging him to set up a separate household. "It is impossible to stay in the same house with your parents anymore," she insisted.

The young man ignored his wife's request, but she was undeterred and began plotting against her in-laws. While he was out, she strewed rubbish around. When he came home, she accused his parents of being messy and dirtying the place.

"It is impossible to keep the house neat and clean," she complained. "This old couple drop food everywhere. I've asked them to be careful, but, whenever I talk to them, they get angry and abuse me. I can't get along with them. They treat me worse than a servant!"

After months of her incessant nagging, the young man grew weary, decided his wife was right, and settled on a plan.

He told his mother and father that he was going to take them to visit some relatives. He put his parents in an ox cart and drove them to the heart of the forest.

Putting the reins into his father's hands, he said, "Father, the oxen will follow the track. I'm getting down to walk ahead. I've heard there are highwaymen in these parts!"

A little later, he disguised his voice and shouted loudly like a band of attacking robbers. His parents were deceived and called out, "Dear son! You are young. Don't worry about us. Save yourself!"

The young man beat his parents to death, abandoned their bodies beside the road, and returned home.

"Bhikkhus," the Buddha concluded, the fruit of this one deed of Moggallana's was suffering in hell for hundreds of thousands of years, followed by a hundred deaths from beatings. Thus, I say that Moggallana's last death was suited to his kamma. Likewise, those who killed him and the ascetics who hired it done have also met an appropriate end, for harming my innocent son." Then the Buddha recited these verses:

> One who strikes another who never strikes;
> One who harms another who does no harm;
> Will quickly suffer one of these ten punishments:
> Severe pain or devastation;
> Disfigurement or grave disease;
> Insanity or legal prosecution;
> The loss of reputation or of relatives;
> Dire poverty or catastrophic fire.
> Then, after death, that fool will be reborn in hell
>
> —Dhammapada Commentary on Verse 137

Nalanda

Venerable Sariputta

Near Nalanda there were two brahmin villages, Upatissa and Kolita. Before the birth of the Bodhisatta in Lumbini, a brahmin woman named Sari, in Upatissa, delivered a son. On the same day, in Kolita, a friend of hers, named Moggalli, also gave birth to a baby boy. The two families were closely connected, and the two boys, named Upatissa and Kolita after their villages, grew up like brothers, playing and studying together.

The two youths remained close even after their education, and they went together to enjoy the entertainment at an annual festival. For two days, sitting in prime seats, they laughed at the comedies and marveled at the spectacular displays of daring. On the third day, as they resumed their seats, Kolita turned to Upatissa and said, "Friend, you seem to be in a strange mood today. You are certainly not as happy as you were yesterday and the day before. What's on your mind?"

"My dear Kolita," Upatissa replied. "What is there to look at here? These shows are stupid and worthless! We ought to seek for a teaching of liberation!"

"Upatissa!" Kolita cried. "I have been thinking exactly the same thing! Before these people reach a hundred years of age they will all be dead. I agree that we should seek for liberation, and, for that, there's nothing to do but to leave home and become ascetics. Under whom shall we study?"

Together, they decided to leave home and to study in Rajagaha with a renowned teacher named Sanjaya. Within a short time, Upatissa and Kolita had mastered Sanjaya's entire teaching. They asked him: "Master, does your teaching go only this far, or is there something more?"

Sanjaya replied: "It goes only this far. You know it all."

"In that case," Upatissa and Kolita thought, "continuing here under him is useless. We left home to seek a teaching of liberation.

Jambudipa is vast; if we wander further afield, we shall certainly find a teacher who can teach us how to achieve liberation."

After that, whenever they heard about a good teacher, they went and talked with him. Unfortunately, they found no one who could answer their questions, whereas they were able to reply satisfactorily to everyone who questioned them.

Having wandered the whole of Jambudipa, they returned to Rajagaha. There they agreed that they should wander separately and that each would immediately inform the other if he found anything promising.

It was about this time that the Buddha returned to Rajagaha, fulfilling the promise he had made to King Bimbisara before his Enlightenment. The Buddha and the Sangha were staying in Veluvana, which had been donated by the king.

One morning, Upatissa happened to see Venerable Assaji, one of the five ascetics, who had become the very first bhikkhus, as he was going for alms in the city. Upatissa was struck by Venerable Assaji's serenity and poise and thought: "I have never before seen such an ascetic. Surely he is an arahat or on the way to becoming so. Should I go closer and ask him who his teacher is?"

Realizing that it was not an appropriate time to ask questions, since the monk was walking for alms, Upatissa followed him discreetly until he had a suitable opportunity to speak. When Venerable Assaji, having finished his almsrounds, prepared to sit down to eat, Upatissa spread his own cloth for him and waited. As soon as Venerable Assaji had finished eating, Upatissa, continuing to perform the duties of a pupil to a teacher, offered him water.

After the usual courtesies, Upatissa said, "Your features are calm, Venerable Sir, and your complexion is clear. Under whom have you gone forth? Who is the master whose teachings you follow?"

Venerable Assaji answered: "I have gone forth under the Great Recluse, scion of the Sakyas. The Blessed One is my teacher; it is his Dhamma that I follow."

"What does this Blessed One teach? What is his Dhamma?"

Before answering, Venerable Assaji thought, "These wandering ascetics are opposed to the Buddha's dispensation. I will show him how profound this teaching is." Then he said aloud, "Friend, it is not long since I left the home life, and only recently have I come to this Dhamma and discipline. I cannot explain the Blessed One's Dhamma in detail to you."

"My name is Upatissa," he replied, and, confident of his own intelligence, he urged Venerable Assaji, "Please tell me what you can. Be it little or much, it will be my task to understand it."

In reply, Venerable Assaji recited this verse:

Of those things that arise from a cause,
The Tathagata has told the cause,
And also what their cessation is.
This is the teaching of the Great Recluse.

As soon as he heard these lines, Upatissa became a stream-enterer and realized that the path to liberation was to be found in this Dhamma.

"Venerable Sir," he said, feeling respect and gratitude to Venerable Assaji, "there is no need to explain the teaching any further. This will suffice! Where does our Master reside?"

"In Veluvana, the Bamboo Grove Monastery, Friend."

"Please go on ahead, Venerable Sir. I have a dear friend with whom I have made a pact that whichever of us should discover the path to liberation first should inform the other. I must go and tell him. Then together we will follow and come into the Teacher's presence."

Prostrating himself at Venerable Assaji's feet, Upatissa took his leave and went to the park of the wandering ascetics to find Kolita.

Kolita saw him approaching and thought, "Today my friend's appearance is changed. I feel sure that he has found liberation!"

Perceiving that thought, Upatissa greeted Kolita, "Yes, dear friend! The Deathless has been found!"

He repeated the verse he had heard from Venerable Assaji, and, by the time he had completed it, Kolita, too, had attained stream-entry. "Where, dear Upatissa," he asked, "does our Master live?"

"Venerable Assaji told me that he is staying at Veluvana, the Bamboo Grove Monastery."

"Let us go there immediately," Kolita suggested.

"No," Upatissa objected. "We should first inform our teacher Sanjaya of what we have learned. Even if he is not able to grasp the teaching immediately, having confidence in our wisdom, he may accompany us to see the Master. When he hears the Buddha's teaching, he, too, may attain liberation."

Kolita agreed and they went to meet Sanjaya. "Dear Teacher," they said, "a Buddha has appeared in the world! His Dhamma is well-proclaimed, and his monks live in a proper way. Let us go together to see the Buddha!"

"What are you saying?" Sanjaya exclaimed. "Just think of the fame you'll enjoy if you stay here and share my place as teacher of all these students!"

The two young men continued to urge their former teacher to join them, and Sanjaya realized that they were determined to follow the Buddha. "Of course, you may go," he said, "but I cannot!"

"Why not, Teacher?" Kolita asked.

"Friends," he replied, "I am the teacher of many. If I were to regress to the status of a pupil, it would be like a vast pond becoming a small pitcher. It is too late for me to become someone else's disciple!"

"Do not think like that, Teacher!" they cried.

"Let it be, my dears. You may go," he repeated, "but I cannot."

"Please reconsider, Teacher!" they urged. "When a Buddha appears in the world, it is natural for people to flock to him, pay him homage, and offer him incense and flowers. We, too, will go there. What will happen to you?"

"My dear students," Sanjaya replied calmly, "what do you think? In this world, which is more numerous, fools or the wise?

"Teacher," they replied, puzzled as to his meaning, "Fools are many, but the wise are few."

"In that case, let the wise ones go to the wise Gotama, and the fools will come to me. You may go, but I will not."

Upatissa and Kolita realized that further pleading was useless, and they departed for Veluvana. Hearing the news, Sanjaya's students began arguing, and many left to follow Upatissa and Kolita. Abandoned by most of his followers, Sanjaya vomited hot blood.

When the Buddha saw the two friends coming, he announced to the bhikkhus, "These two, Upatissa and Kolita, are a blessed pair. They will be my chief disciples."

After Upatissa and Kolita paid their respects, they asked, "Venerable Sir, may we receive the Going Forth under the Blessed One, may we receive Higher Ordination in the Sangha!"

"Come, Bhikkhus!" the Buddha intoned, "Well-proclaimed is the Dhamma. Now live the life of purity to make an end of suffering!" That was sufficient for the two to become bhikkhus and, they were immediately endowed with the eight requisites.

By the time the Buddha had finished his discourse, all who heard, with the exception of two newly ordained bhikkhus, had attained arahatship. It was necessary for those two to make greater attainments to prepare themselves to become the chief disciples and to serve the Buddha in their special roles.

At ordination, Upatissa received the name of Sariputta, and Kolita received the name of Maha-Moggallana.

Seven days later, while Venerable Moggallana was meditating, he became sleepy. The Buddha roused him, helped him overcome his fatigue, and instructed him in meditation on the elements. Through this teaching, Venerable Moggallana attained arahatship along with tremendous supernatural powers and all the qualities requisite to be a Chief Disciple.

Venerable Sariputta spent most of his time near the Buddha in the Boar's Cave on Gijjikuta, Two weeks after his ordination, Venerable Sariputta was standing behind the Buddha and fanning him while the Buddha gave a discourse on the contemplation of feelings to the Venerable Sariputta's nephew, Dighanakha, who was a wandering ascetic. As Venerable Sariputta followed the discourse, he attained arahatship along with the fourfold analytical knowledge. He also achieved the highest level of knowledge for a chief disciple. His understanding and wisdom were second only to the Buddha himself.

That very evening, the Buddha had all the bhikkhus assembled and announced that Venerable Sariputta and Venerable Moggallana had become his Chief Disciples. Some bhikkhus complained that the Buddha was showing favoritism and that he should have given that honor to those who had ordained earlier.

When the Buddha heard about their grumbling, he said, "Bhikkhus, I do not show favoritism, but I acknowledge the aspirations which one has made. For example, in a previous life, Kondañña gave almsfood nine times during a single harvest and made an aspiration was to become the first to attain arahatship in a Buddha Sasana. This he achieved.

"Many aeons ago, Sariputta and Moggallana made aspirations to become chief disciples. Their appointment as chief disciples was not because of any preference of mine. It is the fulfilment of my sons' aspirations. I have simply given them what they wished for."

Throughout his life, Venerable Sariputta showed special respect for Venerable Assaji. As he paid homage in the direction in which Venerable Assaji was staying, he repeated, "This Venerable One was my first teacher. It was through him that I came to know the Buddha's Dhamma."

All of Venerable Sariputta's siblings, three brothers and three sisters, were ordained in the Sangha and attained arahatship. His mother, however, proud of her brahmin caste, remained vociferously hostile to the Buddha and the Sangha. Once, while Venerable Sariputta was staying in his home village with a large group of bhikkhus, he went to his mother's house on his almsrounds. His mother gave him a seat and served him with food, but, all the while, she muttered abusive words. "You eater of others' leftovers!" she cursed. "When you fail to get leavings of sour rice gruel, you go from house to house among strangers, licking the leftovers from the backs of ladles! Was it for this you gave up eighty crores? You abandoned your wealth to became a bhikkhu! You ruined me! Well, go ahead and eat!"

As she served the other bhikkhus, she also reviled them. "You are the ones who have made my son your errand boy!" she mocked. "Go ahead and eat!"

Remaining silent, Venerable Sariputta ate his food and calmly returned to the monastery. Venerable Rahula, who had been present, reported the incident to the Buddha. The other bhikkhus discussed Venerable Sariputta's extraordinary patience, and the Buddha praised him with this verse:

One who is anger-free, dutiful,
Virtuous, and without lust;
One who has gained self-control and destroyed rebirth;
Is one I call a true brahmin.

After serving as Marshall of the Dhamma for many years, Venerable Sariputta reflected on the matter and realized that the chief disciples always pass away before the Buddha. He considered his own life-force and realized that it would sustain him for only one more week.

"Where shall I have my final passing away?" he wondered. "Although my mother gave birth to seven who have become arahats, she has no confidence in the Buddha, the Dhamma, and the Sangha. She has, however, the supportive conditions to acquire that confidence, and I am the only one who can lead her to the path. If I remain indifferent, people may rightly say that Sariputta helped others but failed to remove his own mother's wrong views! Yes! I will pass away in the same room in which I was born."

Venerable Sariputta knelt before the Buddha, paid obeisance, and said, "Venerable Sir, if I have committed any act by speech or body which did not please you, may the Blessed One forgive me! It is now time for me to go. I ask permission of the Blessed One to attain final Nibbana in my home village."

"Sariputta," the Buddha replied, "there has not been a single word or deed of yours that was displeasing to me. Now do what you think is fitting."

When Venerable Sariputta left the monastery, a vast crowd accompanied him. After a while, he ordered the laypeople to turn back. "This is a road that no one can avoid."

In the evening, Venerable Sariputta and the accompanying bhikkhus stopped under a banyan tree near the village gate and happened to meet his nephew, Uparevata. The youth approached, paid his respects, and waited for Venerable Sariputta to speak.

"Please go to your grandmother and announce our coming. If she asks, tell her that I will stay in the village for one day. Ask her to prepare my birth chamber and to provide lodgings for five hundred bhikkhus."

Uparevata did as he was asked.

"Why does my son want me to provide lodgings for so many?" Sari wondered. "Why does he want me to prepare his old room? After having become a monk in his youth, is he going to disrobe in his old age?" Puzzled, she did everything he had requested.

Immediately after entering the room prepared for him, Venerable Sariputta suffered an attack of dysentery. Repeatedly, toilet pails were taken in and carried out, but his mother did not know of his illness.

During the night, the Four Great Kings realized that Venerable Sariputta was in his birth chamber and that his final passing away was quickly approaching. They went there to see him for the last time and offered to take care of him.

He told them that he had Venerable Cunda as his attendant and refused their help. After they left, Sakka and Maha-Brahma also came, and Venerable Sariputta dismissed each of them in the same way.

Venerable Sariputta's mother could not help but see the bright lights appearing in her son's room and wondered what was happening. She went to the door and asked Venerable Cunda if everything was all right, and he let her enter her son's room.

"Why have you come at this late hour?" Venerable Sariputta asked his mother.

"I have come to see you," she replied. "I saw lights. Please tell me who was here earlier."

"It was the Four Great Kings."

"Why? Are you greater than they?"

"From the time that our teacher, the Buddha, was reborn in this world, they have protected him, with swords in hand. They are like temple attendants. They came to pay respects to me."

"Who came after they left?"

"That was Sakka."

"Are you greater than the king of devas?"

"Sakka is like a novice who attends to a bhikkhu's belongings. When the Buddha returned from Tavatimsa, Sakka carried his bowl and robe and descended with him at Sankassa."

"After Sakka left, who came and filled the room with such radiance?"

"Laywoman, that was your own Lord, Maha-Brahma."

"My son, are you greater than even my Lord, Maha-Brahma?"

"Yes, Laywoman. On the day when our teacher was born, four Great Brahmas received him in a golden net."

Hearing this, Sari thought, "If my son is so great that these heavenly being come to pay him their respects, how much greater must be his Master?" At that, her body and mind were thrilled.

"Rapture and joy have arisen in my mother," Venerable Sariputta thought. "Now is the time to preach the Dhamma to her." Aloud he asked, "What were you just thinking, Laywoman?"

"I was thinking, "If my son has such virtue, how great must be his Master?"

Venerable Sariputta replied, "On four occasions—at my Teacher's birth, at his Great Renunciation, at his achieving Enlightenment, and at his first turning of the Wheel of the Law—this ten-thousandfold universe quaked. There is none to equal him in virtue, in concentration, in wisdom, in liberation, and in the knowledge and vision of liberation."

By the time her son had finished teaching, Sari had become a stream-enterer.

"My dear Upatissa," she cried, "why, during all these years, did you not bestow on me this ambrosia, this nectar of the Deathless?"

Venerable Upatissa, satisfied that he had repaid his mother for bringing him up, dismissed her, saying, "You may go now, Upasika."

Then he had Venerable Cunda call the bhikkhus together. When they had gathered, he said to them, "My brothers, for forty-four years I have lived and traveled with you. If any deed or word of mine was unpleasant to you, forgive me."

"Venerable Sir," the bhikkhus replied, "not one of us, who have followed you as closely as your shadow, has ever felt even the slightest displeasure from you. Instead, may you, Venerable Sir, forgive us!"

With that, Venerable Sariputta wrapped his robe around him, covered his face, and lay down on his right side. He passed through successive meditative states, in forward and reverse order, and, as the rising sun appeared over the horizon, he passed away into Nibbana without remnant of clinging.

When his mother entered the room and realized that he had passed away, she fell at his feet, lamenting, "My dear son! Before this, we did not know of your virtue. Because we were unaware, we did not have the good fortune to feed many bhikkhus! We did not have the good fortune to build many monasteries! We learned too late to do many good deeds!"

That morning, Sari opened her treasury. She gave some of her gold to goldsmiths with orders for them to prepare funeral decorations. She used another portion to build a great pavilion of gilded wood where celebrations were held for a full week. On the seventh day, a magnificent pyre of fragrant wood was prepared. Throughout the night of the cremation, devas and humans listened to the Dhamma. After Venerable Anuruddha had extinguished the flames with scented water, Venerable Cunda gathered the relics and placed them in a fine cloth, along with Venerable Sariputta's almsbowl and robes. He carried these things to Savatthi to inform the Buddha of the event.

When Venerable Ananda heard the news, he felt that nothing was clear to him any longer and that his own body had become as weak as a creeper.

"How is this, Ananda?" the Buddha asked. "When Sariputta passed into final Nibbana, did he take from you any portion of your virtue, your concentration, or your knowledge and vision of liberation?"

"No, Venerable Sir," Ananda replied, "but Venerable Sariputta was a mentor, a teacher, and an instructor to me, one who roused, inspired and gladdened. He was untiring in preaching Dhamma and a helper of his fellow monks. We remember how vitalizing, enjoyable, and helpful his Dhamma instructions were."

"Have I not already taught you, Ananda, that it is the nature of all things near and dear to us that we must suffer separation from them? Of that which is born, conditioned, and subject to dissolution, how can it be said that it should not depart? That, indeed, is not possible. As from a mighty hardwood tree a large branch should break off, so has Sariputta, in his final passing away, left this great community of bhikkhus."

Taking up Venerable Sariputta's relics in his hand, the Buddha said, "These, Bhikkhus, are the shell-colored relics of Sariputta, who, not long ago, asked for permission to have his final passing away. He who, for incalculable aeons, had fulfilled the Perfections—this was that bhikkhu. He who obtained the seat next to me—this was that bhikkhu. He who, throughout the ten-thousandfold universe, apart from me, had none equal to him in wisdom—this was that bhikkhu. Of great wisdom was this bhikkhu His wisdom was likewise broad, bright, quick, and penetrative. Few wants had this bhikkhu; he was contented, bent on seclusion, not fond of company, and full of energy. Censuring what is evil, he was an exhorter of his fellow bhikkhus. He who went forth into homelessness, abandoning the great fortune obtained through his merits in five hundred existences—this was that bhikkhu. He who, in my Sasana, was as patient as the earth—this was that bhikkhu. He who was as harmless as a bull whose horns had been cut—this was that bhikkhu. He whose mind was as humble as a Candala boy—this was that bhikkhu."

—Adapted from various sources

The Conch Blower

On one occasion the Blessed One was staying at Pavarika's Mango Grove in Nalanda. At that time, Asibandhakaputta the headman, a lay disciple of the Niganthas, approached the Blessed One, paid his respects, and sat down to one side.

The Blessed One asked him: "Headman, what does Nigantha Nataputta teach his disciples?"

"Venerable Sir, Nigantha Nataputta teaches: 'One who destroys, takes what is not given, engages in sexual misconduct, or speaks falsehood is bound for a state of misery or for hell. One is reborn according to the way in which one usually acts.'"

"If it were true that one is reborn according to the way in which one usually acts, then according to Nigantha Nataputta's word, no one at all would be bound for a state of misery or for hell. What do you think? In the case of a person who destroys life, which is more frequent: the occasions when he is destroying life or those when he is not doing so?"

"In the case of a person who destroys life, Venerable Sir, the occasions when he is destroying life are less frequent than those when he is not doing so."

"Therefore, if it were true that one is reborn according to the way in which one usually acts, then, according to Nigantha Nataputta's word, one who destroys life would not be bound for a state of misery or for hell.

"Is it not the same in the case of a person who takes what is not given, in the case of a person who engages in sexual misconduct, and in the case of a person who speaks falsehood?"

"Yes, Venerable Sir."

"Therefore, if it were true that one is reborn according to the way in which one usually acts, then, according to Nigantha Nataputta's word, no one at all would be bound for a state of misery or for hell.

"Suppose that a teacher believes and teaches: 'One who destroys life, takes what is not given, engages in sexual misconduct, or speaks falsehood is bound for a state of misery or for hell.' A disciple who has full confidence in that teacher might think: 'My teacher believes and teaches: "One who destroys life is bound for a state of misery or for hell." I have destroyed life, so I, too, am bound for a state of misery or for hell.' Thus, he acquires wrong view. If he does not abandon that assertion and that state of mind and relinquish that wrong view, he will be, accordingly, reborn in hell

"He might think in the same way about taking what is not given, engaging in sexual misconduct, or speaking falsehood. In each case, he acquires wrong view. If he does not abandon that assertion and that state of mind and relinquish that wrong view, he will be, accordingly, reborn in hell

"However, suppose that there arises in the world a Tathagata, an arahat, perfectly enlightened, accomplished in true knowledge and conduct, well gone, a knower of worlds, the unsurpassed trainer of people to be tamed, a teacher of devas and humans, enlightened, and blessed. In many ways he criticizes and censures the destruction of life, and he says: 'Abstain from the destruction of life.' He criticizes and censures the taking of what is not given, and he says: 'Abstain from taking what is not given.' He criticizes and censures sexual misconduct, and he says: 'Abstain from sexual misconduct' He criticizes and censures false speech, and he says: 'Abstain from false speech.'

"A disciple who has full confidence in that teacher reflects thus: 'In many ways the Blessed One criticizes and censures the destruction of life, and he says: "Abstain from the destruction of life." I have destroyed life to such and such an extent. That wasn't proper; that wasn't good. Although I feel regret over this, that evil deed of mine cannot be undone.' Having reflected thus, he abandons the destruction of life, and he abstains from the destruction of life in the future. Thus, there comes about the abandoning of that evil deed and the transcending of that evil deed.

"In the same way, he reflects about taking what is not given, sexual misconduct, and false speech. Having reflected thus, he abandons those practices, and he abstains from them in the future. Thus, there comes about the abandoning of those evil deeds and the transcending of them.

"He also abandons and abstains from divisive speech, harsh speech, and idle chatter. Having abandoned covetousness, he is uncovetous. Having abandoned ill-will and hatred, he has a mind without ill-will. Having abandoned wrong view, he is one of right view.

"That noble disciple, who is thus devoid of covetousness and ill-will, unconfused, clearly comprehending, and ever mindful, abides pervading one quarter with a mind imbued with loving-kindness. Likewise, he abides pervading the second quarter, the third quarter, and the fourth quarter Thus, above, below, across, and everywhere, and to all as to himself, he abides pervading the entire world with a mind imbued with loving-kindness, vast, exalted, measureless, without hostility, and without ill-will. Just as a strong conch blower can easily send his signal to the four quarters, when the liberation of mind by loving-kindness is developed and cultivated in this way, any limited kamma that was done does not remain there, does not persist there

"That noble disciple also abides pervading first one quarter and then everywhere with a mind imbued with compassion, with a mind imbued with altruistic joy, and with a mind imbued with equanimity. Just as a strong conch blower can easily send his signal to the four quarters, when the liberation of mind by any of the four Brahma Viharas is developed and cultivated in this way, any limited kamma that was done does not remain there, does not persist there "

When this was said, Asibandhakaputta said to the Blessed One: "Magnificent, Master Gotama! Magnificent, Master Gotama! The Dhamma has been made clear in many ways by Master Gotama, as though he were turning upright what had been turned upside down, revealing what was hidden, showing the way to one who was lost, or holding up a lamp in the dark for those with eyesight to see forms. I go for refuge to Master Gotama, and to the Dhamma, and to the Sangha. Let Master Gotama remember me as a lay follower who from today has gone for refuge for life."

—Samyutta Nikaya 42, 8

Pataliputta

Crossing the Ganges

In Pataligama, the people were excited about the Buddha's arrival. They sent a delegation to invite the Buddha to stay as the first guest in their newly-constructed resthouse, and the Buddha consented by silence. The townspeople hurried to prepare the resthouse, strewing the floor with flowers and incense, preparing the seats, and filling the waterpots and lamps. As soon as everything was ready, they sent a message to the Buddha, and he arrived with the bhikkhus.

Before the Buddha and the bhikkhus entered the hall, the men washed their feet. The Buddha took his seat with his back against the central pillar, facing east. The bhikkhus, arranged themselves at the sides, slightly behind the Buddha, and the laypeople sat facing him.

"Householders, "the Buddha began, "there are five dangers to one of bad morality. First, he suffers great loss of property through neglecting his affairs. Second, he acquires a bad reputation. Third, he is constantly nervous and without self-confidence. Fourth, he dies confused. Fifth, at the breaking up of the body after death, he arises in an evil state, perhaps in hell.

"There are these five advantages to one of good morality. First, through careful attention to his affairs he gains great wealth. Second, he acquires a good reputation. Third, he is always self-confident. Fourth, he dies unconfused. Fifth, at the breaking up of the body after death, he arises in a good place, perhaps in heaven."

The Buddha continued teaching until far into the night, and the laypeople were delighted with his words. Finally, he announced, "Householders, the night is nearly over. It is time for you to do as you think fit."

"Very good, Venerable Sir," they replied. They all paid homage to him and departed. The Buddha spent the remainder of the night in the resthouse.

At dawn, as the Buddha was surveying the world with his divine eye, he saw a lot of activity in the city. "Ananda," he asked, "who is building a fortress in Pataligama?"

"Venerable Sir," Ananda replied, "two of King Ajatasattu's ministers, Sunidha and Vassakara, have brought many other royal ministers to Pataligama. They are fortifying the city to defend it against the Vajjians."

The Buddha declared, "Ananda, it is as if they had taken counsel with the thirty-three gods. I have seen thousands of devas residing here. They have so influenced the Magadhans that the most powerful ministers have chosen the dwelling places of the most powerful devas, and all the other ministers have chosen places corresponding to the respective rank of devas. Ananda, within the realm of Jambudipa and as far as its trade extends, this will become the chief city, and it will be called Pataliputta. In the future, this city will face three perils: fire, water, and internal dissension."

Sunidha and Vassakara called on the Buddha and invited him and the bhikkhus for a meal. The Buddha consented with silence, and the ministers returned home. All in the proper manner, they prepared the food and summoned the Buddha. The Buddha and the bhikkhus arrived, took their assigned seats and were served a delicious meal. Afterward, Sunidha and Vassakara sat down on low stools to one side, and the Buddha offered anumodana:

> Wherever a wise person makes his dwelling, when he
> provides food for the virtuous, the restrained, and
> those who lead the holy life, he should dedicate that
> offering to the devas of that place.

Receiving honor, they will honor him. Being respected,
they will show him respect. They will also feel
sympathy for him, like that of a mother for her child.

For one with whom the devas sympathize, things always
go auspiciously.

Then the Buddha rose from his seat and left.

Sunidha and Vassakara followed closely behind and said: "The gate by which the Buddha leaves our city today shall be henceforth called 'The Gotama Gate.' The ford he uses to cross the Ganges shall be called 'The Gotama Ford.'" Accordingly, one of the city gates became known as "The Gotama Gate."

When the Buddha reached the Ganges River, the water was so high that a crow could drink from it. Many people were gathered on the bank, trying find a means for crossing the river. As swiftly as a strong man might stretch out his flexed arm or flex it again, the Buddha vanished from that side of the Ganges and reappeared with the bhikkhus on the other side.

Then the Buddha declared, "To cross the sea, a lake, or a river, some build a bridge, others search for a boat, and still others make a raft, but the wise have crossed already."

—Digha Nikaya 16

Baranasi

The Case of the Gnawed Leather

It was while staying at Jetavana that the Buddha told this story about acting for the good of relatives.

Long, long ago, when Brahmadatta was reigning in Baranasi, the Bodhisatta was born as a dog. He lived in a great charnel ground as the leader of a pack of several hundred dogs.

One day, the king rode out to his pleasure garden in the royal chariot drawn by milk-white horses. After amusing himself all day in the garden, he returned to the city, well after sunset. Hungry and tired, the king's men hurriedly unhitched the horses, but they left the chariot in the courtyard, with harness and reins still attached. During the night, it rained heavily.

The next morning, the grooms discovered that the leather of the chariot and harness had gotten wet and had been gnawed. They immediately went to the king. "Sire," they reported, "Your Majesty's chariot has been ruined. It seems that, during the night, dogs entered the courtyard through the sewers and gnawed the straps and the beautiful leatherwork covering the chariot."

Enraged, the king shouted, "Kill every dog you see."

The king's soldiers immediately began roaming the streets of the city, killing every dog they found. The dogs were terrified by this wanton slaughter and sought safety in the charnel ground.

"Why are you here in such great numbers?" asked the chief. "What is happening?"

"The king is so infuriated by reports that dogs gnawed the leatherwork and straps of his chariot," they answered, "that he has ordered that all dogs be killed. Throughout the city, dogs are being destroyed wholesale. We are in great danger!"

The leader thought about this and reasoned to himself, "The palace is closely guarded. It would be impossible for an animal from outside to get inside. This must have been done by the king's own purebred dogs, but now innocent creatures are being executed, while there is no punishment for the real culprits. I must try to save the lives of these dogs, my followers."

He comforted his relatives, saying, "Have no fear! I will save you, but, to do it, I must see the king."

Protecting himself with thoughts of loving-kindness and calling to mind the Ten Perfections, the leader stealthily made his way alone into the city. Because of his kindly thoughts, he was able to reach the palace safely without encountering anyone.

He ran straight to the Hall of Justice, where the king was seated, and dived under the throne. The king's servants tried to catch him, but the king stopped them.

Emboldened by this, the great dog emerged from under the throne, bowed to the king, and asked, "Sire, was it you who ordered that all the dogs be destroyed?"

"Yes, it was I."

"What was their offense, Your Majesty?"

"Dogs gnawed the harness straps and the beautiful leatherwork of my chariot and ruined it."

"Do you know which dogs actually did the mischief?"

"No, I do not."

"But, Your Majesty, if you do not know for certain who the real culprits are, is it right to order that every dog be destroyed?"

"It's very simple. Dogs gnawed the leather of my carriage, so I ordered that all dogs be killed. That way, I am sure to punish the guilty dogs."

"Do your men kill all dogs without exception, or are there some dogs who are spared?"

"Some are spared, of course. I am not going to kill the purebred dogs of my own palace."

"Sire, just now, you said that you had ordered the slaughter of all dogs because dogs had gnawed the leather of your chariot. Now you say that the purebred dogs of your own palace are spared. In this, you are following four evil ways—partiality, dislike, ignorance, and fear. Such behavior is wrong, and not king-like. When a king tries a case, he should be as unbiased as the beam of a balance. In this instance, however, you are allowing the royal dogs to go free, while you are mercilessly massacring poor stray dogs. What you are carrying out is not the impartial destruction of all dogs, but rather the slaughter of the poor. Your Majesty is not acting with justice!"

The king listened carefully and replied, "You speak wisely, and I am impressed. Tell me. In your wisdom, do you know who actually gnawed the leather of my chariot?"

"Yes, Sire, I do."

"Who was it?"

"It was the purebred dogs of your palace."

"Can you prove this?"

"I will demonstrate it to you."

"Do so, wise creature."

"Please provide me with a little buttermilk and kusa grass, and send for your dogs."

When this was done, the great dog instructed the king's men to mash the grass, to stir it into the buttermilk, and to feed it to the purebred dogs.

A few minutes after the dogs had drunk the mixture, they began to vomit. When the king's men examined the vomit which the palace dogs had brought up, they discovered bits of leather.

"There is your evidence, Sire!" the wise dog exclaimed.

"What a perfect judgment!" cried the king. He was so pleased that he offered the royal umbrella to the king of the dogs, who established the king in the five precepts. Then he returned the white umbrella of kingship and encouraged the king to be steadfast and righteous.

The king immediately ordered that the slaughter of dogs be stopped and, further, that all dogs be given food fit for the king himself. The king was so moved by the teaching that he also ordered that the lives of all creatures in the realm be protected. He spent the rest of his life in generosity and other good deeds and, when he died, was reborn in heaven. The wise dog lived to a ripe old age before passing away to fare according to his deserts. His teaching endured for ten thousand years.

Having concluded his story, the Buddha identified the birth: "At that time, Ananda was the king, my followers were the dogs of the pack, and I was their wise leader."

—Kukkura Jataka

Savatthi

Visakha

One of the most famous residents of Savatthi was Visakha, who was the Buddha's foremost female devotee.

In Magadha, King Bimbisara's realm, there were a number of millionaires, but, in Kosala, King Pasenadi's realm, there were none. King Bimbisara suggested that Dhananjaya relocate to Kosala, and that rich man agreed. Rather than settling in the city of Savatthi itself, however, Dhananjaya chose to live in Saketa, about seven yojanas from the capital. Dhananjaya and his wife, Sumana Devi, had a daughter named Visakha. When she only seven years old, Visakha had gone to hear the Buddha teach and, by the end of his discourse, had attained stream-entry.

In Savatthi, there was a well-to-do merchant called Migara, with a son named Puññavaddhana. When Puññavaddhana came of age, Migara sent some brahmins to seek throughout the kingdom for a suitable woman of good family with the requisite qualities to marry his son.

The brahmins traveled from one end of Kosala to the other but could find no one satisfactory. They reached Saketa on a public holiday when even usually sequestered young women went to the river to bathe and to celebrate the day.

The brahmins joined the crowd and spied the lovely sixteen-year-old Visakha, who was accompanied by five hundred attendants. Suddenly, a rainstorm came up. Visakha's attendants ran as fast as they could to shelter, but Visakha proceeded at her usual pace. When she reached the hall, her hair and clothing were all wet.

"This young woman is certainly lazy. I'll bet her husband won't even get sour rice gruel to eat," one of the brahmins remarked sarcastically, loud enough for her to overhear.

"What's that you say, sirs?" asked Visakha mildly, in her melodious voice.

"We were talking about you, young lady. We were noticing that, while your attendants hurried here and saved their clothing from getting wet, you didn't quicken your pace at all and got yourself thoroughly soaked needlessly."

"Sirs, I am much faster and stronger than these girls. I had good reason for not hurrying"

"What could that be, Miss?"

"There are four persons who do not appear to advantage while hurrying, but, in addition to that, I have another reason as well."

"Please explain."

"A king in full regalia deserves criticism if he hikes up his robes and runs. People will judge him unfavorably if he acts like a common householder."

"In the same way, the royal elephant when fully caparisoned, a bhikkhu on his almsrounds, and a well-bred lady under any circumstances appear to disadvantage whenever they run. As for the woman, if she takes to her heels, people will say that she is acting like a man."

"Please tell us the other reason you mentioned," they requested.

"Parents bring up a daughter with great care. If she were to fall and break an arm or leg, she would become a burden to them, rather than repaying them for that care. With these considerations in mind, sirs, I never hurry."

Impressed by her poise, beauty, and maturity, the brahmins placed a golden garland around her neck and identified themselves as the emissaries of a family in Savatthi interested in finding a bride. They gave full particulars of the family, and Visakha accepted their proposal. As soon as she had informed her parents of her decision, they also gave their consent. King Pasenadi himself, out of respect for Dhananjaya, accompanied Migara to Saketa to celebrate the match.

Despite her youth, Visakha undertook full responsibility for the arrangements to entertain all the visitors from Savatthi, and she managed everything perfectly. To show their appreciation for

Dhananjaya's hospitality, everyone sent presents to Visakha, according to their ability. Visakha, in turn, redistributed these gifts to the people of Saketa, including a thoughtful message with each gift. Everything was so graciously done that both visitors and residents felt akin to her.

So that his daughter would never lack for anything in her new home, Dhananjaya prepared a dowry of five hundred carts each of coins, gold vessels, silverware, garments, bags of fragrant rice, and jars of ghee. He also gave her a great herd of cattle and many servants. In regard to servants, he chose only those who had true affection for her so that she would be looked after by those who really wanted to be with her.

As a wedding gift, Dhananjaya gave Visakha a magnificent jewel-encrusted gold parure (Mahalatapasadhana), which covered her head and swept to the ground.

The day before the ceremony, Dhananjaya called Visakha and said, "My dear daughter, tomorrow you will leave. I want to give you some advice. There are ten rules you should observe with your husband's family.

"Indoor fire should not be carried outside; outdoor fire should not be carried inside; give only to one who gives in return; do not give to one who does not give in return; give both to one who gives and to one who does not give; sit happily; eat happily; sleep happily; tend the fire; and honor the household deities."

Dhananjaya assigned eight respected citizens of Saketa to accompany Visakha and to serve as her sponsors in Savatthi. "If my daughter is accused of any fault," he instructed them, "clear her name."

Dhananjaya gave permission to those all who so wished to escort his daughter to Savatthi, and such a huge crowd of people followed that Migara was afraid of the expense and forcefully drove most of them back.

At the gate of Savatthi, Visakha stood up in her chariot. When the residents of Savatthi saw her, they cried, "So that is Visakha! She is lovely! Her gold and jeweled parure certainly becomes her! We won't soon forget this sight!"

Migara was devoted to the Niganthas, who were naked ascetics. He had neither interest in nor respect for the Buddha, even though the Teacher was staying in a monastery nearby. One day, Migara invited five hundred naked ascetics for rice porridge. When they were seated, he called Visakha to pay homage to the "arahats."

Delighted to hear that arahats were there, Visakha gladly went to the hall, but she was severely shocked to see those ascetics sitting stark naked. "Such men as these are without modesty!" she cried. "They are not arahats!" Instantly, she turned and left the hall.

Migara was mortified, and the ascetics castigated him. "Why did you choose that woman to be your son's wife?" they asked. "It was a great mistake to bring a follower of Gotama into your family. Throw her out of your house!"

Migara did not know what to do. He realized that it was impossible to send her away because Visakha came from a wealthy and influential family and the king himself had solemnized the marriage.

After the naked ascetics left the house, Migara sat down to eat his own lunch of rich rice porridge from a golden dish, while Visakha fanned him. Just then, a bhikkhu on his almsrounds paused at the door. Visakha saw the bhikkhu but was reluctant to announce his presence. She stepped aside so that Migara could see the bhikkhu, but Migara pretended not to see him and continued eating. Fully grasping the situation, Visakha said to the bhikkhu, "Pass on, Venerable Sir. My father-in-law is eating stale food."

Migara became furious. He ordered servants to remove Visakha from the house. Since all the domestic help had come with Visakha, however, not one of them spoke or made a move.

"My dear father-in-law," Visakha replied calmly, "there is no reason for me to leave your house. I am not a common wench brought here from some bathing place on the river. A young woman who has living parents does not leave her in-laws' home for such a flimsy reason. For just such a situation, my father sent eight respected sponsors from Saketa. Send for these men and let them clear me of the charge."

Migara was forced to admit the truth of Visakha's words. He summoned the men and said, "This young woman told an ascetic that I was eating stale food, although, in fact, I was eating rich rice porridge out of my golden bowl. She insulted me, and I want her expelled from this house!"

"Is what he says true, dear girl?" the sponsors asked.

"Not exactly, sirs. Let me explain. A bhikkhu was walking for alms and stopped at the open door. My father-in-law was eating porridge and completely ignored him. I thought, 'My father-in-law is consuming his past merit but is making no fresh merit.' It was to this I was referring when I said to the bhikkhu, 'Pass on, Venerable Sir. My father-in-law is eating stale food.' My words were apt. What fault is there in that?"

"None at all. What our daughter said was entirely proper. There is no reason to get angry, sir."

Migara grudgingly accepted their judgment but went on to complain that Visakha had once left the house with her servants in the middle of the night for some frivolous reason.

"Is what he says true, dear girl?" the sponsors asked.

"Sirs, shortly after my arrival in Savatthi, my favorite mare delivered a foal, and I was concerned for her safety. Although it was midnight, I gathered a few maids and hurried to the stable to assess the situation. Satisfied with all arrangements, I returned to my own quarters."

"Sir, it seems that our daughter does work in your house which would normally would be expected only of servants. What fault do you find in this?"

"Sirs, I admit that I was wrong in that case, too, but, just before this young woman left Saketa, I happened to be in an adjoining room, and I heard her father give her some very peculiar and suspicious advice. He told her not to give fire from the house to those outside, but we always give fire when asked. Then he said not to take into the house fire from outside. That is sheer nonsense! He advised her to give only to those who give in return, not to give to those who do not give in return, and to give both to him who gives and to him who does not give. That is gobbledegook! He advised her to sit, eat and sleep happily, to tend the fire, and to honor household deities. She agreed to all points, but they make no sense!"

"Is what he says true, dear girl?"

"Sirs, my father's meaning was clear to me, but my father-in-law has failed to understand it. My father's first advice was that if I see any fault in this family which I have married into, I should say nothing about it outside the house because there is no fire like bearing such tales.

"His second advice was not to bring is to bring gossip about my in-laws that I hear from neighbors back into this house, for saying, 'So-and-so said this about you,' is just as dangerous as a fire.

"Giving only to one who gives in return means lending only to those who return borrowed articles. Not giving to one who does not give in return means not lending to one who does not return borrowed articles. Giving both to him who gives and to him who does not give means giving to any poor friend or relative who asks for help, whether or not that person will ever be able to repay.

"When my father told me to sit happily, he meant that a wife should stand when either her mother-in-law or her father-in-law is present. Eating happily means eating only after her mother-in-law and father-in-law have eaten. Sleeping happily means going to bed only after having cared for her parents-in-law and her husband.

"Tending the fire means treating her new family with devotion.

"Finally, honoring the household deities means paying proper respect to her parents-in-law."

Migara was struck dumb and could look neither Visakha nor her sponsors in the eye.

"Sir, is there any other fault you can find with our daughter?"

"No," he said in a low voice, with his head bowed. "There is not."

"In that case, you should not be trying to force her to leave."

Visakha then spoke up with a firm voice. "Friends, being innocent of those charges, it would have been improper for me to have left at my father-in-law's behest. Now, however, I have decided, for my own good reasons, to return to my father's house."

Turning to her servants, she gave the order for them to prepare everything immediately for departure.

Migara was nonplussed and said, "Dear daughter-in-law, please pardon me for my mistakes. I spoke through ignorance. Forgive me!"

"Father-in-law, I certainly pardon you for your accusations. However, I am the daughter of a household which has firm confidence in the Buddha and his Sangha. I cannot stay without an opportunity to serve the bhikkhus. If, however, I am allowed to serve them, according to my inclinations, I will stay."

"Dear daughter-in-law, serve them to your heart's content."

"In that case, let me, with great joy, invite the Buddha and his bhikkhus tomorrow!"

When the Niganthas heard about this, a group of ascetics surrounded the house.

The next morning Visakha sent a message asking her father-in-law to help serve the Buddha, and Migara told the Niganthas about it. They berated him for even considering such a thing. To placate them Migara told her to manage without him. After she had finished offering the rice and curries, she sent a second message to Migara, inviting him to hear the Buddha teach the Dhamma. Migara realized that it would be extremely improper for him not to attend. Moreover, he was curious and even eager to hear the Buddha preach. Finally, the naked ascetics relented, but they made him promise that he would sit behind a curtain to listen.

The Buddha began, "You may sit beyond a curtain or beyond a wall or beyond a mountain, or even beyond the range of mountains that encircles the earth, but I am the Buddha, and I can make you hear my words." With his clear voice, the Buddha taught a gradual discourse of the Dhamma such that Migara felt that the Teacher was speaking to him alone. As he listened, he reflected, and, at the end of the discourse, he attained stream-entry, with unshakable confidence in the Triple Gem.

With tears in his eyes, Migara prostrated himself at the Buddha's feet and declared, "Venerable Sir, all this time, I have not appreciated the splendid results of giving alms to you. Now, because of my daughter-in-law, I understand, and I have escaped from the misery of rebirth in the states of woe. It was for my sake and my liberation that my daughter-in-law came to my house! Today I know where alms yield abundant fruit. My excellent daughter-in-law is my mother!" From then on, Visakha was known as Migaramata, Migara's mother.

Soon, Visakha's mother-in-law also attained stream-entry, and, from that time on, the doors of that house were always open to the Buddha and the Sangha.

Visakha continued giving prodigious alms, feeding five hundred bhikkhus in her home every day. In the afternoon, she visited the Buddha, and, after listening to his teaching, made the rounds of the monastery to find out what was needed. She asked the Buddha for eight boons, and he granted them. She asked to be allowed to provide robes for the Sangha for the rainy season retreat, food for bhikkhus coming into Savatthi, food for those going out, food for those who were sick, food for those who were caring for the sick, medicine for the sick, a constant supply of rice gruel for any needing it, and bathing robes for the bhikkhunis.

Visakha had ten sons, ten daughters, many grandchildren, and even more great-grandchildren. Throughout her long life, she maintained such a youthful appearance that some people could not distinguish her from her descendants. She was noteworthy for her excellent health and her great strength. Because of her reputation for bringing good fortune, all the citizens of Savatthi invited her to their homes on auspicious occasions.

Once, during a festival, Visakha was invited to a friend's house, and she wore her magnificent golden parure over her dress. On her return, she decided to stop at the monastery, but she realized that it would be inappropriate to wear such an elegant ensemble, adorned from head to foot in gold and jewels, while listening to the Buddha, let alone afterwards, while visiting the sick bhikkhus. With her maid's help, she removed the heavy parure, wrapped it neatly, and asked her maid to take care of it. Of course, the maid could not carry the parure around as she waited on Visakha, so she laid it in a corner of the monastery where she was sure it would be safe.

A little later, as Venerable Ananda was inspecting the monastery to see if anything had been left behind, he came upon the parure and informed the Buddha about it.

"Just put it away," the Buddha told Ananda. "She can collect it later."

After Visakha had finished visiting the sick, she left the monastery and, turning to her servant, asked for her parure.

"Dear Mistress, I had forgotten about it. I'll go and get it now."

"Fine," Visakha answered, "but, if Venerable Ananda has put it away for safe keeping, I do not want it back. I freely give it to him."

The maid approached Venerable Ananda and explained that she had left the parure in a bundle in a corner.

"Yes," Venerable Ananda replied. "I found it and hung it by the staircase."

"In that case, Venerable Sir, my noble mistress does not want it back!"

Visakha was delighted to donate the parure, but she immediately realized that such a tremendous amount of gold would be troublesome for the bhikkhus. She resolved to sell it and to offer the proceeds to the Sangha. She took the parure to a goldsmith for appraisal and learned that the gold and jewels alone were worth nine crores, while the superb workmanship was easily worth a hundred thousand more. No one in the entire kingdom could afford to buy it from her. She decided to redeem the parure herself at its true value, and she asked the Buddha how she should donate the money.

In reply, the Buddha suggested a residence for the Sangha in Pubbarama, the park at the eastern gate of Savatthi. Visakha's heart overflowed with delight, and she replied, "Venerable Sir, that would be my great joy!" She immediately purchased a piece of land in Pubbarama and began construction of a monastery.

Shortly after the work started, the rains retreat ended, and the Buddha prepared to leave Jetavana with most of the bhikkhus. Visakha asked him to assign one capable bhikkhu to advise her on the construction project.

"Visakha," the Buddha replied, "take the bowl of whichever bhikkhu you wish to stay."

Visakha was particularly fond of Venerable Ananda, but, realizing that Venerable Moggallana's great skills would make the work much easier, she approached the chief disciple and took his bowl. The Buddha told him to turn back with his five hundred bhikkhus and to remain in Savatthi. Thus, the work progressed smoothly and speedily. The new residence, which was called Migaramatupasada was a magnificent two-story building with five hundred rooms on each floor. Because it was crowned with a brilliant pinnacle of beaten gold, it was also called the Brazen Palace. The monastery was being completed at the beginning of the rains retreat, just as the Buddha returned to Savatthi.

Visakha conducted the Teacher to her new monastery and invited him and the Sangha to stay there. He accepted, and she joyfully offered alms to them every day.

A woman came to the monastery and said, "Dear Visakha, I have made this small rug and would like to put it in the new residence. Please tell me where I can spread it."

Visakha answered, "Friend, if I say: 'There is no room,' you will think, 'Visakha is selfish and doesn't want to give me a space.' Therefore, please look around, both upstairs and down, to see whether there is a place for your beautiful rug."

The woman searched throughout the monastery, but she could not find any spot with a rug of less value than her own. "It is impossible for me," she thought, "to share in the merit of furnishing this residence." She leaned against a staircase and shed tears of disappointment.

Venerable Ananda happened to see her and asked, "Lady, why are you crying?"

She showed him the rug and explained the situation. "Come with me," he said. "I know a suitable place for your rug." He led the woman to the entrance and pointed to a spot which Visakha had overlooked.

"Place your rug here between the place where the bhikkhus wash their feet and the foot of the stairs," he suggested. "After washing his feet, every bhikkhu will step on your rug to wipe them before entering the monastery. In this way you will earn great merit!" The woman did so and was overjoyed.

At last, the monastery was completed, and there was a festival to celebrate the grand offering. That evening, as Visakha was walking around the monastery, accompanied by her children, her grandchildren, and her great-grandchildren, she recalled the aspiration she had made in the distant past, and, in her sweet voice, she intoned this solemn utterance:

When shall I give the gift of a monastery,
a pleasing residence for the Buddha and his Sangha?
Fulfilled is my desire.

When shall I furnish that monastery
with beds, chairs, mats, and pillows?
Fulfilled is my desire.

When shall I give alms,
delicious and wholesome food, to those noble ones?
Fulfilled is my desire.

When shall I give the gift of robes,
fine cotton, linen, and silk,dyed ochre, brown, and saffron?
Fulfilled is my desire.

When shall I give the gift of medicines?
Fulfilled is my desire.

The aspiration which I made long ago
is now entirely fulfilled!

The bhikkhus who saw and heard this went to the Buddha and said, "Surrounded by all of her offspring, Visakha is going around the monastery and singing. We have never known her to sing before. Has she lost her mind?"

"Bhikkhus," the Buddha answered, "my daughter is not singing. Today her heart is filled with joy. She is thinking, 'The earnest wish I made long ago is now completely fulfilled,' and she is making a solemn utterance."

"Venerable Sir, when did she make that wish?" they asked.

Then the Buddha told this story of the past.

Long, long ago—one hundred thousand eons ago—a Buddha named Padumuttara appeared in the world. His lifespan was one hundred thousand years. His father was named Sunanda, and his mother was Sujata Devi. The female lay disciple, who was his principal benefactress and stood in the relation of a mother to him, had obtained from him the eight boons, provided him with the four requisites, and waited upon him both in the evening and in the morning.

Another woman, who frequently accompanied the chief lay disciple to the monastery, saw how intimately her friend conversed with the Buddha and how beloved she was, and, one day, she asked the Buddha, "Venerable Sir, in what relation is this woman to you?"

"She is the foremost of my female lay disciples."

"How does a woman become the foremost of a Buddha's female lay disciples?"

"By making an earnest aspiration and striving toward that goal for many eons."

"Venerable Sir, would it be possible to begin by making such an aspiration at this very time?"

"Yes, that would be possible."

"In that case, Venerable Sir, along with your one hundred thousand bhikkhus, please accept alms from me for seven days." The Buddha consented by remaining silent.

Thus, for seven days, she gave alms to the Buddha and all the bhikkhus. On the last day, as she was offering the requisites, she prostrated herself at the Buddha's feet, and declared: "Venerable Sir, in giving these requisites, I do not seek rebirth in a heavenly realm. Instead, may I receive the eight boons from a Buddha like you, may I stand in the relation of a mother to him, and may I be the foremost female lay disciple in providing him with the four requisites."

The Buddha Padumuttara surveyed the vastness of the future and assured her, "At the end of a hundred thousand eons, a Buddha named Gotama will arise in the world. At that time, you will be a female lay disciple named Visakha. You will receive the eight boons from him, you will stand in the relation of a mother to him, and you will be his foremost female lay disciple."

After spending the remainder of that lifetime in doing good works, that woman was reborn as a deva. After other rebirths in various deva realms and in the human realm, she was reborn in Kasi, during the dispensation of the Buddha Kassapa, as the youngest of the seven daughters of King Kiki. Along with her sisters, she frequently offered alms and performed other meritorious deeds.

One day, she fell at the feet of the Buddha and reiterated her earnest aspiration: "In the future, may I stand in the relation of mother to a Buddha like you, and may I be his foremost female lay disciple."

She was again reborn in deva realms and in the human realm, until, in this present life, she was born in Saketa as the daughter of Dhananjaya.

"Thus, Bhikkhus, my daughter was not singing. She was making a solemn utterance because she had seen the fulfillment of her earnest aspiration."

Then, referring to Visakha's many meritorious deeds, the Buddha recited this verse:

> As from a heap of flowers many garlands can be made,
> Even so should many good deeds be done by one born a mortal.
>
> —Dhammapada Commentary on Verse 53

The Pregnant Doe

It was while staying at Jetavana that the Buddha told this story about Venerable Kumara-Kassapa.

In Rajagaha, a wealthy merchant had a daughter who, even as a child, had been uninterested in frivolous things. Unlike other girls her age, she was disgusted by the usual career of marriage and motherhood and wished to become a bhikkhuni instead. Although she begged to be allowed to take the vows, her parents refused because theirs was a wealthy family and she was the only daughter.

Undeterred, she thought to herself, "After I am married, I will get my husband's consent to become a bhikkhuni."

She did, indeed, marry and become a devoted wife, living a life of goodness and virtue in her new home. After some time, she conceived, although she was unaware of her pregnancy.

Shortly after that, there was a big festival. The city was decorated like heaven itself, and people were enjoying the holiday. Despite the festivities, she continued the same as usual. Noticing this, her young merchant husband said, "Dear wife, everybody has gotten dressed up and is celebrating the holiday. You are still wearing your ordinary clothes. You have not put on any make-up, and you are not wearing any of your beautiful jewelry."

"Husband," she replied, "the body is made up of thirty-two parts. What is the point of adorning it? It comes from a bloody womb, born to parents themselves liable to decay. The body is born to waste away and to expand the graveyard. It is a source of sorrow, subject to innumerable diseases. It is only the repository of the workings of kamma. Foul inside, it seeps and oozes foulness. Why decorate and perfume such a nasty thing?"

"Wife," retorted her husband, "if you think this body is so disgusting, why don't you become a bhikkhuni?"

"If I could, Husband, I would take vows this very day."

"Very well," he agreed. "I will help you enter the Order." He offered hospitality to the Sangha and escorted her to a monastery, where she was ordained under Devadatta. She rejoiced at the fulfillment of her life's desire.

As her pregnancy advanced, the other bhikkhunis noticed the signs and said, "Lady, you seem about to become a mother; what does it mean?"

"I have led a virtuous life."

The bhikkhunis took her to Devadatta. "Venerable Sir," they said, "this young gentlewoman, who became a bhikkhuni with the reluctant consent of her husband, is now expecting a baby. Whether this dates from before her admission to the Order or not, we cannot say. What should we do?"

Not being a Buddha, and lacking generosity and compassion, Devadatta figured that rumors that one of his bhikkhunis was pregnant might cause him damage. "It must not be thought that I condone the offense. My course is clear! I must expel this woman from the Order." Without any enquiry, he had her thrown out immediately.

The bhikkhunis paid their respects to Devadatta and started back to the monastery, but the young woman pleaded with them, saying "Ladies, Devadatta is not the Buddha. My ordination was into the Buddha's Order. Don't deprive me of the vocation which I won with great difficulty. Take me to the Buddha at Jetavana." Moved by her supplications, they accompanied her on the journey of forty-five yojanas from Rajagaha to Savatthi. After paying their respects to the Buddha, they explained the matter to him.

The Buddha listened and thought, "Even though the baby was conceived while she was still a laywoman, unbelievers will talk if I decide by myself to accept a bhikkhuni expelled by Devadatta. In order to avoid such talk, this case must be examined in the presence of the king and his court."

The next morning, he asked King Pasenadi and the great lay disciples, Anathapindika and Visakha, to come to the monastery, along with other influential persons. When all bhikkhus, bhikkhunis, and lay disciples were present, the Buddha instructed Venerable Upali, who was foremost in knowledge of the Vinaya, to clear up the matter of the young bhikkhuni.

First, Venerable Upali called upon Visakha and asked her to determine when the young woman had conceived and whether it had occurred before or after she had joined the Order. Visakha compared the days and months and discovered that the conception had, without doubt, taken place before she had become a bhikkhuni. When this was reported, Upali proclaimed to the assembly that the bhikkhuni was innocent. With her innocence clearly established, she paid her respects to the Buddha and the bhikkhus and returned to her own monastery with her companions.

In due time, she delivered a strong and healthy son, for whom she had prayed at the feet of the Buddha Padumuttara many ages previously. One day, when the king was passing the monastery, he heard an infant's cry. Asking his courtiers to find out the source, he learned that the crying came from the baby which the young bhikkhuni had recently delivered.

"Caring for a child will be a burden to the bhikkhunis in their religious life; let us take charge of him." He offered to take the baby and handed him over to his commander, who gave him to the women of his own family. The baby was named Kumara-Kassapa, Prince Kassapa, and was raised in the king's court as a prince.

At the age of seven, Kumara-Kassapa became a samanera under the Buddha, and, when he was twenty, was fully ordained as a bhikkhu. Venerable Kumara-Kassapa became famous as a preacher of the Dhamma, and the Buddha declared him foremost among the bhikkhus in eloquence. Both he and his mother attained arahatship. One day, the bhikkhus were talking about the attainments of Venerable Kumara-Kassapa and his mother. "Because Devadatta lacked generosity and compassion," one of them said, "he almost ruined Venerable Kumara-Kassapa and his venerable mother. The Buddha, however, perfect in generosity, love, and pity, became their refuge." When the Buddha heard what they were discussing, he said, "This is not the first time, Bhikkhus, that I have been the refuge of these two. Long ago, also, I was their refuge." At the request of the bhikkhus, he told this story of the past.

Long, long ago, when Brahmadatta was reigning in Baranasi, the Bodhisatta was born as a deer. While a fawn, he was a beautiful golden color, with bright eyes, horns like silver, and lacquered hooves. After he matured, he led five hundred deer and was known as King Nigrodha. In the same forest, there was another deer, also with a herd of five hundred. He was called Sakha.

King Brahmadatta demanded meat at every meal and was passionately fond of hunting. He regularly conscripted his subjects, townsfolk and countryfolk alike, to act as beaters for him on his hunting expeditions.

"This king interferes with our work," the people grumbled. While they were discussing the hardship imposed upon them by the king's frequent hunting trips, one of them suggested, "Why don't we sow grass and provide a water supply in the king's own pleasure garden? We can drive deer into the enclosure, and the king can hunt them at his pleasure!"

Everyone agreed that this was a great idea. They chose a suitable corner of the king's pleasure garden, planted it with lush grass, and erected a sturdy fence. With the gate opened wide, they armed themselves with sticks and noise makers and surrounded about a yojana of forest to catch the deer. Their circle included the haunts of the herds of both of the deer kings Nigrodha and Sakha. As soon as the people saw the deer, they beat the trees, bushes, and ground with their sticks. The noise so startled the animals that they all ran, trying to flee. Of course, they ran straight into the enclosure. As soon as all the deer were inside the garden, the men shut the gate.

They chose a spokesman to inform the king, "Sire, your frequent hunting trips have so interrupted our work that we have created a deer park in your pleasure garden. There you may hunt as much you like, and there are plenty of deer for your table." The king inspected the new park and was very pleased. Among the deer, he saw the two golden stags, Nigrodha and Sakha, and granted them immunity.

Thereafter, the king enjoyed hunting without disturbing his subjects, and, at other times, he sent his cook to kill a deer for the meat. At the sight of the bow, the deer would dash off in fear. Sometimes, several deer were injured as they fled. Sometimes, the deer that was shot was able to escape but would later collapse and die. Thus, on some days, many deer were injured, and several died accidentally.

Some of the deer described this to Nigrodha, who sent for Sakha and said, "Friend, our deer know that they cannot escape death, but they are being destroyed in great numbers, and many are being needlessly injured. Let us establish a system whereby the deer go to the block by turns, one day one from my herd, and the next day one from yours. The deer on whom the lot falls must go to the place of execution and lie with its head on the block. In this way, the deer will escape unnecessary suffering." Sakha readily consented. When they understood what their leaders had discussed, the other deer also agreed. Whenever the cook arrived at the park, he found a deer waiting to be slain. He, too, was pleased at how easy his work had become.

One day, the lot fell on a pregnant doe from Sakha's herd. She approached Sakha and said, "Sire, I am with young. After I have delivered my little one, there will be two of us to take our turns. Please allow me to be passed over this time."

"No," he said curtly, "I cannot make your turn another's. You must bear the consequences of your own fate. Go!" Finding no sympathy from him, the doe went to Nigrodha and repeated her story. He immediately told her not to worry and promised that he would get her exempted from the lottery. After reassuring her, Nigrodha himself went to the execution block and placed his head there.

When the cook saw him, he cried out, "Would you look at that! Here's the king of the deer! What can this mean?" He rushed off to tell the king what he had seen. The king immediately mounted his chariot and hurried to his garden, followed by a large retinue. "My friend, king of the deer," he said, "I granted you immunity. Why are you here?"

"Sire, a doe heavy with fawn came to me and begged that she and her unborn young be spared. I promised to spare her, but, not wanting to pass her doom onto another from my herd, I decided to take it upon myself."

"My Lord, golden king of the deer," said the king, "even among men, I have never seen one so abounding in generosity, love, and compassion as you. I am simply delighted! Stand up! Once more, I spare your life, and I spare her life as well."

"Though two be spared, what about the rest, Sire?"

"I spare their lives, too, Your Majesty."

"Sire, only the deer in your pleasure garden will have immunity. What about all the rest?"

"I spare their lives, too!"

"Sire, deer will thus be safe, but what about all the other four-footed creatures?"

"I spare their lives, too, Your Majesty."

"Sire, four-footed creatures will thus be safe, but what about the flocks of birds?"

"They, too, shall be spared."

"Sire, birds will thus be safe, but what about the fish?"

"I spare their lives, also, Your Majesty."

Having thus interceded with the king for the lives of all creatures, Nigrodha arose and established the king in the five precepts. "Walk in righteousness," he advised the king. "Be just toward all so that, when this life ends, you may be reborn in heaven."

The stag Nigrodha remained in the garden for a few more days to instruct the king. Then, with his herd, he returned to the forest. Often, however, the deer, enjoying full immunity, wandered into the farmers' fields and ate their crops. The farmers did not dare hit the deer or drive them away. Unable to endure the depredations wrought by the voracious deer, the men assembled in the king's courtyard and complained.

"When the deer Nigrodha won my favor," the king answered, "I promised him a boon. I would rather lose my kingdom than break my word. My promise stands! Not a man in my kingdom may harm the deer."

When Nigrodha heard about the problem, he called his herd together and instructed them to stop eating men's crops. Then he sent a message to the farmers explaining that he had forbidden his followers to eat their crops. "From this day forward," his message continued, "farmers need not fence their fields. It will be enough to indicate a field by simply tying leaves around it." That was the beginning of the custom of tying up leaves to mark a field, and never was a deer known to trespass on a field so marked. The doe delivered a fair fawn, who sometimes played with Sakha's herd. "My child," his mother warned him, "don't go about with those deer. Stay with Nigrodha's herd. Death in Nigrodha's company is preferable to the longest life with Sakha."

Nigrodha always admonished the members of his herd to be virtuous. At the close of his long life, he passed away to fare according to his deserts. After spending the rest of his life in performing good deeds, according to the teaching of Nigrodha, King Brahmadatta, too, passed away to fare according to his deserts

Having concluded his story, the Buddha taught the Dhamma. Then he identified the birth: "At that time, Devadatta was Sakha, his followers were that deer's herd, the bhikkhuni was the doe, Kumara-Kassapa was her offspring, Ananda was King Brahmadatta, and I was Nigrodha."

—Nigrodha Jataka

Speculative Views

Once, in Jetavana, Venerable Malunkyaputta said to the Buddha, "These views have been left undeclared by the Blessed One, namely: 'The world is either eternal or not eternal'; 'The world is either finite or infinite'; 'Either the soul is the same as the body or the soul is one thing and the body another'; and 'After death, either a Tathagata exists or does not exist, both exists and does not exist, or neither exists nor does not exist.' I do not accept the fact that the Blessed One does not declare these to me. If you declare these things to me, I will lead the holy life under you; if you do not declare them to me, however, I will abandon the training and return to the low life. If the Blessed One knows either that the world is eternal or that the world is not eternal,' let the Blessed One declare it to me. If the Blessed One does not know whether the world is eternal or not eternal,' then it is straightforward to say: 'I do not know.'

"It is the same for all the others."

"Malunkyaputta," the Buddha replied, "did I ever say to you: 'Come, Malunkyaputta, lead the holy life under me and I will declare to you, "The world is eternal," "The world is not eternal," or any of these other speculative views?"

"No, Venerable Sir."

"Did you ever tell me: 'I will lead the holy life under the Blessed One, and the Blessed One will declare these views to me?"

"No, Venerable Sir."

"That being so, misguided man, who are you and what are you abandoning?

"If anyone should say: 'I will not lead the holy life under the Blessed One until the Blessed One declares to me, "the world is eternal," "the world is not eternal," or any of these other speculative views, those views would remain undeclared by the Tathagata, and, meanwhile, that person would die. Suppose, Malunkyaputta, that a man were wounded by an arrow thickly smeared with poison, and that his friends and relatives, brought a surgeon to treat him. Suppose that that man said: 'I will not let the surgeon pull out this arrow until I know whether the man who wounded me is a nobleman, a brahmin, a merchant, or a worker. I will not let the surgeon pull out this arrow until I know the name and clan of the man who wounded me; whether he is tall, short, or of middle height; whether he is dark, brown, or golden-skinned; in which village, town, or city he lives; whether the bow was a long bow or a cross-bow; whether the bowstring was fibre, reed, sinew, or hemp, whether the shaft of the arrow was wild or cultivated; with what kind of feathers the shaft was fitted—those of a vulture, a heron, a hawk, a peacock, or a stork; and with what kind of sinew the shaft was bound—an ox, a buffalo, a deer, or a monkey; whether the arrowhead was spiked, razor-tipped, curved, barbed, calf-toothed, or lancet-shaped.' All this would still not be known to that man, and, meanwhile, he would die. So too, Malunkyaputta, if anyone should say, 'I will not lead the holy life under the Blessed One until the Blessed One declares those speculative views to me, they would still remain undeclared by the Tathagata, and, meanwhile, that person would die.

"Malunkyaputta, if there is the view, 'The world is eternal,' the holy life cannot be lived; and, if there is the view, 'The world is not eternal,' the holy life cannot be lived. Whether there is the view, 'The world is eternal,' or the view, 'The world is not eternal,' there is birth, aging, death, sorrow, lamentation, pain, grief, and despair, the destruction of which I prescribe here and now.

"It is the same for all the other speculative views.

"Therefore, Malunkyaputta, remember what I have left undeclared as undeclared, and remember what I have declared as declared. What have I left undeclared? I have left undeclared all those speculative views you mentioned.

"Why have I left them undeclared? Because they are unbeneficial, they do not belong to the fundamentals of the holy life, they do not lead to disenchantment, to dispassion, to cessation, to peace, to direct knowledge, to enlightenment, to Nibbana. That is why I have left them undeclared.

"What have I declared? I have declared: 'This is suffering,' 'This is the origin of suffering, ' 'This is the cessation of suffering,' and 'This is the way leading to the cessation of suffering.'

"Why have I declared that? Because it is beneficial, it belongs to the fundamentals of the holy life, it leads to disenchantment, to dispassion, to cessation, to peace, to direct knowledge, to enlightenment, to Nibbana.

"Therefore, Malunkyaputta, remember what I have left undeclared as undeclared, and remember what I have declared as declared."

That is what the Buddha said. The Venerable Malunkyaputta was satisfied and delighted in the Buddha's words.

—Majjhima Nikaya 63

The Weaver's Daughter

Once, the Buddha accepted hospitality from the people of Alavi and, in giving anumodana, taught, "Practice meditation on death, reminding yourselves, 'Uncertain is my life. Certain is my death. I will surely die. Death will be the termination of my life. Life is unstable. Death is sure.'

"Those who have not practiced meditation on death will tremble with fear when their last hour comes, just as a man who has no stick with him, when he sees a snake, is terrified.

"Those who have practiced meditation on death will have no fear when their last hour comes, but will be confident, like an experienced man who, seeing a snake, takes it up with his stick and tosses it easily away from him. Therefore, practice meditation on death."

With only one exception, the people who heard those words of the Buddha were untouched by them and continued to live their lives as before. A weaver's daughter, sixteen years old, heard the Buddha and thought to herself, "Marvelous indeed are those words of the Buddha! It behooves me to practice meditation on death." From that time on, she constantly practiced meditation as the Buddha had taught.

From Alavi the Buddha went to Jetavana. For the next three years, though the Buddha did not visit Alavi again, that weaver's daughter diligently practiced meditation on death.

One day, as he was surveying the world before dawn, the Buddha became aware of that weaver's daughter. He realized that, from the day she heard his discourse, she had practiced meditation on death. "I will go back to Alavi," he thought. "When I ask her four questions, she will answer me correctly each time, and I will congratulate her. Because of her, many will also benefit."

Leaving Jetavana with five hundred bhikkhus, the Buddha went to Alavi, and the people offered him hospitality.

The weaver's daughter heard of the Buddha's arrival and was delighted. "My master has come!" she silently rejoiced. "My teacher is here! For the first time in three years, I can see him and hear him teach the sweet Dhamma."

Just then, her father interrupted her reverie. "Daughter, there is a customer's garment still incomplete on the loom at the workshop. I must finish it today. Hurry and replenish the shuttle. Bring it to me as soon as possible."

The weaver's daughter thought, "I really want to hear the Buddha, but my father has given me work to do. If I disobey my father, he will be angry. First, I will replenish the shuttle. Then, I will hear the Dhamma." With that, she sat down and prepared the shuttle.

Meanwhile, in the hall, the Buddha finished his meal, and the people waited for him to give anumodana.

"I came here for the sake of a certain young woman," the Buddha announced. "She is not yet able to be present. When she comes, I will speak." Then he remained in his seat without saying anymore. The people were quiet because, when the Buddha is silent, no one dares to make a sound.

As soon as the weaver's daughter had replenished the shuttle, she put it in a basket and started toward her father's workshop. As she passed by the hall where the Buddha was sitting, she paused at the edge of the crowd and looked in. The Teacher lifted his head and gazed at her. She understood that he wanted her to draw near, so she put down her basket and walked toward him. She paid obeisance and stood respectfully at one side.

The Buddha asked her, "Young woman, where did you come from?"

"I do not know, Venerable Sir."

"Where are you going?"

"I do not know, Venerable Sir."

"Don't you know?"

"Yes, I know, Venerable Sir."

"Do you know?"

"No, I do not know, Venerable Sir."

When the people heard this exchange, they were offended and began grumbling, "Imagine that! This daughter of a weaver says whatever she pleases to the Enlightened One!

"She should have told the Blessed One that she was coming from her father's house and going to his workshop! Then she says she knows and doesn't know! How rude!"

The Buddha immediately signaled to the people to be quiet and asked the young woman, "When I asked you, 'Where did you come from?' why did you say, 'I do not know'?"

"Venerable Sir, I knew that your meaning was, 'Where did you come from before you were reborn here?' As for me, I do not know where I came from before I was reborn here, and, therefore, I said so."

"Well said! Well said, young woman! You correctly answered that question. When I asked you, 'Where are you going?' why did you say, 'I do not know'?"

"Venerable Sir, I knew that your meaning was, 'When you die, where will you be reborn?' As for me, I do not know where I will be reborn when I have passed from this present existence, and, therefore, I said so."

"Well said! Again you correctly answered my question. When I asked you, 'Don't you know?' why did you say, 'I know'?"

"Venerable Sir, I know that I will surely die, and, therefore, I said so."

"Well said! Again you correctly answered my question. When I asked you, 'Do you know?' why did you say, 'I do not know'?"

"I only know, Venerable Sir, that I will surely die; but at what time I will die, whether in the morning, during the day, or at night, I do not know, and, therefore, I said so."

"Well said!" the Buddha praised her. "You answered all four of my questions correctly." Then he addressed the people, saying: "Those of you who failed to understand her words were offended. Those not having the eye of understanding are blind. Only those who possess the eye of understanding can see." Then he recited the verse:

Blind is this world;
There are few here who see.
Those who go to heaven
Are as few as birds who escape from a net.

As soon as the Buddha finished speaking, the weaver's daughter attained stream-entry.

Recollecting her duty, she picked up her basket and hurried to her father's shop. Unaware that he had fallen asleep at the loom, she leaned forward to give him the shuttle. As she did so, the basket hit the tip of the loom and fell with a clatter. Startled, her father awoke and yanked the loom. As he did so, the tip swung around, striking his daughter in the breast, killing her outright, and she was instantly reborn in Tusita Heaven.

Seeing her body lying there, stained with blood, her father was overcome with grief. "No one but the Buddha," he cried, "can ease my sorrow!"

He hurried to the Teacher and related what had happened. "Venerable Sir," he pleaded, "extinguish my suffering!"

"Do not grieve, Disciple," the Buddha comforted him. "In the round of existence, which is without conceivable beginning, you have shed more tears than the water of the four great oceans over the death of your daughter." As he listened to the Buddha, his grief was assuaged, and he asked to be admitted into the Order.

In no long time, he attained arahatship.

—Dhammapada Commentary on Verse 174

Venerable Sariputta's Patience

One day, near Jetavana, while the Buddha was in residence there, some laypeople were discussing Venerable Sariputta's noble qualities, in particular, his remarkable patience.

"Our noble Elder has such great patience that even when people abuse him or strike him, he feels no trace of anger!"

A brahmin overheard them and asked, contemptuously, "Who is this man who never gets angry? I'll bet nobody has ever really provoked him!"

"We are talking about the Venerable Sariputta."

"Well, I'll make him angry! Just watch me!" the brahmin retorted and strode away to find the Elder. Venerable Sariputta had just entered the city on his almsrounds, and the brahmin, approaching from behind, struck him a tremendous blow on the back, almost knocking the Elder over.

"What was that?" Venerable Sariputta asked mildly and, without even turning around, continued on his way.

A wave of remorse swept over the brahmin and he hurried after the Elder. Throwing himself down at Venerable Sariputta's feet, he begged forgiveness.

"For what?"

"In order to test your patience, I just struck you on the back," the mortified brahmin admitted.

"Very well, then. I pardon you."

"Venerable Sir, please take your meal at my house."

He took Venerable Sariputta's bowl, led the way to his house, and served him food.

The onlookers were furious with the brahmin for assaulting Venerable Sariputta and gathered in front of the brahmin's house, armed with sticks and stones, mad enough to kill him.

When Venerable Sariputta stepped out of the house, accompanied by the brahmin, the angry mob shouted, "Venerable Sir, we want that brahmin! Let us have him!"

"Why, lay disciples? What do you want him for?"

"That man struck you, and we're going to give him just what he deserves!"

"What do you mean? Was it you or me that he hit?"

"It was you, Venerable Sir."

"Well then, he apologized, and I have forgiven him. Go on your way."

After allowing the brahmin to return, Venerable Sariputta calmly went back to Jetavana.

When the Buddha learned of this incident, he recited these verses:

No one should strike a brahmin;
Nor in the brahmin struck should anger rise.

Shame on him who strikes a brahmin!
More shame on the brahmin who strikes back
For a brahmin, nothing's better than
Mind-restraint from all that's dear.
As much as the intention to harm decreases,
So much does one's suffering subside.

—Dhammapada Commentary on Verses 389-390

Angulimala

One of the advisors of the King Pasenadi had a son named Ahimsaka. He was an intelligent youth, and, when he was old enough, he was sent to Takkasila for his education. He proved to be an exceptional student; so much so that his fellow students were jealous of him and spread a rumor that he was having an affair with the teacher's wife. The teacher believed the gossip and was enraged. Wanting to have his star student killed, he devised a wicked plan. Rather than accepting money, the teacher told Ahimsaka that the fee for his studies was one thousand fingers, one from each victim that he killed. Bound to his teacher by a pledge of honor, the poor young man could see no alternative but to comply.

Ahimsaka returned to Kosala and began his bloody quest. He became a merciless killer, attacking anyone he could find on the highways outside the capital. Utterly fearless, he was known to attack groups of ten, twenty, or thirty, sparing no one. Villages became deserted, and people were terrified to travel. At first, Ahimsaka hung the fingers on a tree, but crows ate them. In order to keep count of his victims, he started to wear a garland (mala) of fingers (anguli) around his neck, and he became known as Angulimala.

Terrorized, the people finally rose up and demanded that the king catch Angulimala and stop his killing spree. To satisfy them, the king mobilized a force of five hundred soldiers to capture the outlaw.

When Angulimala's mother heard that the king himself intended to catch the murderer, suspecting him to be her own son, she set out to warn him. It so happened that, by this time, Angulimala had collected nine hundred ninety-nine fingers. He needed only one more to reach his goal. When he saw his mother, he decided to kill her as his final victim.

That morning, when the Buddha surveyed the world, he saw the mass murderer, and he knew that Angulimala would attempt to kill his own mother. Knowing that he was ripe for insight but would fall into hell if he committed matricide, the Buddha set out to save him.

When Angulimala saw the Buddha walking alone, he thought it would be very easy to kill him, so he abandoned the idea of killing his mother and ran after the Buddha instead. With his supernatural power, the Buddha prevented Angulimala from catching him, no matter how fast the bandit ran. Frustrated, Angulimala shouted, "Stop, Monk! Stop!"

"I have stopped, Angulimala," the Buddha calmly replied. "Now, you must stop."

Puzzled by this, but knowing that monks told the truth, Angulimala asked, "What do you mean?"

"I have completely stopped all violence toward living beings," the Buddha replied. "You go on killing. I have stopped, Angulimala. You have not stopped."

"At long last, a sage has come to the great forest for my sake!" Angulimala declared. "Having heard your admonition, from now on, I will abandon evil!" He hurled his sword and other weapons over a cliff, paid homage at the Buddha's feet, and asked for ordination.

"Come, Bhikkhu!" the Buddha declared, and Angulimala was instantly provided with all the requisites.

With the newly-ordained Venerable Angulimala as his attendant, the Buddha returned to Jetavana.

On his way to the forest in search of the mass murderer, King Pasenadi, with a brigade of soldiers, stopped at Jetavana to pay his respects to the Buddha. After the king had bowed down to the Buddha and sat at one side, the Buddha asked him, "What is it, Sire? Why have you set out with such a large force? Have you been attacked by one of the neighboring kingdoms?"

"No, Venerable Sir, no hostile king has attacked Kosala. There is a bandit called Angulimala who is terrorizing Savatthi. He has killed hundreds of travelers, showing no mercy to anyone. I am going with these troops to capture him and to stop his killing spree."

"Sire, suppose you were to see Angulimala with his hair and beard shaved off, wearing the yellow robe, having gone forth from the homelife into homelessness, refraining from killing living beings, restraining the senses, and virtuous. What would you do to him?"

"We would bow down to him, Venerable Sir. We would offer him requisites. We doubt, however, that there could be such virtue and restraint in such an unruly and evil character."

With his right arm, the Buddha pointed to a bhikkhu sitting near him and said, "That, Sire, is Angulimala." King Pasenadi was terrified, and his hair stood on end. The Buddha sensed the king's fear and said, "Don't be afraid, Sire. He poses no danger to you."

The king went over to Venerable Angulimala and asked, "Venerable Sir, are you really Angulimala?"

"Yes, Your Majesty."

"Venerable Sir," King Pasenadi said, "please allow me to offer you the requisites for your livelihood."

Since Venerable Angulimala had undertaken the dhutanga practice, including the wearing of robes made of cast-off rags, he replied, "Enough, Sire. My triple robe is complete."

King Pasenadi bowed again to the Buddha and said, "It is wonderful, Venerable Sir, it is marvelous how the Blessed One tames the untamed, brings peace to the unpeaceful, and leads to Nibbana those who have not attained Nibbana. Venerable Sir, we ourselves could not tame him with force and weapons, yet the Blessed One has tamed him without force or weapons. And now, Venerable Sir, we must depart. We are busy and have much to do."

One morning, as Venerable Angulimala was walking for alms he saw a woman in difficult and painful labor. When he saw this, he thought: "How beings are afflicted!" After his meal, he went to the Blessed One, paid homage to him, sat down at one side, and said: "Venerable Sir, As I was walking for alms this morning, I saw a woman in difficult and painful labor, and I thought: 'How beings are afflicted!'"

"In that case, Angulimala, go into Savatthi and say to that woman: 'Sister, since I was born, I do not recall that I have ever intentionally deprived a living being of life. By this truth, may you be well, and may your infant be well!'"

"Venerable Sir, wouldn't I be telling a deliberate lie, for I have intentionally deprived many living beings of life?"

"Then, Angulimala, say: 'Sister, since I was born with the noble birth, I do not recall that I have ever intentionally deprived a living being of life. By this truth, may you be well, and may your infant be well!'"

"Yes, Venerable Sir," Venerable Angulimala replied. Then he went into Savatthi and repeated to that woman what the Buddha had taught him. Consequently, the woman easily delivered a healthy baby.

Before long, dwelling alone, withdrawn, diligent, ardent, and resolute, Venerable Angulimala, by realizing for himself with direct knowledge, there and then, entered upon and abided in that supreme goal of the holy life for the sake of which clansmen rightly go forth from the home life into homelessness. He directly knew: "Birth is destroyed, the holy life has been lived, what had to be done has been done, there is no more coming to any state of being." And Venerable Angulimala became one of the arahats.

On another morning, as Venerable Angulimala was walking for alms in Savatthi, someone threw a clod of dirt and hit him. Someone else threw a stick, someone else threw a shard of pottery, and these, too, hit him. With blood running from his cut head, with his bowl broken, and with his outer robe torn, Venerable Angulimala went to the Buddha, who saw him coming in the distance and said: "Bear it, Angulimala! Bear it! You are experiencing here and now the result of deeds because of which you might have been tortured in hell for many years, for many hundreds of years, for many thousands of years."

Later, while Venerable Angulimala was alone in retreat, experiencing the bliss of liberation, he uttered this exclamation:

One who was negligent,
But now has gained mindfulness;
One who reveled in evil deeds,
But now has gained virtue;

One who devotes himself
To the Buddha's Teaching;
Illumines the world
Like the moon freed from clouds.

May my enemies listen to the Dhamma,
May they, like me, take refuge in the Buddha.
May they make offerings to the Sangha.
And observe the Noble Precepts.

Thus, abandoning ill-will toward me,
They will erase all anger from their minds,
Then, with loving-kindness toward all beings,
May they find that all-embracing peace.
Canal builders guide water;
Fletchers straighten arrows;
Carpenters straighten beams;
But the wise tame themselves

Once I was bloody-handed
And a Finger-garland bandit,
But now "Harmless" is the name I bear,
And true to that I swear to be.

The evil I was once so guilty of
Comes back to me as kamma does,
And would have condemned me to hell,
Had not the Buddha shown me the way.

May none give way to negligence
Nor seek for sensual pleasure.
May all strive on with diligence
And gain that perfect bliss.
Having taken refuge in the Buddha

In the Dhamma and the Sangha,
I have done what must be done;
Rebirth is mine no more.

—Majjhima Nikaya 86 and Introduction to Maha-Sutasoma Jataka

Hunger

Early one morning, as the Buddha sat in his Perfumed Chamber at Jetavana Monastery, he surveyed the world and recognized that a poor man in Alavi had the potential to attain stream-entry.

With five hundred bhikkhus, the Buddha walked to Alavi, and the residents of the town immediately invited him for a meal.

The poor man heard the news that the Buddha had arrived and wanted to listen to him teach the Dhamma. Unfortunately, the man's only ox had strayed overnight. Although he briefly debated whether to hunt for his ox first or to go to hear the Buddha, necessity dictated that he search for his ox without delay.

The people served the Buddha and the bhikkhus, and, after the meal, took the Buddha's bowl, expecting him to offer anumodana.

The Buddha gently announced, "The man for whose sake I came has gone to the jungle to look for his ox. I will not teach the Dhamma until he comes." Then he remained silent.

As the daylight faded, the poor man found his ox, led it back to its enclosure, and gave it food and water. Despite suffering severe hunger pangs himself, he decided to go to the monastery and, at least, pay his respects to the Buddha.

Seeing the man, the Buddha asked the steward, "Is there any almsfood left over from the monks' meal?"

"Yes, Venerable Sir, there is.

"Then serve that poor man some food."

The steward gave the man left-over rice porridge and curries. When the man finished his meal, he rinsed his mouth. As soon as the man's physical suffering was relieved, his mind became calm. Then the Buddha taught the Dhamma, and, as he finished, the poor man became a stream-enterer.

Finally, the Buddha offered anumodana, stood up, and left. The people walked behind him a little ways, then turned back.

Some of the bhikkhus were indignant and grumbled, "Just think, Friend, what the Teacher did today! Nothing of that sort has ever happened before. Seeing a poor man, the Buddha asked about leftovers and instructed that food be given to him."

The Buddha stopped, turned around, and asked, "Bhikkhus, what are you talking about?"

When he heard what it was, he told them, "That's right, bhikkhus. I came here for the sole purpose of teaching that poor man, who had the potential to attain stream-entry. He spent the whole day searching for his lost ox, so, when he finally came to listen to me, he had not eaten. I knew that, if I were to teach Dhamma to him while he was suffering pangs of hunger, he could not have comprehended it. Therefore, I did what I did. There is no affliction like the affliction of hunger."

Then the Buddha recited this verse:

Hunger is the greatest disease,
Conditioned things are the greatest suffering.
For one who has known this as it is
Nibbana is the greatest bliss.

— Dhammapada Commentary on Verse 203

Sankassa

From a Few Words

It was while staying at Jetavana that the Buddha told this story about the wisdom of Venerable Sariputta.

In the seventh year after the Buddha's Enlightenment, a rich man of Rajagaha placed an expensive sandalwood almsbowl on the top of a high pole and issued a challenge to ascetics to get it down. Encouraged by Venerable Moggallana, Venerable Pindola used his supernatural power to rise into the air and to retrieve the bowl.

Many people were impressed, and the followers of other ascetics chided their teachers, "Why didn't you use your supernatural powers and get the bowl?"

Those ascetics scoffed and belittled the feat. "Such a thing means nothing to us. Why should we display our true abilities for the sake of a small wooden bowl? The greedy Sakyan bhikkhus were just showing off!"

The Buddha rebuked Venerable Pindola for using his powers in performing a tawdry magic trick for such an unworthy end. The bowl was forfeited to the Sangha to be ground into sandalwood powder, and bhikkhus were thereafter forbidden to display any supernatural powers they might possess.

When the ascetics from other sects heard about this, they thought, "Since Gotama has prohibited the use of supernatural powers, he will not perform any miracles himself." They began to speak differently about such feats. "Actually," they said to their followers, "our supernatural powers are much greater than those of Gotama's disciples. If we wanted to, we could very easily outdo any of them. We could even outdo Gotama himself! In fact, we challenge him! If he performs even one miracle, we will perform one twice as difficult, twice as amazing!" When bhikkhus reported this to the Buddha, he calmly replied, "I will accept their challenge."

When King Bimbisara heard about this, he asked the Buddha, "Will you perform a miracle, Venerable Sir?"

"Yes, Sire, I will."

"Wasn't a prohibition placed on the display of supernatural powers?" the king asked.

"The prohibition was given to my disciples. No such rules limit what a Buddha may or may not do. Although others are forbidden to pick flowers and fruit in your royal park, Sire, certainly that rule does not apply to you!"

"Where do you intend to perform your miracle, Venerable Sir?"

"In Savatthi, under a Ganda mango tree."

"What must I do?" asked the king.

"Nothing is needed, Sire."

The next morning, while the Buddha and the bhikkhus were walking for alms, people asked the bhikkhus what the Buddha was going to do. "Under a Ganda mango tree, near the city gate of Savatthi," the bhikkhus replied, "the Blessed One will perform a twofold miracle which will confound the ascetics of other sects."

People began talking excitedly, "This miracle is going to be fantastic! I mustn't miss it! Let's go to Savatthi!" Many locked their doors and followed the Buddha out of the city. Rival ascetics and their disciples also joined the throng. They declared to any who would listen that they, too, would perform a miracle in the same place.

In Savatthi, King Pasenadi asked the Buddha, "Is it true, Venerable Sir, that you are going to perform a miracle here?"

"Yes, it is true," the Buddha replied.

"When?"

"One week from today, on the full-moon day of Asalha."

"Shall I prepare a pavilion for you, Venerable Sir?"

"That will not be necessary. In the place where I will perform my miracle, Sakka will prepare a jeweled pavilion twelve yojanas in diameter. You need do nothing on that account."

"Shall I announce the event, Venerable Sir?"

"Proclaim it widely if you wish, Sire."

Every day for seven days, the king sent his royal crier throughout the city on a richly caparisoned elephant to announce, "On the full-moon day of Asalha, under a Ganda mango tree near the gate of Savatthi, the Buddha will perform a twofold miracle, which will utterly confound all rival ascetics!"

No one knew what a Ganda mango tree was, but, in order to prevent any miracle, the rival ascetics ordered their followers to cut down every mango tree of any kind in and around the city of Savatthi.

When the proclamation was made on the last day, Sakka used his power to extend its range so it could be heard far beyond Savatthi. He also shortened the distance so that everyone who wanted to attend would be able to reach the city gate in time to see the event.

On the morning of the day appointed, the royal gardener was taking an exceptionally large, ripe, and flawless golden mango to the palace for the king's breakfast. When he saw the Buddha on his almsrounds at the city gate, he thought, "This fruit is worthy of the Blessed One!" He offered it to the Buddha, who immediately sat down and ate it. When he finished, he handed the seed to Venerable Ananda and said, "Give this seed to the gardener. Let him plant it at this spot. Because his name is Ganda, the tree that grows here will be known as the Ganda mango tree." As soon as Ganda had smoothed the earth over the seed, a red shoot burst through the soil. As a crowd watched, the shoot grew into a magnificent tree with a straight and sturdy trunk and thick branches full of dark green leaves. When it reached one hundred hatthas in height, tiny flowers bloomed on every branch, and bees swarmed around the tree. The flowers quickly became small green fruit, which swelled into golden mangoes. A slight breeze arose, and the newly ripened fruit began falling to the ground. Bhikkhus picked up some of the luscious mangoes and carried them back to the monastery.

That evening, Sakka summoned Vissakamma and ordered him to create the magnificent jeweled pavilion. A vast crowd filled the pavilion, which was, as the Buddha had told the king it would be, twelve yojanas long. Myriads of devas who had come to witness the miracle hovered in the air above the pavilion.

As the full moon rose, the Buddha appeared and stood beneath the branches of the tree. Suddenly, water gushed from the upper part of his body, and flames shot out from the lower part. Then he reversed the order. Next, flames shot out from his right side, and water gushed from the left. Then he reversed that order, as well. The fire and water never mingled. Every pore of his body emitted rays of six colors creating a resplendence beyond words. That marvelous light reached up to the Brahma heavens and down to the hells. As the Buddha preached to the devas and the people, he walked up and down a jeweled walkway which he had created in the air. The Buddha also multiplied himself innumerable times in the branches of the tree such that each listener was able to see and to hear according to his own particular disposition and level of understanding. All those who had not had faith in the Buddha before this became his followers, while those who had already had faith became more zealous in their practice of the Noble Eightfold Path and in their desire for Nibbana.

Every Buddha performs this twin miracle, and it is the tradition that, after performing it, he goes to Tavatimsa. Thus, did the Buddha disappear from Savatthi and, in only three steps, reach Tavatimsa, where he spent the rains retreat, preaching the Abhidhamma to devas, including his mother, who had descended from Tusita in order to hear the Teaching. Just before the end of the rains retreat, Venerable Moggallana went to Tavatimsa to confer with the Buddha about the ceremony marking the end.

"Where is Sariputta spending the rains retreat?" the Buddha asked.

"Venerable Sir, after witnessing the great twin miracle, he went to Sankassa and has remained there."

"Moggallana, in one week's time, I will descend from this heaven to Sankassa, near the city gate. Let those who wish to behold the Tathagata descending gather there." Venerable Moggallana informed the people of Savatthi and, at the appointed time, transported a multitude to Sankassa, thirty yojanas away, in an instant.

When the Buddha informed Sakka that it was time for him to return to the realm of men, the king of the devas ordered Vissakamma to build a staircase. Vissakamma created a triple staircase. The center stairs were bejeweled, with silver and gold stairs on either side. The top rested on the peak of Sineru in Tavatimsa, and the foot was positioned beside the gate of Sankassa. The Buddha descended the center stairs. On one side, Sakka was carrying the Buddha's robe and bowl, and, on the other, Brahma was holding an umbrella. Many other devas paid their respects with divine garlands and heavenly perfumes. When the Buddha reached the bottom step, Venerable Sariputta greeted him at the head of the great assembly.

The Buddha thought, "Moggallana has amply demonstrated his supernatural power. Upali has been recognized as thoroughly versed in the Vinaya, but Sariputta's wisdom, which is second only to mine, has not yet been adequately shown. Let me allow him to demonstrate the brilliance of his wisdom!"

First, the Buddha asked a question which even ordinary people could answer. Then he asked a question which could be answered only by those who had attained at least the first path. Successively, he asked questions requiring the attainment of the second, third, and fourth paths. After asking a question which Venerable Moggallana could answer, the Buddha asked a question which only Venerable Sariputta could understand, and that great disciple answered it with ease.

The entire assembly marveled at the depth of Venerable Sariputta's understanding. Thenceforth, everyone recognized the excellence of the wisdom of the Captain of the Teaching.

Next, the Buddha asked Venerable Sariputta another question, which required the understanding of a Buddha: "Some are on the way, and some have reached the goal. What are the manners and the conversation of each?"

Venerable Sariputta immediately understood that the Blessed One was asking him to describe the proper deportment of bhikkhus as they progress toward arahatship, but he was not sure on what the Buddha wanted him to base his answer—the five aggregates, the four elements, or the organs and objects of sense. The Buddha realized Venerable Sariputta's hesitation and knew that with only one hint, Venerable Sariputta would be able to expound the answer. "Sariputta," he said, "consider 'this being'! Venerable Sariputta immediately understood that he was to base his answer on the aggregates, and he completely and perfectly formulated the answer to the Buddha's question. Finally, Venerable Sariputta posed a question, which opened the way for the Buddha to teach the Dhamma with great eloquence to the assembly, which extended for twelve yojanas and comprised thirty crores of beings, including both devas and men, and all, without exception, were satisfied with his teaching.

When his discourse was finished, the Buddha left Sankassa and proceeded to Savatthi. The next day, the bhikkhus were talking about Venerable Sariputta's wisdom and how skillfully he had explained in full what the Buddha had asked in brief. When the Buddha heard what they were discussing, he said, "This is not the first time, Bhikkhus, that Sariputta has answered at length a question briefly put. He did the same before." Then he told this story of the past.

Long, long ago, when Brahmadatta was reigning in Baranasi, the Bodhisatta was a handsome stag in the forest.

King Brahmadatta was extremely fond of hunting. He was a very good hunter, and he judged other men on their skill in hunting.

One day, he went with a large party to the forest and told his courtiers, "Anyone who lets a deer get past him will be punished!"

The men realized that the deer had to go toward the king, so they placed him at the head of the path. They surrounded a great thicket and began beating the ground. The mighty stag leaped from the thicket and tried to flee. He darted here and there, looking for an escape route, but, on three sides, archers were standing at the ready. The deer ran toward the king, who was standing a little apart as his men had planned. When the king saw the powerful stag with blazing eyes rushing toward him, he was so dazzled he could hardly see. He shot his arrow, but the stag was quicker, and the arrow missed its mark. The stag burst free, found a clear path, and bounded away like a cloud before the wind.

The courtiers began to make sport of the king, laughing and joking about the deer that got away. This made the king furious. "I'll show you!" he shouted. "I'll catch that stag if it's the last thing I do!" Grabbing his sword, he tore off on foot after the deer. He ran for three yojanas without losing sight of the stag. When the animal plunged back into the deep forest, the king was following closely behind. Right in the middle of the path was a deep pit, formed when the roots of an ancient tree that had fallen rotted away. The pit was full of water. Even before it saw the pit, the great deer sensed water and swerved to avoid it. The king was oblivious to the danger and fell in.

Realizing that he was no longer being pursued, the great deer stopped and turned back. He cautiously approached the pit and saw the king, struggling to keep his head above the water. Although he knew that the king had tried to slay him, the stag felt no malice toward him, but only compassion. "I will not allow this king to die in this wild spot," he resolved. "I will deliver him from this great peril!' Aloud he shouted, "Don't be afraid, Sire! I will rescue you from the pit!"

Working as earnestly as he would for his own son, the great deer managed to free the king from what otherwise would have been his muddy unmarked grave. When, at last, the king was safely out of the watery pit, the deer rested briefly. Then, placing the king on his back, he transported him back to within hailing distance of his hunting party. Before returning him to the courtiers, the stag admonished the king to rule righteously and established him in the five precepts.

The king was so pleased with the teaching that he did not want to part from his rescuer. "King of the deer," he begged, "please come to Baranasi with me! You may rule my kingdom!"

"Sire," the stag replied, "I am an animal! I have no use for a kingdom! If you have any affection for me, keep the precepts I have taught you, and instruct your subjects to keep them as well. Do good deeds, and be generous. Rule wisely and with righteousness." Bidding farewell, the stag returned to the forest.

Even after the king had returned to the city, the recollection of the noble qualities of the great stag who had saved his life filled his eyes with tears. He immediately mounted his royal elephant and, surrounded by a division of his army, led a procession around the city. To the accompaniment of a drum, a crier read out his proclamation: "From this day on, all the inhabitants of Baranasi are to observe the five precepts!" He did not tell anyone, however, of the great kindness that had been done to him by the stag.

At daybreak the next morning, after a good night's sleep on his gorgeous couch, the king again remembered the stag's noble qualities and sat up cross-legged. With a joyful heart, he began singing:

> Never give up hope, my good man! Be wise, and keep up
> your courage! I, indeed, have reached my goal!
>
> Never give up hope, my good man! Be wise, and keep your
> spirits up, no matter how pressed! I fought the waves
> and reached the shore!
>
> Strive on, my good man! Be wise, and keep up your
> courage! I, indeed, have reached my goal!

Strive on, my good man! Be wise, and keep your spirits up,
no matter how pressed! I fought the waves and
reached the shore!

One who is wise, though overwhelmed with pain, never
gives up hope that bliss will come again.

Men have many feelings of both joy and woe, but,
unaware and heedless, they march on straight to death!

The unexpected happens, while what one expects does
not; just wishing does not make one happy.

Just as the king had begun singing, his chief advisor had arrived at the door and was about to go in. Not wishing to disturb the king, however, he had hesitated, unannounced, and stood at the door listening so that he heard all that the king sang. As soon as the king finished, he tapped lightly. "Who is there?" asked the king.

"It is I, Sire," replied the advisor.

"Come in, Teacher," the king called.

"Long live the king!" the advisor said, as he entered. "I am very pleased that your hunting trip yesterday was so rewarding. I'm very sorry that you missed the deer and that the others mocked you so mercilessly. You must have been very tired after chasing the stag for such a long way. Perhaps that is why you fell into the pit. How marvelous that the magnificent stag, feeling compassion, rescued you from drowning! That was very kind and courageous of the animal! It is wonderful that he was completely free from thoughts of anger and vengeance! It is also wonderful that you, in recollecting his magnanimity, would sing such beautiful words of praise!"

"Teacher!" exclaimed the king. "You may have heard about my missing the deer from some of the courtiers, but I have told no one about my falling into the pit and my encounter with the stag. How did you know? Were you there yesterday? Have you met a witness that I did not see?"

"No, Sire, I was not there," the advisor assured him. "Nor have I heard about your hunting trip from anyone else. I happened to overhear your song just now, and I understood clearly everything that happened. From your own sweet words, I understood exactly what you were describing. Thus, can a wise man discern the full meaning of what he hears in brief."

The king was delighted at his advisor's mental acuity and rewarded him handsomely.

Encouraged by the teaching of the deer, King Brahmadatta devoted himself to almsgiving and to good deeds. Following his exhortation and example, the citizens of Baranasi also practiced morality and generosity, and many were reborn in heaven. Sakka noticed the sudden increase in arrivals in Tavatimsa and understood the cause. He decided to test the king.

One day, the king and the chief advisor went to the royal park for target practice. As the king was about to shoot, Sakka caused the magnificent stag to appear between the king and the target. Recognizing the king of the deer, the king froze and could not release his arrow. Sakka caused the advisor to say, "Sire, your arrow has been certain death to many powerful foes! Why do you hesitate now? Certainly, venison is proper meat for warriors like you. Prove your skill and kill that deer!"

"Of course, a stag is a suitable target for a warrior's bow," replied the king, "but I am grateful to this animal, and I dare not think of killing it."

"Actually, Your Majesty," the advisor continued, speaking for Sakka, "if you kill it, thereby fulfilling your obligation as a warrior, you will become king of the devas. On the other hand, if you hesitate from mere sentimentality, you doom yourself to hell and to judgment by King Yama."

"So be it!" the king declared. "Even to escape from King Yama's wrath, I will not harm this deer. When I was helpless, without hope, and drowning in that pit, it was this very stag who saved my life! How could I kill my benefactor, who showed me such mercy and forgiveness?"

After hearing those brave words, Sakka revealed himself and stood poised in the air. "Long live the righteous King Brahmadatta!" he proclaimed. "This ruse, including the words your advisor spoke, constituted a test, and you have nobly proved your gratitude and virtue. May you continue to rule your kingdom with wisdom and righteousness. Continue to guide your subjects along the path of generosity, and your kingdom will be at peace. Live blamelessly, and you will be reborn in heaven!" The stag vanished, and Sakka himself returned, with great glory, to Tavatimsa.

Having concluded his story, the Buddha identified the birth: At that time, Ananda was King Brahmadatta, Sariputta was the chief advisor, and I was the noble stag.

—Sarabha-Miga Jataka

Kosambi

The Eternal Law of Peace

It was while staying at Jetavana that the Buddha told this story about quarrelsome bhikkhus in Kosambi.

In Kosambi, there were two senior bhikkhus staying in the same monastery. One was well-versed in the Vinaya, and the other was an expert in the suttas,.

One day, after the sutta expert had finished in the lavatory, he left water in a vessel for rinsing the mouth. The Vinaya specialist noticed the water and asked the other if he was the one who had left it there.

The bhikkhu admitted that he had left it, and the Vinaya specialist scolded him, "Didn't you know that that is a breach of the rules?"

"No. I had no idea it was wrong."

"Well, it is wrong."

"Then I will confess it."

"Oh, well, if you did it from carelessness, it is not really an offence."

Thus, the sutta expert thought no more about his mistake.

The Vinaya expert, however, began telling his students, "That bhikkhu, who considers himself a sutta expert, violates the rules without being aware of it."

These students repeated this accusation to the students of the sutta expert.

When the sutta expert heard this, he told his students, "That Vinaya specialist told me that what I had done was not an offence. Now he says that it is. He is a liar!"

These students in turn said to the others, "Your master is a liar!

The quarrel quickly escalated, and the Vinaya specialist demanded that the sutta expert be disrobed and expelled from the Sangha for refusing to acknowledge his offence. At this point, all the unenlightened followers of the Buddha in that area, including bhikkhus, bhikkhunis, lay followers, and even the gods, sided with one group or the other and argued forcefully about the expulsion.

When the Buddha learned of the impending schism, he confronted the two groups and attempted to restore harmony. "Enough, Bhikkhus," he said. "Let us have no quarreling."

A bhikkhu from one of the groups replied, "Let the Blessed One not bother about this. Let the Blessed One stay comfortably. This is our problem. We take full responsibility for making ourselves notorious, but we must settle this altercation!"

Without saying anything further, the Buddha left and went to the Parileyyaka forest, where he spent the rains retreat. During that time, he was looked after by the elephant Parileyya and a monkey. After the monks, pressured by their lay followers, had reconciled their differences, they went to Savatthi to ask the Buddha's forgiveness.

"Bhikkhus," the Buddha admonished them, "you are my heirs in this Sasana. Children should not go against the counsel given them by their father, but you did not follow my advice. Long ago, a wise young prince, having resolved, 'I will not trample on the counsel given me by my father,' did not kill the one who had slain his parents and seized their kingdom. Even when the culprit, who was undeniably guilty, fell into his hands, the wise young man remembered his father's advice and refrained from violence." Then the Buddha told this story of the past.

Long, long ago, when Brahmadatta was reigning in Baranasi, the capital of the kingdom of Kasi, Dighiti was the king of Kosala. At that time, Kasi was rich and powerful, but Kosala was very weak. When Brahmadatta attacked Kosala, Dighiti fled with his wife, and Kosala fell without a fight.

King Dighiti and his queen wandered incognito, finally ending up in a potters' village just outside Baranasi. Not long afterwards, the exiled queen gave birth to a son whom they named Dighavu. When Dighavu was old enough to look after himself, his parents sent him to live and to study in a safe place.

A few years later, King Dighiti's former barber, who had come to serve King Brahmadatta, happened to see the exiled king in the potters' village and recognized him in spite of his disguise. He hurried to inform King Brahmadatta about his enemy.

King Brahmadatta immediately ordered soldiers to arrest King Dighiti and his queen, to bind them tightly, to march them through the town, and to execute them at the southern gate.

It so happened that, on that same day, Prince Dighavu returned to visit his parents, whom he had not seen for a long time. As he entered Baranasi, he heard the beat of a harsh-sounding drum and saw his dear parents cruelly tied with ropes and being marched to the southern gate. Of course, he started toward them. King Dighiti saw his son coming and stopped him, shouting with a clear voice: "Dear Dighavu! Don't be far-sighted! Don't be near-sighted. Vengeance is not settled through vengeance. Vengeance is settled through non-vengeance." The people in the crowd heard King Dighiti's words and mocked him, shouting, "Have you gone crazy? You're talking nonsense. Who is Dighavu? What do you mean?"

The king replied, "I'm neither crazy nor talking nonsense. He who knows will understand."

Then a second time and a third time, he cried, "Dear Dighavu, don't be far-sighted! Don't be near-sighted. Vengeance is not settled through vengeance. Vengeance is settled through non-vengeance."

The people jeered. "This King Dighiti has gone crazy. He's talking gibberish!"

Again the king retorted, "I'm not crazy, nor am I talking gibberish. He who knows will understand."

When the soldiers reached the southern gate, they executed the king and queen, cut their bodies into four pieces, and buried the pieces in four different holes.

That night, Prince Dighavu bought some liquor and got the guards drunk. Solemnly he gathered sticks and pieces of wood to make a funeral pyre. He exhumed his parents' bodies and respectfully cremated them. King Brahmadatta happened to be standing on the balcony of his palace, and he saw the prince circumambulating a fire where the king and queen had been executed. The king wondered who it was but gave it no more thought.

A few days later, the prince went to the king's elephant stable in the palace compound and said to the chief mahout, "Sir, I want to learn your craft."

The mahout accepted him and was pleased with his new helper. One night, Prince Dighavu was sitting near the stable and singing as he accompanied himself on the lute. The king heard him and called his page, "What an incredibly sweet voice that is! Who is singing and playing the lute in the elephant stable? I've never heard that before."

"Your Majesty, it is a young man who came recently. The elephant trainer has taken him on as an apprentice."

"Bring him to me."

The page fetched Prince Dighavu. The king was impressed with the young man and asked him to serve in the palace. Prince Dighavu soon gained such favor that he became a personal attendant to the king. Never revealing his background, the prince always spoke politely to the king and faithfully did whatever the king ordered. It was not long before King Brahmadatta gave the prince a position of trust and kept him by his side almost constantly.

One day, King Brahmadatta said to Prince Dighavu, "Harness the chariot. I'm going hunting."

"As you wish, Your Majesty."

King Brahmadatta mounted the chariot but gave the reins to the prince and asked him to drive. At first, the hunting party stayed together, but, then the prince turned the horses aside so that the chariot became separated from the rest. After they had ridden quite a while, the king said that he was tired and wanted to rest. He ordered Prince Dighavu to stop and to unharness the horses.

"As you wish, Your Majesty."

The king lay down and put his head in the prince's lap. Soon, he was fast asleep.

The prince looked at the king and thought, "This King Brahmadatta has done us great harm. He seized our kingdom and executed my parents. Here he lies, completely in my power. Now is my chance for revenge! I will slay the villain who killed my dear mother and father and cut their bodies into pieces!" Silently, he drew his sword. As he raised his weapon to strike the king, however, he remembered what his father had said, "Dear Dighavu, don't be far-sighted! Don't be near-sighted. Vengeance is not settled through vengeance. Vengeance is settled through non-vengeance." Quietly, he replaced his sword in its sheath. "Even though I lose my own life," he vowed, "I will not disobey my father's words."

A few minutes later, as the king continued sleeping quietly, the prince again drew his sword. Again he remembered what his father had said, and he put away his sword. A third time he pulled out his sword. A third time he recollected his father's words and put away his sword. Suddenly, frightened and alarmed, King Brahmadatta jumped to his feet.

"What is the matter, Your Majesty?" asked the prince.

"Just now I dreamed that the son of Dighiti, king of Kosala, killed me with his sword."

The prince quickly grabbed King Brahmadatta by the hair with his left hand and with his right hand drew his sword. "Your Majesty," he shouted, "I am Prince Dighavu, son of Dighiti, king of Kosala. You did great harm to my family. You seized our kingdom and killed my dear parents. Now I will have my vengeance!"

King Brahmadatta wept, helpless before the prince. "Please don't kill me, Dighavu! Please spare my life, Prince Dighavu!"

"In the hour of death, Sire," Dighavu replied softly, slightly relaxing his grip on the king's hair, "one's wealth is of no use at all!

Only good deeds done and good words spoken can bring any comfort. 'This man abused me. That man struck me. That other man robbed me long ago.' Those who harbor such thoughts will never overcome their anger. Only by giving up such thoughts can we appease our anger and hatred. Hatred is never appeased by hatred. Hatred is appeased only by love. This is the eternal law of peace."

The prince released his hold on the king and held out his sword. "Take my sword, Your Majesty," he said. "Who am I to give you your life? Slay me, or give me my life."

"In that case, Dighavu," the king replied in a tremulous voice, as he grasped the prince's hand, "you have given me my life, and I give you your life." King Brahmadatta and Prince Dighavu embraced and vowed never to harm one another.

"Now, my dear Dighavu," the king said, "harness the chariot. We will go back."

They rejoined the hunting party and returned to Baranasi. The king summoned his court and asked, "If you were to see Prince Dighavu, son of King Dighiti, what would you do?"

From various corners the cries went up, "We would cut off his hands, Your Majesty!" "We would cut off his feet!" "We would execute him at the southern gate!"

"This," the king announced, "is Prince Dighavu, the son of King Dighiti, You are not to harm him in any way. He gave me my life, and I have given his life to him."

"Now, Prince," the king continued, turning to Dighavu, "as your father was about to die, he kept repeating these sentences: 'Dear Dighavu, don't be far-sighted! Don't be near-sighted. Vengeance is not settled through vengeance. Vengeance is settled through non-vengeance.' Please tell us what he meant by that."

"When my father said, 'Don't be far-sighted,' he was telling me not to hold a grudge for a long time, not to seek revenge. When he said, 'Don't be near-sighted,' he was telling me not to be quick to break with a friend. When he said, 'Vengeance is not settled through vengeance. Vengeance is settled through non-vengeance,' he was expressing an eternal law. He knew that if I were to kill you as you killed my parents, your friends would kill me. Then my friends would kill your friends. In this way, vengeance, hatred, and killing would go on endlessly. But, by swearing friendship, you have given me my life, and I have given you your life. Hatred and vengeance have ceased."

"Wonderful! Wonderful!" King Brahmadatta exclaimed. "It's amazing how wise this Prince Dighavu is! He was able to understand in full what his father said in brief!"

To demonstrate to all that he was sincere in his vow of friendship, King Brahmadatta restored to Prince Dighavu the entire kingdom of Kosala—capital, palace, army, fields, villages, and all its wealth. He also offered his own daughter to the prince in marriage.

The prince accepted all the gifts and established himself as the king of Kosala with his new queen. The two kings lived the rest of their lives in harmony and peace.

Having concluded his story, the Buddha identified the birth: "My parents were King Dighiti and his queen, and I was Prince Dighavu."

—Dighiti-Kosala Jataka

Kesariya

When You Know for Yourself

On one occasion, the Blessed One was wandering on tour together with a large number of bhikkhus.

The Kalamas learned of the Buddha's arrival and were eager to meet him. They had heard that he was the son of a Sakyan king and had gone forth. They had also heard that he was an arahat, perfectly enlightened, accomplished in true knowledge and conduct, fortunate, a knower of worlds, the unsurpassed leader of persons to be tamed, a teacher of devas and humans, the Enlightened One, and the Blessed One. "Master Gotama," they said to each other, "having realized with his own direct knowledge this world with its devas, Maras, and Brahmas, ascetics, brahmins, and other humans, makes it known to others. He teaches a Dhamma that is good at the beginning, good in the middle, and good at the end, with the right meaning and expression. He reveals a spiritual life that is perfectly complete and purified.' It is good to see such arahats."

Thus, the Kalamas of Kesaputta approached the Blessed One. Some paid homage to him, some paid respect, some exchanged greetings with him, and some remained silent. After they had all sat down to one side, they said to the Blessed One, "Venerable Sir, some ascetics and brahmins who come to Kesaputta explain and elucidate their own doctrines, but disparage and revile the doctrines of others. Then, other ascetics and brahmins come and explain and elucidate their own doctrines, but disparage and revile the doctrines of the others. For us, Venerable Sir, there is perplexity and doubt as to which of these good ascetics speak truth and which speak falsehood."

"It is fitting for you to be perplexed, Kalamas. It is fitting for you to be in doubt. Doubt has arisen in you about a perplexing matter. Come, Kalamas. Do not go by oral tradition, by lineage of teaching, by hearsay, by a collection of texts, by logic, by inferential reasoning, by reasoned cogitation, by the acceptance of a view after pondering it, by the seeming competence of a speaker, or because you think, 'The ascetic is our teacher.' When you know for yourselves, 'These things are unwholesome; these things are blamable; these things are censured by the wise; these things, if undertaken and practiced, lead to harm and suffering,' you should abandon them.

"What do you think, Kalamas? When greed, hatred, and delusion arise in a person, is it for his welfare or harm?"

"For his harm, Venerable Sir."

"Kalamas, a person who is greedy, hating, and deluded, overpowered by greed, hatred, and delusion, his thoughts controlled by them, will destroy life, take what is not given, engage in sexual misconduct, and tell lies; he will also prompt others to do likewise. Will that conduce to his harm and suffering for a long time?"

"Yes, Venerable Sir."

"Are these things wholesome or unwholesome?

"Unwholesome, Venerable Sir."

"Blamable or blameless?"

"Blamable, Venerable Sir."

"Censured or praised by the wise?"

"Censured, Venerable Sir."

"Undertaken and practiced, do they lead to harm and suffering or not?"

"To harm and suffering, Venerable Sir."

"It was for this reason that I said, 'Do not go by oral tradition or by any of the other things I enumerated.' When you know for yourselves, 'These things are unwholesome; these things are blamable; these things are censured by the wise; these things, if undertaken and practiced, lead to harm and suffering,' then you should abandon them.

"When non-greed, non-hatred, and non-delusion arise in a person, is it for his welfare or harm?"

"For his welfare, Venerable Sir."

"Kalamas, a person who is without greed, without hatred, without delusion, not overpowered by greed, hatred, and delusion, his thoughts not controlled by them, will abstain from the destruction of life, from taking what is not given, from sexual misconduct, and from false speech; he will also prompt others to do likewise. Will that conduce to his welfare and happiness for a long time?"

"Yes, Venerable Sir."

"Are these things wholesome or unwholesome?"

"Wholesome, Venerable Sir."

"Blamable or blameless?"

"Blameless, Venerable Sir."

"Censured or praised by the wise?"

"Praised, Venerable Sir."

"Undertaken and practiced, do they lead to welfare and happiness or not?"

"To welfare and happiness, Venerable Sir."

"It was for this reason that I said, 'Do not go by oral tradition, by lineage of teaching, by hearsay, by a collection of texts, by logic, by inferential reasoning, by reasoned cogitation, by the acceptance of a view after pondering it, by the seeming competence of a speaker, or because you think, "The ascetic is our teacher." When you know for yourselves, 'These things are unwholesome; these things are blamable; these things are censured by the wise; these things, if undertaken and practiced, lead to harm and suffering,' you should abandon them.

"Then, Kalamas, this noble disciple, who is thus devoid of covetousness and ill-will, unconfused, clearly comprehending, and ever mindful, abides pervading one quarter with a mind imbued with loving-kindness. Likewise, he abides pervading the second quarter, the third quarter, and the fourth quarter Thus, above, below, across, and everywhere, and to all as to himself, he abides pervading the entire world with a mind imbued with loving-kindness, vast, exalted, measureless, without hostility, and without ill-will.

"In the same way, he dwells pervading first one quarter and then everywhere with a mind imbued with compassion, with a mind imbued with altruistic joy, and with a mind imbued with equanimity.

"When, Kalamas, this noble disciple has thus made his mind free of enmity, free of ill-will, uncorrupted, and pure, he has won four assurances in this very life.

"The first assurance he has won is: 'If there is another world and if good and bad deeds yield results, it is possible that, with the breaking up of the body after death, I shall arise in a good destination, in a heavenly world.'

"The second assurance he has won is: 'If there is no other world and if good and bad deeds do not yield results, still, right here, in this very life, I live happily, free of enmity and ill-will.

"The third assurance he has won is: 'If evil befalls the evil-doer, in that I do not intend evil for anyone, suffering will not afflict me, who does no evil deed.'

"The fourth assurance he has won is: 'If evil does not befall the evil-doer, I see myself, right here, purified in both respects.'

"When, Kalamas, this noble disciple has thus made his mind free of enmity, free of ill-will, uncorrupted, and pure, he has won these four assurances in this very life."

"So it is, Venerable Sir! Magnificent, Venerable Sir! The Blessed One has made the Dhamma clear in many ways, as though he were turning upright what had been overthrown, revealing what was hidden, showing the way to one who was lost, or holding up a lamp in the darkness so those with good eyesight can see forms. We now go for refuge to the Blessed One, to the Dhamma, and to the Sangha. Let the Blessed One accept us as lay followers who have gone for refuge from today until life's end."

—Anguttara Nikaya 3, 65

Lauriya Nandangar

The Sound the Hare Heard

It was while staying at Jetavana that the Buddha told this story about ascetics of different sects.

One morning, while some bhikkhus were on their almsrounds in Savatthi, they passed some ascetics of different sects practicing austerities. Some of them were naked and lying on thorns. Others sat around a blazing fire under the burning sun.

Later, while the bhikkhus were discussing the ascetics, they asked the Buddha, "Lord, is there any virtue in those harsh ascetic practices?"

The Buddha answered, "No, Bhikkhus, there is neither virtue nor any special merit in them. When they are examined and tested, they are like a path over a dunghill or like the sound the hare heard."

Puzzled, the bhikkhus said, "Venerable Sir, we do not know about that sound. Please tell us what it was." Then the Buddha told them this story of the distant past.

Long, long ago, when Brahmadatta was reigning in Baranasi, the Bodhisatta was born as a lion in a forest near the Western Ocean. In one part of that forest there was a grove of palms mixed with bael trees. A hare lived in that grove beneath a palm sapling at the foot of a bael tree.

One day, the hare lay under the young palm tree, idly thinking, "If this earth were destroyed, what would become of me?" At that very instant, a ripe bael fruit happened to fall and hit a palm frond making a loud "Thud!"

Startled by this sound, the hare leapt to his feet and cried, "The earth is collapsing!" He immediately fled, without even glancing back.

Another hare, seeing him race past, as if for his very life, asked, "What's wrong?" and started running, too.

"Don't ask!" panted the first. This frightened the second even more, and he sprinted to keep up.

"What's wrong?" he shouted again.

Pausing for just a moment, the first hare cried, "The earth is breaking up!" At this, the two of them bolted off together.

Their fear was infectious, and other hares joined them until all the hares in that forest were fleeing together. When other animals saw the commotion and asked what was wrong, they were breathlessly told, "The earth is breaking up!" and they, too, began running for their lives. In this way, the hares were soon joined by herds of deer, boars, elk, buffaloes, wild oxen, rhinoceroses, a family of tigers, and some elephants.

When the lion saw this headlong stampede of animals and heard the cause of their flight, he thought, "The earth is certainly not coming to an end. There must have been some sound which they misunderstood. If I don't act quickly, they will be killed. I must save them!"

Then, running as fast as only he could run, he got in front of them and roared three times. At the sound of his mighty voice, all the animals stopped in their tracks. Panting, they huddled together in fear. The lion approached them and asked why they were running away.

"The earth is collapsing," they all answered.

"Who saw it collapsing?" he asked.

"The elephants know all about it," some animals replied.

When he asked the elephants, they said, "We don't know. The tigers know."

The tigers said, "The rhinoceroses know."

The rhinoceroses said, "The wild oxen know."

The wild oxen said, "The buffaloes know."

The buffaloes said, "The elk know."

The elk said, "The boars know."

The boars said, "The deer know."

The deer said, "We don't know. The hares know."

When he asked the hares, they pointed to one particular hare and said, "This one told us."

The lion asked him, "Is it true, sir, that the earth is breaking up?"

"Yes, Your Majesty, I saw it," said the hare.

"Where were you when you saw it?"

"In the forest in a palm grove mixed with bael trees. I was lying there under a palm at the foot of a bael tree, thinking, 'If this earth were destroyed, what would become of me?' At that very moment, I heard the sound of the breaking up of the earth, and I fled."

From this explanation, the lion realized exactly what had really happened, but he wanted to verify his conclusions and to demonstrate the truth to the other animals. He gently calmed the animals and said, "I will take the hare and go to find out whether or not the earth is coming to an end where he says it is. Until we return, stay right here!"

Placing the hare on his tawny back, he raced with great speed back to that grove. Then he put the hare down and said, "Come, show me the place you meant."

"I don't dare, My Lord," said the hare.

"Don't be afraid," said the lion.

The hare, shivering with fear, would not risk going near the bael tree. He could only point and say, "Over there, sir, is the place of dreadful sound."

The lion went to the place the hare indicated. He could make out where the hare had been lying in the grass, and he saw the ripe bael fruit that had fallen on the palm frond. Having carefully ascertained that the earth was not breaking up, he placed the hare on his back again and returned to the waiting animals. He told them what he had found and said, "Don't be afraid. The earth is not breaking up."

Reassured, all the animals went back to their usual places and resumed their routines.

Those animals had placed themselves in great danger because they listened to rumors and unfounded fears rather than trying to find out the truth themselves. Truly, if it had not been for the lion, all of them would have rushed into the sea and perished. It was only because of the lion's wisdom and compassion that they escaped death.

Having concluded his story, the Buddha identified the birth: "At that time, I was the lion."

—Duddubha Jataka

Vesali

The Discourse on Jewels

At one time, Vesali was plagued by famine, disease, and non-human beings. The Buddha taught this sutta so that its recitation would free the city of these troubles.

Whatever beings are assembled here, whether terrestrial or celestial, may they be happy. Let them attentively listen to these words.

Beings, please pay attention! Radiate loving-kindness towards mankind, who day and night bring offerings to you. Protect them with earnestness.

Whatever treasure there be, either here or in the other world; whatever precious jewel there be in the heavenly worlds; there is none comparable to the Tathagata. This precious jewel is in the Buddha. By this truth may there be peace!

The sage of the Sakyas, with a tranquil mind, realized that cessation which is passionless, immortal, and excellent. There is nothing equal to that state. This precious jewel is in the Dhamma. By this truth may there be peace!

The supreme Buddha praised pure meditation which gives immediate results. There is nothing equal to that meditation; This precious jewel is in the Dhamma. By this truth may there be peace!

Eight individuals are praised by good people. They constitute the four pairs. These disciples of the Buddha are worthy of offerings. Whatever is offered to them yields abundant fruit. This precious jewel is in the Sangha. By this truth may there be peace!

Those who are freed from desires, with firm minds, are well-established in the teaching of Gotama. They have attained that which should be attained—deathless Nibbana. This peace is freely obtained. This precious jewel is in the Sangha. By this truth may there be peace!

Just as the post of a city gate fixed in the earth is not shaken by the winds from the four directions, even so, I declare a good person to be one who thoroughly perceives the noble truths. This precious jewel is in the Sangha. By this truth may there be peace!

Those who comprehend clearly the noble truths well-taught by him who is endowed with profound wisdom, however exceedingly heedless they may be, will experience no more than seven births. This precious jewel is in the Sangha. By this truth may there be peace!

Three conditions are forsaken by one at the instant of gaining insight: self-delusion, doubt, and the indulgence in rites and rituals. That person is incapable of committing any act for which one must suffer in hell, nor will he ever suffer in any of the four states of misery. This precious jewel is in the Sangha. By this truth may there be peace!

Whatever evil deed such a person commits, by his body, speech, or thought, he or she is incapable of concealing it. For it has been said that such an act is impossible for one who has seen the path. This precious jewel is in the Sangha. By this truth may there be peace!

As a clump of trees whose tops are blossoming during the first heat of the summer months, so the sublime doctrine leading to Nibbana was taught for the highest goal. This precious jewel is in the Buddha. By this truth may there be peace!

The excellent one, the knower of the excellent, the giver and bringer of the excellent, has expounded the excellent doctrine. This precious jewel is in the Buddha. By this truth may there be peace!

With the old kamma extinct, no new kamma arising, and their minds detached from future birth, they have destroyed the seeds of existence. Their desires do not spring up again, and those wise ones go out even as this lamp. This precious jewel is in the Sangha. By this truth may there be peace!

Whatever beings are assembled here, whether terrestrial or celestial, let us pay respect to the Buddha. The Tathagata is honored by gods and men! May there be peace!

Whatever beings are assembled here, whether terrestrial or celestial, let us pay respect to the Dhamma. The Tathagata is honored by gods and men! May there be peace!

Whatever beings are assembled here, whether terrestrial or celestial, let us pay respect to the Sangha. The Tathagata is honored by gods and men! May there be peace!

—Sutta Nipata 2,1

The Courtesan Ambapali

During his last tour, the Buddha arrived in Kotigama, near Vesali, with a large number of bhikkhus. To prepare the bhikkhus, the Buddha cautioned them, "Be mindful. While you are in the world, overcome the grief which arises from bodily craving, from the lust of sensations, and from the errors of wrong reasoning. Whatever you do, act always in full presence of mind. Be thoughtful in eating and drinking, in walking and standing, in sleeping and waking, and while talking and being silent."

The courtesan, Ambapali was delighted to hear of the Buddha's arrival, and she was eager to meet him. Extremely beautiful, she was also scrupulous about religious matters, so she dressed simply without jewelry, climbed into her carriage, set out, and rode as far as she could. Then she got down and walked to where the Buddha was sitting. She paid obeisance and sat respectfully at one side.

When the Buddha saw her, he thought, "This woman moves in worldly circles and is a favorite of kings and princes, but her heart is calm and composed. She is young, rich, and surrounded by pleasures, but she is thoughtful and steadfast. This, indeed, is rare in the world.

Some women are vain and frivolous, but this courtesan, although living in luxury, has acquired the wisdom of a master. She delights in piety and is able to perceive the truth fully."

The Buddha gave a discourse which greatly gladdened and aroused Ambapali. As she listened to the Dhamma, her face became bright with joy. After the Buddha had concluded his teaching, Ambapali asked, "Will the Blessed One do me the honor of taking his meal, together with the Sangha, at my house tomorrow?" The Buddha consented with silence.

A short time later, a messenger arrived at the palace of the Licchavis, the ruling family of Vesali, and announced, "The Buddha has arrived in Vesali and is staying at Kotigama." The princes, gorgeously dressed in bright silk garments and wearing costly jewels, mounted their magnificent chariots and set out.

Along the way, they encountered Ambapali, who drove her carriage, axle to axle and wheel to wheel against the head chariot of the Licchavis. "Ambapali!" the prince in that chariot shouted. "Why are you driving your carriage against us in this way?"

"My lords," she replied, "I have just invited the Buddha and the Sangha for tomorrow's meal."

"Ambapali!" another prince shouted. "We will give you one hundred thousand coins if you will let us have this meal."

"My lords," Ambapali scoffed, "even if you offered me all of Vesali, I would not give up so great an honor!"

Paying her no more attention, the Licchavis continued toward the grove. When the Buddha saw them approaching, he said to the bhikkhus, "Let those who have never seen the devas gaze upon this company of Licchavis, for they are dressed as gorgeously as the inhabitants of Tavatimsa!"

Having ridden as far as they could, the Licchavis alighted and walked to the grove. They paid obeisance to the Buddha and sat respectfully at one side. The Buddha delivered a discourse which greatly gladdened them. When the Buddha had concluded his lesson, one of the princes asked, "Will the Blessed One do us the honor of taking his meal, together with the Sangha, at our palace tomorrow?"

"Licchavis," the Buddha replied, "I have promised Ambapali that I will take a meal from her tomorrow."

"We understand," the princes said. They rose from their seats, paid homage to the Buddha, and departed, keeping him on their right. As soon as they arrived back at their palace, they threw up their hands and cried, "We have been beaten by a mango lass! Left behind by a mere mango lass!"

That night, Ambapali prepared food and decorated her mansion. The next morning, she sent a messenger to the grove. "Venerable Sir," the messenger announced, "the hour has come, and the meal is ready!"

The Buddha took his bowl and went with the Sangha to Ambapali's mansion. She seated them, placed the sweet rice and cakes before them, and served them as much of the delicious curries as they would eat.

After the Buddha had finished his meal, Ambapali had a low stool brought and sat down. "Venerable Sir," she said, "I would like to offer this mansion and my mango grove to the Sangha, of which the Blessed One is the chief."

The Buddha accepted the gift, and, after instructing, arousing, and gladdening her with another discourse, he rose from his seat and departed.

Ambapali's son, Vimala, was so impressed by the Buddha's teaching that he entered the Sangha and soon attained arahataship. Ambapali herself became a bhikkhuni, and it was a discourse taught by her son that led her to attain insight and arahatship.

—Compiled from various sources

Kusinara

Mahaparinibbana

The Buddha said: "Ananda, let us go to the Mallas' sal grove in Kusinara."

"Very good, Venerable Sir," said Ananda. With a large company of bhikkhus, the Buddha went to the sal grove. There, he said: "Ananda, prepare me a bed between these twin sal trees with my head to the north. I am tired and want to lie down."

"Very good, Venerable Sir," said Ananda, and he did so. Then the Buddha lay down on his right side in the lion posture, placing one foot on the other, mindful and fully aware.

Those twin sal trees burst forth into an abundance of unseasonable blossoms, which fell upon the Tathagata's body, sprinkling it and covering it in homage. Divine coral-tree flowers and divine sandalwood powder fell from the sky, sprinkling and covering the Tathagata's body. Divine music sounded from the sky in homage to the Tathagata.

The Buddha said: "Ananda, never before has the Tathagata been so honored, revered, esteemed, worshiped, and adored, but any bhikkhu, bhikkhuni, or male or female lay follower who dwells practicing the Dhamma properly and perfectly follows the path of the Dhamma honors the Tathagata and pays him supreme homage. Therefore, Ananda, your watchword must be, 'We will dwell practicing the Dhamma properly and will perfectly follow the path of the Dhamma.'"

Venerable Upavana was standing in front of the Buddha, fanning him. The Buddha told him to move, and Venerable Ananda thought: "Venerable Upavana has for long been the Blessed One's attendant. Now, in his last hour, the Blessed One tells him to stand aside and not to stand in front of him. Why does he do that?"

He asked the Buddha about this, and the Buddha replied, "Ananda, the devas from ten world-spheres have gathered to see the

Tathagata. For a distance of twelve yojanas around the Mallas' sal grove there is not a space you could touch with the tip of a hair that is not filled with mighty devas, and they are grumbling: 'We have come a long way to see the Tathagata. It is rare for a Tathagata, a fully-enlightened Buddha, to arise in the world, and tonight, in the last watch, the Tathagata will attain final Nibbana, and this mighty bhikkhu is standing in front of the Blessed One, preventing us from getting a last glimpse of the Tathagata!'"

"But, Venerable Sir, what kind of devas can you perceive?"

"Ananda, there are both sky devas and earth devas whose minds are earth-bound, who are weeping and tearing their hair, raising their arms, throwing themselves down, twisting, turning, and crying: 'All too soon the Blessed One is passing away! All too soon the Well-Farer is passing away! All too soon the Eye of the World is disappearing!' There are also those whose minds are earth-bound, who do likewise. But those devas who are free from craving endure patiently, saying: 'All compounded things are impermanent—what is the use of this?'"

"Venerable Sir, formerly, bhikkhus who had spent the rains retreat in various places came to see the Tathagata, and we welcomed them, so that such well-trained bhikkhus might see you and pay their respects. But with the Blessed One's passing, we shall no longer have a chance to do this."

"Ananda, there are four places, the sight of which should arouse emotion in the faithful. Which are they? 'Here the Tathagata was born' is the first. 'Here the Tathagata attained supreme enlightenment' is the second. 'Here the Tathagata set in motion the Wheel of Dhamma' is the third. 'Here the Tathagata attained the Nibbana-element without remainder' is the fourth.

"Furthermore, Ananda, faithful bhikkhus, bhikkhunis, and male and female lay followers will visit those places. Any who die while making the pilgrimage to these shrines with a devout heart will, at the breaking up of the body after death, be reborn in a heavenly world."

"Venerable Sir, what shall we do with the Tathagata's remains?"

"Ananda, they should be dealt with like the remains of a wheel-turning monarch."

"And how is that, Venerable Sir?"

"Ananda, the remains of a wheel-turning monarch are wrapped in a new linen cloth. This is wrapped in teased cotton wool, and this is wrapped in a new cloth. Having done this five hundred times each, the king's body is enclosed in an oil vat of iron, which is covered with another iron pot. Then, on a funeral pyre of all manner of perfumes, the king's body is cremated, and a stupa is raised at a crossroads. That, Ananda, is what is done with the remains of a wheel-turning monarch, and the Tathagata's body should be dealt with in the same way. Whoever, with a devout heart, lays wreaths or puts sweet perfumes and colors at that stupa, will reap benefit and happiness for a long time."

Venerable Ananda went into his lodging and, leaning on the doorpost, lamented, "Alas. I am still a learner with much to do, but the Teacher, who was so compassionate to me, is passing away!"

The Buddha asked where Ananda was, and the other bhikkhus told him. The Buddha turned to one of them and said, "Go, Bhikkhu, and say to Ananda from me: 'Friend Ananda, the Teacher summons you.'"

"Very good, Venerable Sir," said the bhikkhu, and he did so.

"Very good, Friend," Ananda replied. He went to the Buddha, paid respect, and sat down to one side.

"Enough, Ananda," the Buddha said. "Do not weep and wail! Have I not already told you that all things that are pleasant and delightful are changeable, subject to separation and becoming other? Therefore, how could it be, Ananda—since whatever is born, become, and compounded, is subject to decay—how could it be that it should not pass away? For a long time, Ananda, you have been in the Tathagata's presence, showing loving-kindness in acts of body, speech, and mind, beneficially, blessedly, wholeheartedly, and unstintingly. You have achieved much merit, Ananda. Make the effort, and, in a short time, you will be free of the corruptions.

"Bhikkhus," the Buddha continued, "all those who were arahats, fully-enlightened Buddhas in the past, have had just such a chief attendant as Ananda, and so, too, will those Buddhas who come in the future. Bhikkhus, Ananda is wise. He knows when it is the right time for bhikkhus to come to see the Tathagata. He also knows when it is the right time for bhikkhunis, for male lay followers, for female lay followers, for kings, for royal ministers, for leaders of other schools, and for their pupils.

"Ananda has four remarkable and wonderful qualities. What are they? If a company of bhikkhus comes to see Ananda, they are pleased at the sight of him. When he speaks Dhamma to them, they are pleased, and, when he is silent, they are disappointed. It is the same with bhikkhunis, with male lay followers, and with female lay followers."

After this, Venerable Ananda said: "Venerable Sir, may the Blessed One not pass away in this miserable little town of daub and wattle, right in this remote jungle! Venerable Sir, there are great cities, such as Campa, Rajagaha, Savatthi, Saketa, Kosambi, and Baranasi. In those places there are wealthy khattiyas, brahmins, and householders who are devoted to the Tathagata, and they will provide for the Tathagata's funeral in proper style."

"Ananda, don't call it a miserable little town of daub and wattle, in the remote jungle!

"Long ago, Ananda, King Mahasudassana was a rightful and righteous king and a wheel-turning monarch, who had conquered the land in four directions, ensured the security of his realm, and possessed the seven treasures. This very town of Kusinara, which was then called Kusavati, was King Mahasudassana's capital. And it was twelve yojanas long from east to west and seven yojanas wide from north to south.

The royal city of Kusavati was rich, prosperous, full of people, and well-stocked with food, the same as the deva city of Alakamanda. At that time, Kusavati was never free, neither by day nor at night, of the ten sounds of elephants, horses, carriages, kettledrums, sidedrums, lutes, singing, cymbals and gongs, and cries of "Eat, drink and be merry!"

"Now, Ananda, go to Kusinara and announce to the Mallas: "Tonight, Vasetthas, in the last watch, the Tathagata will attain final Nibbana. Approach him, Vasetthas, approach him, lest later you should regret it, saying: 'The Tathagata passed away in our realm, but we did not take the opportunity to see him for the last time!'"

"Very good, Venerable Sir," Ananda replied, and, taking robe and bowl, he went with a companion to Kusinara.

Ananda found the Mallas assembled in their meeting hall and delivered the Buddha's words.

When they heard them, the Mallas and their families were struck with anguish and sorrow. Their minds were so overcome with grief that they wept and tore their hair. Then they all went to the sal grove.

Ananda thought: "If I allow the Mallas of Kusinara to pay respect to the Blessed One individually, the night will have passed before they have all paid homage. I had better have them pay homage family by family." As each family approached, Ananda announced: "Venerable Sir, the Malla so-and-so, with his children, his wife, his servants, and his friends, pays homage at the Blessed One's feet."

Thus, he allowed all the Mallas of Kusinara to pay homage to the Buddha in the first watch.

At that time, a wanderer called Subhadda was in Kusinara, and he heard that the ascetic Gotama was to attain final Nibbana in the final watch of that night. He thought: "I have heard from venerable wanderers, advanced in years, teachers of teachers, that a Tathagata, a fully-enlightened Buddha, only rarely arises in the world. Tonight, the ascetic Gotama will attain final Nibbana. Now a doubt has arisen in my mind, and I feel sure that the ascetic Gotama can dispel that doubt."

Subhadda went to the Mallas' sal grove, told Ananda what he had thought, and asked, "Venerable Ananda, may I be permitted to see the ascetic Gotama?"

Ananda replied, "Enough, friend Subhadda, do not disturb the Tathagata for he is weary." Subhadda made his request a second and a third time, but still Ananda refused it.

The Buddha overheard this conversation and called to Ananda: "Enough, Ananda, do not hinder Subhadda, let him see the Tathagata. For, whatever Subhadda asks me, he will ask in quest of enlightenment and not to annoy me, and what I say in reply to his questions he will quickly understand."

Then Ananda said: "Go, friend Subhadda, the Blessed One gives you leave."

Subhadda approached the Buddha, exchanged courtesies with him, sat down to one side, and said: "Venerable Gotama, all those ascetics and brahmins who have orders and followings, who are teachers, well-known and famous as founders of schools, and popularly regarded as saints, like Purana Kassapa, Makkhali Gosala, Ajita Kesakambali, Pakudha Kaccayana, Sanjaya Belatthaputta, and the Nigantha Nataputta, have they all realized the truth as they claim, or have none of them realized it, or have some realized it and some not?"

"Enough, Subhadda, never mind whether all, or none, or some of them have realized the truth. I will teach you Dhamma, Subhadda. Listen, pay close attention, and I will speak."

"Yes, Venerable Sir."

"More than fifty years ago, when I was twenty-nine, I left home to seek the Truth. On my own I discovered the Noble Eightfold Path which leads to liberation. In whatever doctrine and discipline the Noble Eightfold Path is not found, no ascetic is found to have attained the first, the second, the third, or the fourth path. However, ascetics who have attained the first, the second, the third, and the fourth path can be found in a doctrine and discipline where the Noble Eightfold Path is found. Now, Subhadda, in this Dhamma and Discipline the Noble Eightfold Path is found, and in it are to be found ascetics who have attained the first, the second, the third, and the fourth path. Those other schools are devoid of ariyans, noble ones, but, if in this one the bhikkhus live the life to perfection, the world will not lack for arahats."

At this, the wanderer Subhadda said: "Excellent, Venerable Sir, excellent! It is as if someone were to set up what had been knocked down, or to point out the way to one who had got lost, or to bring an oil lamp into a dark place, so that those with eyes could see what was there. Just so the Blessed One has expounded the Dhamma in various ways. And I, Venerable Sir, go for refuge to the Buddha, the Dhamma, and the Sangha. May I receive the going forth in the Blessed One's presence! May I receive ordination!"

"Subhadda, whoever, coming from another school, seeks the going forth and ordination in this Dhamma and Discipline, must wait four months on probation. At the end of four months, those bhikkhus who are established in mind may let him go forth and give him ordination to the status of a bhikkhu. However, there can be a distinction of persons."

"Venerable Sir, if those coming from other schools must wait four months on probation, I will wait four years, and then let them give me ordination!"

"Let Subhadda go forth!" the Buddha said to Ananda.

"Very good, Venerable Sir," Ananda replied.

Then Subhadda received the going forth and the ordination in the Buddha's presence. In a short time, Venerable Subhadda, alone, secluded, unwearying, zealous, and resolute, attained to that for which young men of good family go forth from the household life into homelessness, that unexcelled culmination of the holy life. By his own insight and dwelling therein, he realized here and now: "Birth is destroyed, the holy life has been lived, what had to be done has been done, there is nothing further to be done." Thus, Venerable Subhadda became another of the arahats. He was the last personal disciple of the Buddha.

Then the Buddha said: "Ananda, it may be that you will think: 'The Teacher's instruction has ceased; now we have no teacher!' It should not be seen like this, Ananda, for what I have taught and explained to you as Dhamma and Discipline will, at my passing, be your teacher."

"It may be, Bhikkhus," the Buddha continued, "that some bhikkhu has doubts or uncertainty about the Buddha, the Dhamma, the Sangha, or about the path or the practice. Ask, Bhikkhus! Do not afterwards feel remorse, thinking: 'The Teacher was there before us, and we failed to ask the Blessed One face to face.'"

At these words the bhikkhus were silent. The Buddha repeated his words a second and a third time, and still the bhikkhus were silent. Then the Buddha said: "Perhaps, Bhikkhus, you do not ask out of respect for the Teacher. Then, Bhikkhus, let one friend tell it to another."

Still they were silent.

Then Venerable Ananda said: "It is wonderful, Venerable Sir, it is marvelous! I clearly perceive that in this assembly there is not one bhikkhu who has doubts or uncertainty."

"You, Ananda, speak from faith. But the Tathagata knows that in this assembly there is not one bhikkhu who has doubts or uncertainty about the Buddha, the Dhamma or the Sangha, or about the path or the practice. Ananda, the least one of these five hundred bhikkhus is a stream-enterer, incapable of falling into states of woe, certain of Nibbana."

"Now, Bhikkhus," he continued, "I declare to you: all conditioned things are of a nature to decay. Strive on with diligence." These were the Tathagata's last words.

Then the Buddha entered the first jhana. Leaving that, he entered the second, the third, and the fourth jhana. Then, leaving the fourth jhana, he successively entered the Sphere of Infinite Space, the Sphere of Infinite Consciousness, the Sphere of Nothingness, the Sphere of Neither-Perception-Nor-Non-Perception. Then he attained the Cessation of Feeling and Perception.

Then Venerable Ananda said, "Venerable Anuruddha, the Blessed One has passed away."

"No, friend Ananda, the Blessed One has not passed away, he has attained the Cessation of Feeling and Perception."

Then the Buddha returned, successively entering the Sphere of Neither-Perception-Nor-Non-Perception, the Sphere of Nothingness, the Sphere of Infinite Consciousness, the Sphere of Infinite Space, the fourth jhana, the third jhana, the second jhana, and the first jhana. Then he again entered the second, the third jhana, and the fourth jhana. From the fourth jhana, the Buddha finally passed away.

At the Buddha's final passing there was a great earthquake, terrible and hair-raising, accompanied by thunder.

Brahma Sahampati declared, "All beings in the world, all bodies, must break up, even the Teacher, peerless in the human world. The Blessed One, the perfect Buddha, has passed away."

Sakka declared, "Impermanent are all compounded things. Having arisen, they're destroyed; their passing is the highest bliss."

Venerable Anuruddha declared, "Breathing neither in nor out, but with a steadfast heart, the Sage who's free from lust has passed away to peace. With mind unshaken, he endured all pains. By Nibbana the Illumined One's mind is freed."

Venerable Ananda declared, "Terrible was the quaking—men's hair stood on end—when the all-accomplished Buddha passed away."

Those bhikkhus who had not yet overcome their passions wept and tore their hair. Raising their arms, throwing themselves down, and twisting and turning, they cried: "Too soon the Blessed One has passed away, too soon the Well-Farer has passed away, too soon the Eye of the World has disappeared!"

Those bhikkhus, however, who were free from craving endured mindfully and said: "All compounded things are impermanent—what is the use of this?"

Then the Venerable Anuruddha said: "Friends, enough of your weeping and wailing! Has not the Buddha already told you that all things that are pleasant and delightful are changeable, subject to separation and to becoming other? Thus, friends, why all of this? Whatever is born, become, and compounded is subject to decay. The devas are grumbling."

"Venerable Anuruddha, what kind of devas are you aware of?" Ananda asked.

"Friend Ananda, there are both sky devas and earth devas whose minds are earth-bound who are weeping and tearing their hair. Those devas who are free from craving, however, endure patiently and are saying, 'All compounded things are impermanent. What is the use of this?'"

Venerable Anuruddha and Venerable Ananda spent the rest of the night discussing Dhamma. Then Venerable Anuruddha said: "Now, friend Ananda, go to Kusinara and announce to the Mallas: 'Vasetthas, the Blessed One has passed away. Now is the time to do as you think fit.'"

The Mallas were again assembled in their meeting hall, and Venerable Ananda delivered the message. When they heard it, the Mallas were again struck with anguish and sorrow, and they tore their hair.

They ordered their men to bring perfume and wreaths and to gather all the musicians together. With the perfume and wreaths, the musicians, and five hundred sets of garments, the Mallas went to the sal grove. They paid respects and honored, worshiped, and adored the Buddha's body with garlands and scents, music, song, and dance. They erected awnings and circular tents and spent the day there. Every day, they thought: "It is too late to cremate the Buddha's body today; we shall do so tomorrow." Thus, paying homage in the same way, they waited a second, a third, a fourth, a fifth, and a sixth day.

On the seventh day, they thought: 'We have paid sufficient honor to the Buddha's body. Now we shall carry him out by the south gate and burn his body." Eight Malla chiefs washed their heads, put on new clothes, and declared: "Now we will lift up the Buddha's body." They were unable, however, to do so. They went to the Venerable Anuruddha and told him about this.

"Vasetthas, your intention is one thing, but the intention of the devas is another."

"Venerable Sir, what is the intention of the devas?"

"Vasetthas, your intention is, having paid homage to the Buddha's body with song and dance, to carry him out by the south gate and to burn his body there. But the devas' intention is, having paid homage to the Buddha's body with heavenly song and dance, to carry him to the north of the city, to bring him in through the north gate, to bear him through the middle of the city and out through the eastern gate to the Mallas' shrine of Makuta-Bandhana, and to burn his body there."

"Venerable Sir, if that is the devas' intention, so be it!"

At that time, even the sewers and rubbish heaps of Kusinara were covered knee-deep with coral tree flowers. Both the devas and the Mallas of Kusinara honored the Buddha's body with divine and human song and dance. They carried the body to the north of the city, brought it in through the north gate, bore it through the middle of the city and out through the eastern gate to the Mallas' shrine of Makuta-Bandhana, and set it down there.

Then they asked the Venerable Ananda: "Venerable Sir, how should we deal with the body of the Tathagata?"

Venerable Ananda repeated what the Buddha had told him about treating the body of a wheel-turning monarch.

The Mallas ordered their men to bring all that was necessary, and they dealt with the Buddha's body accordingly.

At that time, Venerable Maha-Kassapa was traveling toward Kusinara with about five hundred bhikkhus. While he was resting under a tree, an Ajivika happened to pass by on his way to Pava, carrying a coral tree flower which he had picked in Kusinara. When Venerable Maha-Kassapa saw him from afar, he asked the Ajivika, "Friend, do you know our Teacher?"

"Yes, Friend, I do. The ascetic Gotama passed away a week ago. I picked this coral tree flower there."

Those bhikkhus who had not yet overcome their passions wept and tore their hair. Raising their arms, throwing themselves down, and twisting and turning, they cried: "Too soon the Blessed One has passed away, too soon the Well-Farer has passed away, too soon the Eye of the World has disappeared!"

Those bhikkhus, however, who were free from craving endured mindfully and said: "All compounded things are impermanent—what is the use of this?"

Sitting in the group was one bhikkhu called Subhadda, who had gone forth late in life, and he said to those bhikkhus: "Enough, Friends, do not weep and wail! We are well rid of the Great Ascetic. We were always bothered by his saying: 'It is fitting for you to do this; it is not fitting for you to do that!' Now we can do what we like, and not do what we don't like!"

Then the Venerable Maha-Kassapa said: "Friends, enough of your weeping and wailing! Has not the Buddha already told you that all things that are pleasant and delightful are changeable, subject to separation and to becoming other? Thus, friends, why all of this? Whatever is born, become, and compounded is subject to decay.

Meanwhile, four Malla chiefs, having washed their heads and put on new clothes, announced: "We will light the Buddha's funeral pyre," but they were unable to do so. They went to the Venerable Anuruddha and asked him why this was.

"Vasetthas, your intention is one thing, but that of the devas is another."

"Well, Venerable Sir, what is the intention of the devas?"

The devas' intention is this: "Venerable Maha-Kassapa is coming from Pava to Kusinara with five hundred bhikkhus. The Buddha's funeral pyre will not be lit until the Venerable Maha-Kassapa has paid homage with his head to the Buddha's feet."

"Venerable Sir, if that is the devas' intention, so be it!"

Then Venerable Maha-Kassapa went to the funeral pyre. After covering one shoulder with his robe, he joined his hands in respect, circumambulated the pyre three times, uncovered the Buddha's feet, and, with his head, paid homage to the feet. The five hundred bhikkhus did likewise. When this was done, the funeral pyre ignited by itself.

All parts of the body, except the bones, vanished, and not even ashes or dust remained. Just as when butter or oil is burned, no ashes or dust remain, so it was with the Buddha's body; only the bones remained. All the five hundred garments, even the innermost and the outermost cloth, were also completely burned. Then a shower of water fell from the sky, and a second shower bursting from the sal trees extinguished the funeral pyre. The Mallas further extinguished the fire by pouring perfumed water over it. Then the Mallas created a latticework of spears and encircled the pyre with a wall of bows. For seven days, they honored the relics in their assembly hall with garlands, music, singing, and dancing.

When King Ajatasattu of Magadha heard that the Buddha had passed away at Kusinara, he sent a message to the Mallas of Kusinara: "The Blessed One was a khattiya, and I am a khattiya. I am worthy to receive a share of the Blessed One's remains. I will make a great stupa for them." The Licchavis of Vesali, the Sakyas of Kapilavatthu, the Bulayas of Allakappa, the Koliyas of Ramagama, and the Mallas of Pava sent the same message. The chieftain of Vethadipa also sent a message: "The Blessed One was a khattiya; I am a brahmin. I am worthy to receive a share of the Blessed One's remains. I will make a great stupa for them."

The Mallas of Kusinara replied: "The Blessed One passed away in our territory. We will not give away any share of the Blessed One's remains."

At this, the brahmin Dona declared, "Listen, Sirs, to my proposal. Forbearance is the Buddha's teaching. It is not right that strife should come from sharing the remains of the best of men. Let's all be joined in harmony and peace, in friendship sharing these eight portions. Let stupas be erected far and wide that all may see and gain in faith!"

"Well then, Brahmin, please divide the remains of the Blessed One's in the best and fairest way!"

"Very well, friends," Dona replied. He divided the relics fairly into eight portions and then said to the assembly, "Sirs, please give me the urn, and I will build a great stupa for it." They agreed and gave Dona the urn.

The Moriyas of Pipphalavana also sent the same message, but they were told, "The Buddha's remains have been completely divided up, and nothing is left. You must take the embers." They took the embers.

Eight stupas were built for the Buddha's relics. King Ajatasattu built one in Rajagaha, the Licchavis built one in Vesali, the Sakyans built one in Kapilavatthu, the Bulayas built one in Allakappa, the Koliyas built one in Ramagama, the chieftain of Vethadipa built one in Vethadipa, the Mallas of Pava built one in Pava, and the Mallas of Kusinara built one in Kusinara. The brahmin Dona built a stupa for the urn, and the Moriyas built one for the embers in Pipphalavana.

—Digha Nikaya 16

Part 2
Daily Meditation

The Three Refuges

Namo tassa bhagavato arahato samma sambuddhassa. (3 times)

Homage to the Exalted One, the Blessed One, the Perfectly Enlightened One.

Buddham saranam gacchami.
Dhammam saranam gacchami.
Sangham saranam gacchami.

I go for refuge to the Buddha.
I go for refuge to the Dhamma.
I go for refuge to the Sangha.

Dutiyampi Buddham saranam gacchami.
Dutiyampi Dhammam saranam gacchami.
Dutiyampi Sangham saranam gacchami.

A second time I go for refuge to the Buddha.
A second time I go for refuge to the Dhamma.
A second time I go for refuge to the Sangha.

Tatiyampi Buddham saranam gacchami.
Tatiyampi Dhammam saranam gacchami.
Tatiyampii Sangham saranam gacchami.

A third time I go for refuge to the Buddha.
A third time I go for refuge to the Dhamma.
A third time I go for refuge to the Sangha.

The Five Precepts

Panatipata veramani sikkhapadam samadiyami.
Adinnadana veramani sikkhapadam samadiyami.
Kamesu micchacara veramani sikkhapadam samadiyami.
Musavada veramani sikkhapadam samadiyami.
Sura-meraya majja pamadatthana veramani sikkhapadam samadiyami.

I undertake the training rule to abstain from taking life.
I undertake the training rule to abstain from stealing.
I undertake the training rule to abstain from sexual misconduct.
I undertake the training rule to abstain from false speech.
I undertake the training rule to abstain from intoxicating drinks and drugs causing heedlessness.

The Eight Precepts

Panatipata veramani sikkhapadam samadiyami.
Adinnadana veramani sikkhapadam samadiyami.
Abrahmacariya veramani sikkapadam samadiyami..
Musavada veramani sikkhapadam samadiyami.
Sura-meraya majja pamadatthana veramani sikkhapadam samadiyami.
Vikala-bhojana veramani sikkhapadam samadiyami.
Nacca gita vadita visuka dassana mala gandha vilepana dharana mandana vibhusanatthana veramani sikkhapadam samadiyami.
Ucca-sayana maha-sayana veramani sikkhapadam samadiyami.

I undertake the training rule to abstain from taking life.
I undertake the training rule to abstain from stealing.
I undertake the training rule to abstain from all sexual indulgence.
I undertake the training rule to abstain from false speech.
I undertake the training rule to abstain from intoxicating drinks and drugs causing heedlessness.
I undertake the training rule to abstain from taking food after noon.
I undertake the training rule to abstain from dancing, singing, music
and unseemly shows; from the use of garlands, perfumes and unguents; from things that tend to beautify and adorn the person.
I undertake the training rule to abstain from using high and luxurious beds and seats.

Homage to the Triple Gem

Homage to the Buddha

Iti pi so bhagava araham samma sambuddho vijja carana sampanno sugato lokavidu anuttaro purisa damma sarathi sattha deva manussanam buddho bhagava ti.

The Blessed One is an arahat, perfectly enlightened, accomplished in true knowledge and conduct, well-gone, a knower of worlds, the unsurpassed trainer of people to be tamed, a teacher of devas and humans, enlightened, and exalted.

Homage to the Dhamma

Svakkhato bhagavata dhammo sanditthiko akaliko ehipassiko opanayiko paccatam veditabbo viññuhi ti.

The Dhamma is well-expounded by the Blessed One, directly visible, immediately effective, inviting one to come and see, leading onwards, to be realized personally by the wise.

Homage to the Sangha

Supatipanno bhagavato savakasangho. Ujupatipanno bhagavato savakasangho. Ñayapatipanno bhagavato savakasangho. Samicipatipanno bhagavato savakasangho. Yadidam cattari purisa yugani, attha purisa puggala, esa bhagavato savakasangho, ahuneyyo pahuneyyo, dakkhineyyo, anjalikaraniyo, anuttaram puññakkhettam lokassa ti.

The Order of the Blessed One's disciples is practicing the good way. The Order of the Blessed One's disciples is practicing the straight way. The Order of the Blessed One's disciples is practicing the true way. The Order of the Blessed One's disciples is practicing the proper way. That is, the four pairs of persons, the eight types of individuals—this Order of the Blessed One's disciples is worthy of gifts, worthy of hospitality, worthy of offerings, worthy of reverential salutation; it is the unsurpassed field of merit for the world.

Day One

Reading

Four Wonderful Things

"Bhikkhus," the Buddha said, "on the appearance of the Tathagata, the Arahat, the Perfectly Enlightened One, four wonderful and marvelous things appear.

"People, for the most part, delight and rejoice in attachment, but, when the Dhamma of nonattachment is taught by the Tathagata, they wish to listen to it, lend an ear, and try to understand it. This is the first wonderful and marvelous thing that appears on the manifestation of the Tathagata.

"People, for the most part, delight and rejoice in conceit, but, when the Dhamma is taught by the Tathagata for the abolition of conceit, they wish to listen to it, lend an ear, and try to understand it. This is the second wonderful and marvelous thing that appears on the manifestation of the Tathagata.

"People, for the most part, delight and rejoice in restlessness, but, when the Dhamma of peace is taught by the Tathagata, they wish to listen to it, lend an ear, and try to understand it. This is the third wonderful and marvelous thing that appears on the manifestation of the Tathagata.

"People, for the most part, live in ignorance and are blinded and fettered by ignorance, but, when the Dhamma is taught by the Tathagata for the abolition of ignorance, they wish to listen to it, lend an ear, and try to understand it. This is the fourth wonderful and marvelous thing that appears on the manifestation of a Tathagata.

"On the appearance of the Tathagata, the Arahat, the Perfectly Enlightened One, these four wonderful and marvelous things appear."

—Anguttara Nikaya 4, 128

Reflection

The Best Refuge

To sacred hills, woods, and groves,
To sacred trees and shrines,
Do people go, gripped by fear.
But those are not safe refuges,
They are not the best refuge;
Not by going there
Is one freed from all suffering.
But whoever takes refuge
In the Buddha, the Dhamma, and the Sangha
Will understand with wisdom
The Four Noble Truths:
Suffering, its cause, its overcoming,
And the Noble Eightfold Path,
Leading to its overcoming.
This is a safe refuge;
It is the best refuge.
Having taken refuge here,
One is freed from all suffering.

—Dhammapada 188-192

Day Two

Reading

The Most Beautiful Girl of the Land

The Buddha said, "Suppose that, on hearing, 'The most beautiful girl of the land!' a great crowd of people were to assemble. Then, that most beautiful girl would dance and sing exquisitely. On hearing, 'The most beautiful girl of the land is dancing and singing!' an even larger crowd of people would assemble. Then, suppose that a man, loving life and not wishing to die, were to come along. Now, suppose that someone gave him a bowl filled to the brim with oil and said, 'My good man, you must carry this bowl of oil through the crowd in front of the most beautiful girl of the land. Right behind you, a man with a drawn sword will be following. If you spill even a single drop of oil, he will immediately cut off your head.'

"Would that man be negligent of that bowl of oil and turn his attention elsewhere?"

"No, Venerable Sir."

"Here is the meaning of this simile: 'The bowl filled to the brim with oil' is a designation for mindfulness of the body. Therefore, you should train yourselves thus: 'We will develop and cultivate mindfulness of the body, make it our basis, and fully perfect it.' Thus, should you train yourselves."

—Samyutta Nikaya 47, 20

Reflection

The Brahma Viharas

Metta

Loving-kindness is characterized as promoting the welfare of others. Its function is to desire welfare. It is manifested as the removal of annoyance. Its proximate cause is seeing the loveableness in beings. It succeeds when it makes ill-will subside, and it fails when it gives rise to selfish affection.

Karuna

Compassion is characterized as promoting the removal of others' suffering. Its function is not enduring the suffering of others. It is manifested as kindness. Its proximate cause is seeing helplessness in those overwhelmed by suffering. It succeeds when it makes cruelty subside, and it fails when it gives rise to sorrow.

Mudita

Sympathetic joy is characterized as joy in the success of others. Its function is being free from envy. It is manifested as the elimination of aversion. Its proximate cause is seeing other beings' success. It succeeds when it makes aversion subside, and it fails when it gives rise to merriment.

Upekkha

Equanimity is characterized as promoting equipoise towards beings. Its function is to see the equality in beings. It is manifested as quieting liking and disliking. Its proximate cause is seeing the ownership of deeds thus: "Beings are heirs to their deeds. Whose, if not theirs, is the choice by which they will become happy, or will be free from suffering, or will not fall away from the success they have reached?" It succeeds when it makes liking and disliking subside, and it fails when it gives rise to the indifference of mundane ignorance.

—Visuddhimagga 318

Day Three

Reading

The Three Divine Messengers

The Buddha said, "There are three divine messengers.

"Imagine a person of bad conduct in body, speech, and mind. On the dissolution of the body, after death, he is reborn in hell, where the warders of hell seize him by both arms and take him before Yama, the King of Death. 'Your Majesty,' they announce, 'this man had no respect for father and mother, nor for ascetics and brahmins. He did not honor the elders of the family. May Your Majesty inflict due punishment on him!'

"King Yama asks him, 'My good man, didn't you see the first divine messenger appearing among humankind?'

"'No, Sire,' he replies, 'I did not.'

"'Didn't you ever see a woman or a man, eighty, ninety, or a hundred years old, frail, bent like a roof bracket, crooked, leaning on a stick, shakily going along, ailing, youth and vigor gone, with broken teeth, with gray hair or bald, and with wrinkled and spotted skin?'

"'Yes, Sire, I saw that.'

"'Didn't it ever occur to you, an intelligent and mature person, "I, too, am subject to old age and cannot escape it. Let me now do noble deeds by body, speech, and mind"?'

"'o, Sire, it did not. I was negligent.'

"'Well, you will be treated as befits your negligence.'

"Then King Yama asks, 'My good man, didn't you see the second divine messenger?'

"'No, Sire, I did not.'

"'Didn't you ever see a woman or a man who was sick and in pain, seriously ill, lying in his own filth, and having to be lifted up by some and put to bed by others?'

"'Yes, Sire. I saw that.'

"'Didn't it ever occur to you, "I, too am subject to illness and cannot escape it. Let me now do noble deeds"?'

"'No, Sire. It did not. I was negligent.'

"'Well, you will be treated as befits your negligence.'

"Then King Yama asks, 'My good man, didn't you see the third divine messenger?'

"'No, Sire. I did not.'

"'Didn't you ever see a woman or a man, one, two, or three days dead, the corpse swollen, discolored, and festering?'

"'Yes, Sire, I saw that.'

"'Didn't it ever occur to you, "I, too, am subject to death and cannot escape it. Let me now do noble deeds '?'

"'No, Sire, It did not. I was negligent.'

"'Through negligence, my good man, you failed to do noble deeds by body, speech, and mind. Well, you will be treated as befits your negligence. That evil action of yours was not done by mother, father, brothers, sisters, friends, or companions, nor by relatives, devas, ascetics, or brahmins. You alone did that evil deed, and you will have to experience the fruit!'"

—Anguttara Nikaya 3, 35

Reflection

Subduing Anger

When anger arises, there are five ways by which one can subdue it, and by which he should wipe it out completely.

When anger arises, one should develop loving-kindness toward the other person.

When anger arises, one should develop compassion for the other person.

When anger arises, one should develop equanimity toward the other person.

When anger arises, one should ignore the other person and not pay any attention to him.

When anger arises, one should direct one's thoughts to the fact of the other person's being the product of his kamma: "This person is the owner of his kamma, heir of his kamma, born of his kamma, related to his kamma, and abides supported by his kamma. Whatever kamma he does, for good or for evil, to that he will be the heir."

These are five ways by which one can subdue anger whenever it arises and by which one should wipe it out completely.

—Anguttara Nikaya 5, 161

Day Four

Reading

The Bamboo Acrobat

The Buddha said, "Once, an acrobat set up his bamboo pole and said to his apprentice, 'Come, dear Medakathalika, climb the bamboo pole and stand on my shoulders.'

"'Yes, Teacher,' replied the apprentice. Then he climbed the bamboo pole and stood on the teacher's shoulders.

"The acrobat then said, 'You protect me, dear lad, and I'll protect you. Thus, protected by one another, we'll display our skills, collect our fee, and complete our act safely.'

"'No, Teacher,' the apprentice replied. 'That's not the way it should be done. You protect yourself, and I'll protect myself. Thus, each self-protected, we'll display our skills, collect our fee, and complete our act safely.'

"That is the proper method," the Buddha said. "It's just as the apprentice said to the teacher. 'I will protect myself.' Thus, should the foundations of mindfulness be practiced. 'I will protect others.' Thus, should the foundations of mindfulness be practiced. Protecting oneself, one protects others; protecting others, one protects oneself."

"How does one protect others by protecting oneself? By the cultivation of the four foundations of mindfulness.

"How does one protect oneself by protecting others? By developing patience, harmlessness, loving-kindness, and sympathy."

—Samyutta Nikaya 47,19

Reflection

All Tremble at Violence

All tremble at violence; all fear death. Putting oneself in the place of another, one should not kill nor cause another to kill.

All tremble at violence; life is dear to all. Putting oneself in the place of another, one should not kill nor cause another to kill.

One who, while himself seeking happiness, oppresses with violence other beings who also desire happiness, will not attain happiness hereafter.

One who, while himself seeking happiness, does not oppress with violence other beings who also desire happiness, will find happiness hereafter.

—Dhammapada 129-132

Day Five

Reading

Friendship

Once, in the Sakyan country, Venerable Ananda said to the Buddha, "Venerable Sir, good friendship is half of the holy life."

"Not so, Ananda!" the Buddha replied. "Good friendship is the entire holy life.

"When one has a good friend, it is to be expected that he will develop and cultivate the Noble Eightfold Path—Right view, Right intention, Right speech, Right action, Right livelihood, Right effort, Right mindfulness, and Right concentration—each stage is based upon seclusion, dispassion, and cessation, maturing in release.

"By relying upon me as a good friend, Ananda, beings are freed from birth, from aging, from illness, from death, and from sorrow, lamentation, pain, displeasure, and despair. Thus, Ananda, it may be understood how the entire holy life is good friendship.

"Therefore, you should train yourself thus: 'I will be one who has good friends.'

"When you have good friends, you should dwell with one thing for support: diligence in wholesome states—avoiding unwholesome states not yet arisen, abandoning unwholesome states already arisen, developing wholesome states, and maintaining wholesome states.

"When you are thus dwelling diligently, those around you will think, 'Let us also dwell diligently, with diligence for support.'

"In this way, you will be guarded and protected."

—Samyutta Nikaya 3, 18

Reflection

One Person

There is one person whose birth into the world is for the welfare of the many, for the happiness of the many, for the good, the welfare, and the happiness of devas and humans, out of compassion for the world.

There is one person whose presence is hard to encounter in the world, whose teaching is seldom heard, and whose face is rarely gazed upon.

There is one person whose appearance in the world is unique, unequaled, incomparable, unparalleled, without counterpart, matchless, unrivaled, and who lifts up the hearts of devas and humans.

The passing away of one person from the world is regretted by the many and causes sorrow. Even though he admonished, "After I have passed away, let the Dhamma be your teacher," still his passing away is regretted.

Who is that person? It is the Tathagata, the Arahat, the fully Enlightened Buddha.

—Anguttara Nikaya 1,13

Day Six

Reading

Giving

The Buddha said, "A donation may be endowed with six factors—three factors of the donor and three factors of the recipients. What are those six factors?

"Before giving, the donor is glad; while giving, the donor's mind is bright and clear; and after giving, the donor is gratified. These are the three factors of the donor.

The recipients are free of passion or are practicing for the subduing of passion; they are free of aversion or practicing for the subduing of aversion; and they are free of delusion or practicing for the subduing of delusion. These are the three factors of the recipients.

"It is not easy to measure the merit of a donation which is endowed with these six factors. One cannot say that this is a great amount of merit which will result in a heavenly rebirth. One can say only that the merit of such a donation is incalculable and immeasurable.

"It is not easy to measure the water in the ocean as 'This many buckets of water, this many hundreds of buckets of water, this many thousands of buckets of water, or this many hundreds of thousands of buckets of water.' One can say only that it is an incalculable and immeasurable mass of water. In the same way, as for the merit of a donation endowed with those six factors, one can say only that it is incalculable and immeasurable."

—Anguttara Nikaya 6, 37

Reflection

Blessings

May you receive all blessings. May the devas protect you.

Through the power of the Buddha, the Dhamma, and the Sangha, may you enjoy well-being.

Day Seven

Reading

The Discourse on Loving-Kindness

Once, while the Buddha was staying at Savatthi, a group of bhikkhus, having gotten suitable subjects of meditation from him, went to a forest to spend the rainy season. While the bhikkhus were in the forest, the tree devas living there felt obliged to descend from their tree abodes and to stay on the ground. Hoping that the bhikkhus would soon leave, the devas became very upset when they learned that the bhikkhus intended to stay for three months. They tried to scare the bhikkhus away by harassing them in various ways, especially at night.

The bhikkhus found it impossible to meditate under such conditions, so they went to the Buddha and told him about their difficulties. The Buddha immediately taught them the Metta Sutta and advised them to return, armed with this protective sutta to use on the hostile devas.

When the bhikkhus went back to the forest, they recited the sutta and radiated the whole area with thoughts of loving-kindness. The devas were so affected by the power of the bhikkhus' metta that they allowed them to meditate in peace.

This is what the Buddha taught the bhikkhus:

One who is skilled in goodness and who wishes to attain that state of perfect peace, should be able, honest, truly upright, gentle, and humble.

He should be contented, easy to support, not burdened with responsibilities, frugal, tranquil, prudent, courteous, and undemanding.

He should refrain from any action for which the wise would blame him.

He should always think, "May all beings be well and secure! May all beings be happy!

"Whatever living beings there be, without exception—weak or strong; long or short; stout, middle-sized, or thin; large or small; seen or unseen; living near or far; born or yet to be born—may all beings be happy!

"Let none deceive another nor despise anyone at all. In either anger or ill-will, may none wish harm upon another."

Just as with her own life a mother protects her only child, one should cultivate boundless loving-kindness toward all beings.

He should radiate boundless loving-kindness throughout the universe—above, below, and all around—unhindered, without the slightest ill-will, and without a trace of enmity.

While standing, walking, sitting, or lying down—whenever awake—he should develop this mindfulness. This is what is called divine abiding.

Not holding on to wrong views, being virtuous, endowed with insight, and with sense desires restrained, he will never again be reborn in a womb.

—Sutta Nipata 1, 8

Reflection

Daily Reflection

I am of the nature to age. I am subject to aging. I have not got beyond aging.

I am of the nature to sicken. I am subject to illness. I have not got beyond illness.

I am of the nature to die. I am subject to death. I have not got beyond death.

Separation from what is pleasing and beloved will definitely happen to me.

I am the owner of my kamma, the heir of my kamma; born of my kamma, related to my kamma, and I abide supported by my kamma. Whatever kamma I do, for good or for evil, to that I will be the heir.

These things should be frequently recollected.

Day Eight

Reading

Hungry Ghosts

They stand outside the walls and at the crossroads. Having come to their former homes, they stand in the doorways, but, when abundant food and drink is prepared, no one remembers them. Such is the kamma of living beings.

If, however, when a timely donation of food and drink is made, those who are compassionate think, "May this be for our relatives. May they be happy!" the assembled hungry ghosts who have gathered there, will receive the food and will thankfully give their blessing. They will say, "May our relatives, because of whom we have gained this gift, live long. We have been honored, and the donors are not without reward!"

In their realm there is no farming, no herding of cattle, no commerce, no trading with money. Those hungry ghosts live on what is given here.

As rain falling on a hill flows down to the valley, what is given here benefits the dead. As rivers full of water fill the ocean, what is given here benefits the dead.

As one gives gifts, he should remember what relatives have done in the past and think, "He gave to me, he worked for me, he was my relative, my friend, my companion."

No tears, no grief, nor any other lamentations are of any use to the departed, but a gift that has been properly given to the Sangha is of benefit to them immediately and for a long time.

This is the proper way to repay obligations to one's relatives. This is how to do great honor to the departed and to give strength to the Sangha. The merit you thus receive is not small.

—Khuddakapatha 7

Reflection

The Futility of Worldly Gains

I see men wealthy in the world, who yet
From ignorance give not their gathered wealth.
Greedily they hoard away their riches
Longing still for further sensual pleasures.

Most other people, too, not just a king,
Encounter death with craving unabated;
With plans still incomplete they leave the corpse;
Desires remain unsated in the world.

Clad in a shroud, he leaves his wealth behind,
Prodded with stakes he burns upon the pyre.
And as he dies, no relatives or friends
Can offer him shelter and refuge here.

While his heirs take over his wealth, this being
Must pass on according to his actions;
And as he dies nothing can follow him;
Not child nor wife nor wealth nor royal estate.

Longevity is not acquired with wealth
Nor can prosperity banish old age;
Short is this life, as all the sages say,
Eternity it knows not, only change.

—Majjhima Nikaya 82

Day Nine

Reading

Bhadraka

Once, the Buddha was staying in the Mallan town of Uruvelakappa. At that time, the headman, Bhadraka, said, "It would be good, Venerable Sir, if the Blessed One would teach me about the origin and the passing away of suffering."

"Headman," the Buddha replied, "if I were to teach you about the origin and the passing away of suffering with reference to the past or the future, you would become confused. Instead, I will teach you about the origin and the passing away of suffering at this moment. Listen and attend closely."

"Yes, Venerable Sir," Bhadraka replied.

"Are there any people in Uruvelakappa on whose account pain and sorrow would arise in you if they were to be severely punished or executed?"

"There are such people, Venerable Sir."

"Are there any people in Uruvelakappa on whose account pain and sorrow would not arise in you in such an event?"

"There are such people, Venerable Sir."

"Why would pain and sorrow arise in you on account of some people but not on account of others?

"There are, Venerable Sir, people for whom I have desire and attachment, but there are also people for whom I have no desire and attachment."

"Headman, apply this principle that you have just stated to the past and to the future thus: 'Whatever suffering arose in the past arose rooted in desire, for desire is the root of suffering. Whatever suffering will arise in the future will arise rooted in desire, for desire is the root of suffering.'"

"It is wonderful, Venerable Sir! It is amazing, Venerable Sir! How well that has been stated by the Blessed One: 'Whatever suffering arises is rooted in desire, for desire is the root of suffering.' Venerable Sir, I have a boy named Ciravasi, who stays in another place. Every morning I send a man to find out how Ciravasi is. Until that man returns, Venerable Sir, I am anxious, hoping that Ciravasi has not met with any affliction!"

"If Ciravasi were to be severely punished or executed, would pain and sorrow arise in you?"

"Venerable Sir, if Ciravasi were to be severely punished or executed, my whole life would be upset, so how could pain and sorrow not arise in me?"

"In this way too, it can be understood: 'Whatever suffering arises is rooted in desire, for desire is the root of suffering.'

"Headman, before you knew Ciravasi's mother, did you have any desire, attachment, or affection for her?"

"No, Venerable Sir."

"Then was it because of knowing her that this desire, attachment, and affection arose in you?"

"Yes, Venerable Sir."

"If Ciravasi's mother were to be severely punished or executed, would pain and sorrow arise in you?"

"Venerable Sir, if she were to be severely punished or executed, my whole life would be upset, so how could pain and sorrow not arise in me?"

"In this way too, it can be understood: 'Whatever suffering arises is rooted in desire, for desire is the root of suffering.'"

—Samyutta Nikaya 42, 11

Reflection

Divine Abidings

Metta

May I be free from sorrow and always be happy. May those who desire my welfare, those who are indifferent towards me, and those who hate me also be happy.

May all beings who live in this vicinity and those who live in other kingdoms in this world-system be happy.

May all beings living in every world-system and each element of life within such a system be happy and achieve the highest bliss.

Likewise, women, men, the noble and ignoble ones, devas, humans, those in woeful states, and those living in the ten directions—may all those beings be happy.

Karuna

May all those who are in pain, in trouble, facing hardship and suffering find relief. May their troubles be over. May they find happiness.

Mudita

May all those who are well, successful, healthy, and prosperous, maintain themselves happily.

Upekkha

All beings are the owners of their kamma, heirs of their kamma, born of their kamma, related to their kamma, and abide supported by their kamma. Whatever kamma they do, for good or for evil, to that they will be the heir.

Day Ten

Reading

Tranquillity and Insight

Two things are conducive to knowledge: tranquillity and insight. If tranquillity is developed, what profit does it bring? The mind is developed. If the mind is developed, what profit does it bring? All lust is abandoned. If insight is developed, what profit does it bring? Wisdom is developed. If wisdom is developed, what profit does it bring? All ignorance is abandoned.

A mind defiled by lust is not freed, and a mind defiled by ignorance cannot develop wisdom. Thus, with the fading of lust comes the liberation of the mind, and with the fading of ignorance comes the liberation by wisdom.

—Anguttara Nikaya 2, 32

Reflection

The Chariot

One who has faith and wisdom yoked in harness,
With conscience as the pole, the mind as reins,
And mindfulness as watchful charioteer,
Rides in a chariot of morality.
Its axle is meditation; energy, its wheels;
And equipoise its balanced shaft.
Clothed in freedom from desire
Defended by non-hatred, harmlessness,
And detachment of the mind,
He wears a leather coat of patience.
Furnished thus, this chariot
Rolls on from slavery to freedom.
This noble chariot, the best of vehicles,
Is built by oneself alone.
It carries the wise from this world
On to certain victory.

—Samyutta Nikaya 45, 4

Day Eleven

Reading

Wood from a Pyre

"There are four kinds of people in the world. One who is engaged in promoting neither his own good nor the good of another, one who is engaged in promoting another's good but not his own, one who is engaged in promoting his own good but not that of another, and one who is engaged in promoting both his own good and that of another.

"A person who is engaged in promoting neither his own good nor the good of another is just like a piece of wood from a pyre, burnt at both ends and in the middle fouled with dung, which serves neither for fuel nor for lumber.

More worthy than that person is one who is engaged in promoting another's good but not his own. More worthy than either of them is the person who is engaged in promoting his own good but not that of another. Foremost, however, is the person who is engaged in promoting both his own good and that of another. Of these four individuals he is the supreme.

"Just as from a cow comes milk; from milk, cream; from cream, butter; from butter, ghee; and from ghee, the skimmings of ghee, which is considered the best; among these four kinds of people, the person who is engaged in promoting both his own good and the good of another is the foremost and the supreme."

—Anguttara Nikaya 4, 95

Reflection

Understanding Death

Death can be understood by the shortness of the lifespan. Many die at birth or in their youth. Those who live to fifty years, live long. Fewer live to be seventy or eighty. Rare, indeed, are those who live to ninety or one hundred.

Know death by the weakness of the life force. Life needs water and food. Life is dependent upon air.

Understand death by knowing that this body is shared by many others. It is a home to many others.

Understand death by its absence of signs. There is no sign to indicate when death will come—in the morning, in the afternoon, or at night. There is no sign to tell us where one will die—at home or away from home; in the air, on earth, or in the water. The way death will come is also unknown—from illness, by accident, or by an enemy's hand.

Understand death by knowing that all health ends in sickness, that all strength ends in weakness, and that all success ends in failure.

Know that death comes to all. The most powerful ruler, the richest person, the general, the head of a great family, and even the Buddha himself must die, so how can I hope to be spared?

As a turning wheel touches the earth at only one point, so, too, should life be understood. The present moment arises, persists, then passes away. Death comes to each moment, and, likewise, to each life, which arises, stays a bit, then passes away.

Day Twelve

Reading

Worshiping the Six Directions

One morning,, a young man named Sigalaka got up early and went outside Rajagaha. With wet clothes and hair, he began a ceremony of paying homage. At the same time, the Buddha left the Squirrel's Sanctuary of Veluvana and began walking toward Rajagaha for alms, When he saw the young man, he stopped and asked, "Young man, why are you paying homage like that?"

"Venerable Sir," Sigalaka answered, "As my father was dying, he told me that I should get up early to pay homage to the six directions—the east, the south, the west, the north, the nadir, and the zenith. It is out of respect for my father's words, that I honor and hold sacred, that I am doing this."

"That is not the right way to pay homage to the six directions."

"Well,
Venerable Sir, it would be good if the Blessed One would teach me the proper way."

"Then listen carefully, and I will speak."

"Yes, Venerable Sir," Sigalaka replied."These six things are to be regarded as the six directions. The east denotes mother and father. The south denotes teachers. The west denotes wife and children. The north denotes friends and companions. The nadir denotes servants, workers, and helpers. The zenith denotes ascetics and brahmins.

"There are five ways in which children should attend to their parents as the eastern direction. Having been supported by their parents, they should support them, perform their duties to them, keep up the family tradition, be worthy of their heritage, and, after their parents' deaths, distribute gifts on their behalf.

"There are five ways in which the parents, so attended to by their children, should reciprocate. They should restrain them from evil, support them in doing good, teach them a skill, find them suitable partners, and, in due time, hand over their inheritance to them.

"In this way, the eastern direction is covered, making it at peace and free from fear.

"There are five ways in which students should attend to their teachers as the southern direction. They should rise to greet them, wait on them, be attentive, serve them, and master the skills they teach.

"There are five ways in which the teachers, thus attended to by their students, should reciprocate. They should give thorough instruction, make sure the students have grasped what should be grasped, give them a thorough grounding in all skills, recommend them to their friends and colleagues, and provide them with security in all directions.

"In this way, the southern direction is covered, making it at peace and free from fear.

"There are five ways in which a husband should attend to his wife as the western direction. He should honor her, praise her, be faithful to her, give authority to her, and provide for her security.

"There are five ways in which a wife, thus attended to by her husband, should reciprocate. She should properly organize her work, be kind to the servants, be faithful to her husband, protect his property, and be skillful and diligent in her duties.

"In this way, the western direction is covered, making it at peace and free from fear.

"There are five ways in which a person should attend to friends and companions as the northern direction. One should give gifts, use kind words, look after their welfare, treat them like oneself, and keep one's word.

"There are five ways in which friends and companions, thus attended to by a person, should reciprocate. They should look after him when he is inattentive, look after his property when he is careless, be a refuge when he is afraid, stand by him when he is in trouble, and show concern for his children.

"In this way the northern direction is covered, making it at peace and free from fear.

"There are five ways in which a master should attend to his servants and workers as the nadir. He should arrange their work according to their strength, supply them with food and wages, look after them when they are ill, share special delicacies with them, and let them off work at the right time.

"There are five ways in which servants and workers, thus attended to by their master, should reciprocate. They should get up before him, go to bed after him, take only what they are given, do their work properly, and be bearers of his praise and good repute.

"In this way, the nadir is covered, making it at peace and free from fear.

"There are five ways in which a person should attend to ascetics and brahmins as the zenith. One should be kind in deed, speech, and thought, keep open house for them, and supply their bodily needs.

"There are five ways in which ascetics and brahmins, thus attended to by a person, should reciprocate. They should restrain him from evil, encourage him to do good, be compassionate toward him, teach him what he has not heard, and point out to him the way to heaven.

"In this way, the zenith is covered, making it at peace and free from fear."

—Digha Nikaya 31

Reflection

Reflections on Grief

Observe how others, born into this world according to their kamma, tremble under the specter of death.

However people think, things turn out to be otherwise. Such is the opposite nature of things. Observe thus the nature of the world.

Even if a person were to live a hundred years or more, he must still yield his life, at last bereft of friends and relatives.

Therefore, listening to the wise and the holy and seeing a deceased friend or relative, control your weeping.

Reflect on the departure of your beloved ones by thinking that separation is natural.

Just as one would douse a burning house with water, let one who is steadfast and wise remove grief, as quickly as the wind disperses a handful of cotton.

Let a person, desirous of his own welfare, pluck out the shafts of wails and grief, which he himself planted.

Having plucked out these shafts, and having attained mental peace, one becomes blessed and free from grief, overcoming all sorrows.

—Sutta Nipata 3,8

Day Thirteen

Reading

Families

Once, the Buddha was staying at Pavarika's Mango Grove in Nalanda at a time when the city was in the grip of a severe famine.

At the same time, Nigantha Nataputta was also staying in Nalanda, and Asibandhakaputta, one of his lay disciples, visited him. "Come," Nigantha Nataputta said to him, "refute the doctrine of the ascetic Gotama. Then people will say, 'Asibandhakaputta the Headman has refuted the doctrine of the ascetic Gotama, who is so powerful and mighty.'"

"How, Venerable Sir, shall I refute the doctrine of the ascetic Gotama?"

"Approach the ascetic Gotama," Nigantha Nataputta instructed, "and ask him, 'Venerable Sir, doesn't the Blessed One praise compassion towards families and the protection of families?' If he answers, 'Yes,' you should say to him: 'Then why, Venerable Sir, is the Blessed One wandering with a large Sangha of bhikkhus at a time of famine? The Blessed One is practicing for the destruction of families.' When the ascetic Gotama is posed this dilemma by you, he will be able neither to throw it up nor to gulp it down."

Asibandhakaputta agreed to do this, paid his respects to Nigantha Nataputta, and went to see the Buddha. After paying homage, he sat down to one side and asked, "Venerable Sir, doesn't the Blessed One praise compassion towards families and the protection of families?"

"Yes, Headman, the Tathagata praises compassion towards families and the protection of families."

"Then why, Venerable Sir, is the Blessed One wandering with a large Sangha of bhikkhus at a time of famine? The Blessed One is practicing for the destruction of families."

"Headman," the Buddha replied, "I recollect ninety-one eons back, but I do not recall any family that has ever been destroyed merely by offering cooked almsfood. On the contrary, every rich family whatsoever has become so from giving, from truthfulness, and from self-control.

"There are eight causes for the destruction of families—thieves, fire, water, not finding treasure they may have hidden or stored, mismanagement of business, a family member becoming a wastrel, and, finally, impermanence. While these eight causes for the destruction of families exist, if anyone who accuses the Tathagata of practicing for the destruction of families does not abandon that assertion and relinquish that view, then, according to his deserts, he will be reborn in hell."

When this was said, Asibandhakaputta praised the Buddha and took refuge in the Triple Gem.

—Samyutta Nikaya 42, 9

Reflection

Generosity

The Buddha said: "If beings knew, as I know, the results of sharing gifts, they would not enjoy their use without sharing them with others, nor would the taint of stinginess obsess the heart and stay there. Even if it were their last morsel of food, they would not enjoy it, without sharing it, if there were anyone to receive it."

—Itivuttaka 26

Day Fourteen

Reading

A Handful of Leaves

Once, in a grove of simsapa trees in Kosambi, the Buddha picked up a few leaves in his hand and asked the bhikkhus, "Which is more, the few leaves that I have picked up in my hand or those on the trees?"

"The leaves that the Blessed One has picked up in his hand are few; those on the trees are far more."

"So, too, the things that I have known by direct knowledge are more; the things that I have told you are only a few. Why have I not told them? Because they bring no benefit, no advancement in the spiritual life. They do not lead to dispassion, to fading, to ceasing, to stilling, to direct knowledge, to enlightenment, and to Nibbana. That is why I have not told them.

"What have I told you? 'This is suffering; this is the origin of suffering; this is the cessation of suffering; and this is the way leading to the cessation of suffering.' That is what I have told you. Why have I told it? Because it brings benefit, and advancement in the spiritual life. It leads to dispassion, to fading, to ceasing, to stilling, to direct knowledge, to enlightenment, and to Nibbana. Therefore, let your task be this: 'This is suffering; this is the origin of suffering; this is the cessation of suffering; and this is the way leading to the cessation of suffering.'"

—Samyutta Nikaya 51, 31

Reflection

Advice to Rahula

Develop the meditation on loving-kindness, for, by so doing, hatred will be got rid of.

Develop the meditation on compassion, for, by so doing, cruelty will be got rid of.

Develop the meditation on sympathetic joy, for, by so doing, discontent will be got rid of.

Develop the meditation on equanimity, for, by so doing, aversion will be got rid of.

Develop the meditation on the impure, for, by so doing, attachment will be got rid of.

Develop the meditation on the perception of impermanence, for, by so doing, the conceit "I am" will be got rid of.

—Majjhima Nikaya 62

Day Fifteen

Reading

A Rainless Cloud

The Buddha said, "There are three kinds of persons in the world. What three? One who is like a rainless cloud, one who rains locally, and one who rains everywhere.

"What kind of person is like a rainless cloud? A certain person never gives to anyone. He does not give food, drink, clothing, garlands, incense, medicine, lodging, or lamps to ascetics, the poor, or the needy. This kind of person is like a rainless cloud.

"What kind of person rains locally? A certain person gives to some but not to others. He gives food, drink, clothing, garlands, incense, medicine, lodging, and lamps only to some ascetics and to some of the poor and the needy, but not to others. This kind of person rains locally.

"What kind of person rains everywhere? A certain person gives to all. He gives food, drink, clothing, vehicles, garlands, incense, medicine, lodging, and lamps to all ascetics and to the poor and the needy. This kind of person rains everywhere.

"These are the three kinds of persons in the world."

—Itivuttaka 75

Reflection

The Four Dhamma Summaries

The world is swept away. It does not endure.

The world offers no shelter. There is no one in charge.

The world has nothing of its own. One has to pass on, leaving everything behind.

The world is insufficient, insatiable, and a slave to craving.

—Majjhima Nikaya 82

Day Sixteen

Reading

The Simile of the Six Animals

The Buddha said, "One should develop restraint of the six senses.

"Suppose that a man caught six animals: a snake, a crocodile, a bird, a dog, a jackal, and a monkey, tied each of them by a strong rope, and tied the six ropes together in a knot at the center. Then he let go of the ropes. Those six animals, having different domains and different feeding grounds would pull in six different directions. The snake would pull one way, thinking, 'Let me enter an anthill.' The crocodile would pull another way, thinking, 'Let me enter the water.' The bird would pull another way, thinking, 'Let me fly up into the sky.' The dog would pull another way, thinking, 'Let me enter the village.' The jackal would pull another way, thinking, 'Let me enter the charnel ground.' The monkey would pull another way, thinking, 'Let me enter the forest.'

"When these six animals became worn out, they would be dominated by the one among them that was strongest. They would submit to it and come under its control. In the same way, when one has not developed and cultivated mindfulness directed to the body, the eye pulls in the direction of agreeable forms and is repelled by disagreeable forms. The ear pulls in the direction of agreeable sounds, …. The nose pulls in the direction of agreeable odors, …. The tongue pulls in the direction of agreeable tastes, …. The body pulls in the direction of agreeable tactile objects, …. The mind pulls in the direction of agreeable mental phenomena, and is repelled by disagreeable mental phenomena.

"So it is with nonrestraint. When one sees a form with the eye, if he is intent upon a pleasing form and repelled by a displeasing form, he dwells without having set up mindfulness of the body, and he does not understand as it really is that liberation of mind by wisdom, wherein those evil unwholesome states cease without remainder. It is the same for hearing a sound with the ear, smelling an odor with the nose, tasting a flavor with the tongue, feeling a tactile object with the body, and cognizing a mental phenomenon with the mind.

Now suppose that a man caught those six animals and tied each of them by a strong rope. Then he tied the six ropes to a strong post in the center. Those six animals would again each pull in the direction of its own feeding ground and domain.

"When they became worn out, however, they would move close to the post and rest. In the same way, when one has developed mindfulness directed to the body, the eye does not pull in the direction of agreeable forms, nor are disagreeable forms repulsive. The ear does not pull in the direction of agreeable sounds, ... The nose does not pull in the direction of agreeable odors, ... The tongue does not pull in the direction of agreeable tastes, ... The body does not pull in the direction of agreeable tactile objects, ... The mind does not pull in the direction of agreeable mental phenomena, nor are disagreeable mental phenomena repulsive.

"So it is with restraint. When one sees a form with the eye, if he is not intent upon a pleasing form and repelled by a displeasing form, he dwells having set up mindfulness of the body, and he understands as it really is that liberation of mind by wisdom, wherein those evil unwholesome states cease without remainder. It is the same for hearing a sound with the ear, smelling an odor with the nose, tasting a flavor with the tongue, feeling a tactile object with the body, and cognizing a mental phenomenon with the mind.

"The strong post represents mindfulness directed to the body. Therefore, you should train yourselves thus: 'We will develop and cultivate mindfulness directed to the body. We will make it our vehicle and our basis. We will exercise ourselves in it and fully perfect it.'"

—Samyutta Nikaya 35, 247

Reflection

Be Familiar with Death

Understand death. Be familiar with death.

Death approaches. Just as each step a calf takes toward the slaughterhouse takes him closer to death, so death approaches with each passing day.

Death is inevitable, like the sun, after rising in the east, moves steadily to set in the west.

Death is like a river, always flowing, rushing downstream.

Death is like the drop of water on the tip of a blade of grass, evaporated by the sun.

Death is like the stream that dries up in the summer, leaving only its banks, bereft of water.

Death is like water poured into the sand, disappearing without a trace.

Death is like the overripe fruit that finally falls from the tree.

Death is like the clay vessel which the potter smashes with his hammer.

Just as a mushroom emerges with a cap of soil, when we are born, we carry our death with us.

Day Seventeen

Reading

Grasping and Worry

What is grasping and worry? An ordinary person thinks, "This body is mine; I am this; this is myself." Then, when the body changes, grief, suffering, and despair arise. It is the same with feelings, perception, mental formations, and consciousness.

What is freedom from grasping and worry? An instructed noble disciple thinks, "This body is not mine; I am not this; this is not myself." Then, even though the body changes, grief, suffering, and despair do not arise. It is the same with feelings, perception, mental formations, and consciousness.

—Samyutta Nikaya 22, 7

Reflection

The Mountains

Like gigantic boulders,
Mountains reaching to the sky,
Moving in from the four directions
And crushing all in their path,
In the same way, aging and death
Roll over living beings:
Noble warriors, priests, merchants,
Workers, outcastes, and scavengers.
These mountains spare no one;
They trample everyone.
Here elephants can hold no ground
Neither can chariots, infantry,
A battle of spells, nor wealth win out.
Thus, a wise person,
Seeing his own good,
Establishes firm conviction
In the Buddha, the Dhamma, and the Sangha.
One who practices the Dhamma
In thought, word, and deed,
Receives praise here on earth
And, after death, rejoices in heaven.

—Samyutta Nikaya 3, 25

Day Eighteen

Reading

The Blind Men and the Elephant

One day, in Jetavana, after finishing their meal, some bhikkhus approached the Buddha, paid homage to him, sat down to one side, and said, "Venerable Sir, sometimes, on our almsrounds, we see wanderers of other sects, living around Savatthi, who hold various views, beliefs, and opinions and who propagate those views. They are quarrelsome and disputatious and wound each other with verbal darts, such as, "The Dhamma is like this! It is not like that!" and "The Dhamma is not like this! It is like that!"

The Buddha said: "Bhikkhus, wanderers of other sects are blind and sightless. They do not know what is beneficial and harmful. They do not know what is the Dhamma and what is not the Dhamma.

"Formerly, there was a king in Savatthi who asked a man to round up all the people in the city who were blind from birth. When the man had done so, the king asked him to show the blind men an elephant. To each of the blind men the man presented only one part of the elephant's body, but to all of them he said, 'This is an elephant.'

"Then the king went to the blind men and said, 'Tell me, blind men, what is an elephant like?'

"Those who had been shown the head of the elephant replied, 'An elephant, Your Majesty, is like a water jar.' Those who had been shown the ear replied, 'An elephant is like a winnowing basket.' Those who had been shown the tusk replied, 'An elephant is like a spear.' Those who had been shown the trunk replied, 'An elephant is like a snake.' Those who had been shown the body replied, 'An elephant is like a storeroom.' Those who had been shown the tail replied, 'An elephant is like a rope.' Those who had been shown the tuft of the tail replied, 'An elephant is like a brush.'

"The blind men began fighting with each other, shouting, 'An elephant is like this! It is not like that!' They even resorted to fighting with fists. Seeing this, the king was delighted. In the same way, the wanderers of other sects are blind and sightless, and, thus, they become quarrelsome, disputatious, and wrangling, and they wound each other with verbal darts."

—Udana 6, 4

Reflection

The Thirty-two Parts of the Body

This body is made up of:

hair of the head, hair of the body, nails, teeth, skin;
flesh, sinew, bone, marrow, kidneys;
heart, liver, diaphragm, spleen, lungs;
intestine, mesentery, stomach, excrement, brain;
bile, phlegm, pus, blood, sweat;
lymph, tears, serum, saliva, nasal mucous;
synovial fluid, urine.

Urine, synovial fluid;
nasal mucous, saliva, serum, tears, lymph;
sweat, blood, pus, phlegm, bile;
brain, excrement, stomach, mesentery, intestine;
lungs, spleen, diaphragm, liver, heart;
kidneys, marrow, bone, sinew, flesh;
skin, teeth, nails, hair of the body, hair of the head.

Know that here there is nothing pure, lasting, or reliable.
All is subject to change and to dissolution.

Day Nineteen

Reading

The Merit of Giving

One day, King Pasenadi asked the Buddha, "Venerable Sir, how should a gift be given?"

"One should give with his mind full of confidence, great king."

"How, Venerable Sir, does giving bear great fruit?"

"This, great king, is a very different question from your first. Giving to one who is virtuous bears great fruit, but giving to one who is immoral does not. Now, great king, let me ask you a question on this point. Suppose you are at war and a battle is about to take place. A khattiya youth, untrained, unskillful, inexperienced, and cowardly, arrives. Would you employ that man as an archer?"

"Surely not, Venerable Sir."

"If he were a brahmin. Would you employ him?"

"Surely not, Venerable Sir."

"What if he were a vessa or a sudda. Would you employ him?"

"Surely not, Venerable Sir."

"Now suppose you are at war and a battle is about to take place. A khattiya youth, trained, skillful with bow and arrow, experienced, and brave, arrives. Would you employ that man as an archer?"

"Surely I would, Venerable Sir."

"If he were a brahmin. Would you employ him?"

"Surely I would, Venerable Sir."

"What if he were a vessa or a sudda. Would you employ him?"

"Surely I would, Venerable Sir."

"In the same way, great king, when a person has gone forth from the household life into homelessness, no matter from which social class, if he has abandoned five factors and possesses five factors, giving to him bears great fruit. What five factors have been abandoned? Sensual desire, ill-will, sloth and torpor, restlessness and worry, and doubt have been abandoned. What five factors does he possess? He possesses proficiency in virtue, concentration, wisdom, liberation, and the knowledge and vision of liberation. Giving to one who has abandoned these five factors and who possesses these five factors bears great fruit."

The Buddha concluded this lesson with this simile, "Just as a king would hire, as an archer, the youth who possesses skill, persistence, and strength, rather than one of noble birth, who is perhaps a coward, so, too, should one honor the wise of noble conduct, in whom patience and gentleness are established, even though they be of lowly birth.

"Build pleasant hermitages with tanks and walking paths and invite the learned to stay there. With calm awareness provide the requisites for those of upright character. As a mighty cloud produces thunder and lightning and pours refreshing rain upon the earth, filling the streams and gullies, one of confidence provides food and drink to mendicants. 'Give! Give!' he cries, like thunder from the clouds. And in return rains down on him the merit from his gifts!"

—Samyutta Nikaya 3, 24

Reflection

The Three Characteristics

All that is conditioned is impermanent;
When with wisdom one sees this,
One tires of suffering—
This is the path to purity.

All that is conditioned is suffering;
When with wisdom one sees this,
One tires of suffering—
This is the path to purity.

All phenomena are non-self;
When with wisdom one sees this,
One tires of suffering—
This is the path to purity.

Day Twenty

Reading

Bringing Tranquillity to the Land

One day, the brahmin Kutadanta addressed the Blessed One: "Master Gotama, I have heard that you understand how to conduct the triple sacrifice successfully with its sixteen requisites. I want to make just such a big sacrifice, but I do not know how to do it. It would be good if Master Gotama would explain this to me."

"Listen, Brahmin," the Buddha answered. "Pay proper attention, and I will explain."

"Yes, Master Gotama," replied Kutadanta.

"Brahmin," the Buddha continued, "long ago there was a very wealthy king called Mahavijita. One day, as this king was reflecting in private, the thought came to him: 'I have acquired extensive wealth, I occupy a wide extent of land which I have conquered. Let me now make a great sacrifice.' He called his spiritual advisor and asked, 'How can I make a great sacrifice which will be of lasting benefit to me and ensure my happiness?'

"'Your Majesty,' the advisor replied, 'your country is beset by outlaws, who are ravaging villages and towns. The countryside is infested with brigands. It would not be right for Your Majesty to tax this region. Your Majesty might think, "I will get rid of this plague of robbers by executions and imprisonment, or by confiscation, threats, and banishment." In that way, however, the problem would not be properly resolved. Those who survived would later harm Your Majesty's realm. There is, however, a plan by which you can completely eliminate the lawlessness. To those in the kingdom who are engaged in cultivating crops, let Your Majesty distribute grain. To those who are raising cattle, give fodder. To those in trade, give capital. To those in government service, assign proper living wages. In this way, thievery will disappear, and Your Majesty's revenues will certainly increase.'

"'So be it!' cried the king, and he did exactly as his advisor had suggested. As a result, all of his subjects became intent on their own occupations, and no one harmed the kingdom. Not only did thievery disappear and the king's revenues increase, but the land became tranquil, and the people, with joy in their hearts, playing with their children, dwelled in open houses."

—Digha Nikaya 5

Reflection

An Auspicious Day

Don't dwell on the past;
Don't long for the future.
The past is gone;
The future is yet to come.

With mindfulness be aware
Of every present moment,
Training the mind with
Diligence and steadfastness.

Who knows when death may come?
Perhaps tomorrow he will strike.
There is no bargaining
With him or with his army.

For one who practices in this way,
Both ardent and untiring,
Everyday, the Buddha taught,
Is an auspicious day.

—Majjhima Nikaya 131

Day Twenty-one

Reading

Gratitude

The Blessed One said: "A person of no integrity is ungrateful and does not acknowledge the help given to him. This ingratitude is second nature to rude people. It is the mark of a person of no integrity.

A person of integrity is grateful and acknowledges the help given to him. This gratitude is second nature to fine people. It is the mark of a person of integrity.

There are two people who are not easy to repay—your mother and father. Even if you were to carry your mother on one shoulder and your father on the other shoulder for one hundred years and to look after them by bathing and massaging their limbs and they were to defecate and urinate on you, you would not be repaying your parents. Even if you were to establish them in abundant wealth of the seven treasures and in sovereignty over the entire world, you would not be repaying your parents. Why not? Mother and father do so much for their children! They care for them, nourish them, and introduce them to this world. However, one who rouses his unbelieving parents and establishes them in the Dhamma, rouses his unvirtuous parents and establishes them in virtue, rouses his stingy parents and establishes them in generosity, and rouses his foolish parents and establishes them in wisdom, is, to that extent, repaying one's mother and father.

—Anguttara Nikaya 2, 31-32

Reflection

Advisory Stanzas

Viewing indolence as something frightful, as the root of all defilements and the destroyer of all good, and treating effort, its opposite, as the remover of all dangers, be energetic at all times—this is the advice of the Buddhas.

Viewing confrontation as something frightful and treating non-confrontation, its opposite, as a haven, seek peace at all times—this is the advice of the Buddhas.

Viewing negligence as something frightful and treating diligence, its opposite, as a haven, practice the Noble Eightfold Path—this is the advice of the Buddhas.

—Cariya Pitaka

Day Twenty-two

Reading

A Lump of Foam

Seated on the bank of the Ganges, the Buddha said, "Suppose that this river Ganges is carrying along a great lump of foam. A person with good eyesight inspects it and carefully investigates it, and it appears to be void, hollow, and insubstantial, for what substance can there be in a lump of foam? So, too, whatever kind of form there is, whether past, future, or present, internal or external, gross or subtle, inferior or superior, or far or near: one inspects it and carefully investigates it, and it appears to be void, hollow, and insubstantial, for what substance can there be in form?

"Suppose that, in the autumn, when it is raining and big rain drops are falling, a water bubble forms and bursts on the surface of the water. A person with good eyesight carefully investigates it, and it appears to be insubstantial, for what substance can there be in a water bubble? So, too, whatever kind of feeling there is, one carefully investigates it, and it appears to be insubstantial, for what substance can there be in feeling?

"Suppose that, in the last month of the hot season, at high noon, a shimmering mirage appears. A person with good eyesight carefully investigates it, and it appears to be insubstantial, for what substance can there be in a mirage? So, too, whatever kind of perception there is, one carefully investigates it, and it appears to be insubstantial, for what substance can there be in perception?

"Suppose that a person, seeking heartwood, takes a sharp axe and enters a forest. That person finds and cuts down a large and straight plantain tree. Upon unrolling the coils of the trunk, there is found to be no softwood, let alone heartwood. It appears to be insubstantial, for what substance can there be in the trunk of a plantain tree? So, too, whatever kind of volitional formations there are, one carefully investigates them, and they appear to him to be insubstantial, for what substance can there be in volitional formations?

"Suppose that a magician displays a magical illusion at a crossroads. A person with good eyesight inspects it and carefully investigates it, and it appears to be void, hollow, and insubstantial, for what substance can there be in a magical illusion? So, too, whatever kind of consciousness there is, whether past, future, or present, internal or external, gross or subtle, inferior or superior, or far or near, one inspects it and carefully investigates it, and it appears to be void, hollow, and insubstantial, for what substance can there be in consciousness?

"Seeing thus, the instructed noble disciple experiences revulsion toward form, revulsion toward feeling, revulsion toward perception, revulsion toward volitional formations, revulsion toward consciousness. Experiencing revulsion, one becomes dispassionate. Through dispassion the mind is liberated. When it is liberated, there comes the knowledge: 'It's liberated.' One understands: 'Destroyed is birth; the spiritual life has been lived; what had to be done has been done; there is no more for this state of being.'"

—Samyutta Nikaya 22, 95

Reflection

No Cause for Grief

Uncalled, he hither came,
Without leave, departed, too;
Even as he came, he went.
What cause is there for woe?
No friend's lament can touch the ashes of the dead.
Why should I grieve?
He fares the way he had to tread.

Though I should fast and weep,
How would it profit me?
My kith and kin, alas, would more unhappy be!
No friend's lament can touch the ashes of the dead.
Why should I grieve?
He fares the way he had to tread.

—Uraga Jataka

Day Twenty-three

Reading

Be Your Own Island

Once, not long after Venerable Sariputta and Venerable Moggallana had attained final Nibbana, the Buddha was staying among the Vajjians on the bank of the river Ganges, with a large number of bhikkhus.

The Buddha surveyed the bhikkhus, who were all silent, and said, "This assembly appears to me empty now that Sariputta and Moggallana have attained final Nibbana. It is wonderful that, when my disciples act in accordance with the Teacher's instructions, they will be revered and esteemed by the fourfold Sangha. It is wonderful that, when such a pair of disciples has attained final Nibbana, there is no sorrow or lamentation in the Tathagata.

"Suppose that the largest branches of a mighty tree were to break off. That is how it is for the Tathagata that Sariputta and Moggallana have attained final Nibbana. One may wish: 'May what is born, come to be, conditioned, and subject to disintegration not disintegrate!' but that is impossible.

"Therefore, dwell with yourself as your own island, with yourself as your own refuge, with no other refuge, and with the Dhamma as your refuge, with no other refuge. How does one dwell with oneself as one's own refuge?

"One dwells ardent, clearly comprehending, and mindful, having subdued longing and dejection in regard to the world.

"One dwells contemplating the body in the body, ardent, clearly comprehending, and mindful, having subdued longing and dejection in regard to the world.

"One dwells contemplating feelings in feelings, in the same way.

"One dwells contemplating the mind in the mind, in the same way.

"One dwells contemplating phenomena in phenomena, in the same way.

"One who dwells with oneself as one's own island, with oneself as one's own refuge, with no other refuge, and with the Dhamma as one's refuge, with no other refuge, will be for me foremost of those keen on the training."

—Samyutta Nikaya 47, 14

Reflection

Again and Again

One morning, in Savatthi, the Buddha dressed, took his bowl and robe, and approached the residence of the brahmin Udaya. Udaya filled the Buddha's bowl with rice. The next morning, the Blessed One again went to Udaya's residence, and the brahmin filled the Buddha's bowl with rice a second time. The next morning, the Buddha again went to Udaya's residence, and, after the brahmin Udaya had filled the Buddha's bowl with rice a third time he said, "This pesky ascetic Gotama keeps coming again and again."

The Buddha recited these verses:

Again and again, they sow the seed.
Again and again, the sky-king rains.
Again and again, the farmers plough the fields.
Again and again, the land produces grain.
Again and again, the beggars come and beg.

Again and again, the generous donors give.
Again and again, when many gifts are given,
Again and again, the donors reach the heavens.
Again and again, the dairymen milk the herds.
Again and again, the calf goes to its mother.
Again and again, we tire and we toil.
Again and again, the heedless come to birth.
Again and again, comes birth, and dying follows.
Again and again, we are carried to the grave.
Only by gaining the path for non-returning,
Is a person of wisdom not, again and again, reborn

Hearing this, Udaya took refuge in Buddha, the Dhamma, and the Sangha.

—Samyutta Nikaya 7, 12

Day Twenty-four

Reading

The Four Similes for Nutriment

The Buddha said, "There are these four kinds of nutriment for the maintenance of beings: edible food, contact, mental volition, and consciousness.

"As for the nutriment edible food, suppose a husband and wife have taken limited provisions and are traveling through a desert. They have with them their only son, dearly beloved. In the middle of the desert, their provisions have been used up. In desperation, the husband and wife think: 'Alas! We must kill our dearly beloved son and prepare dried meat. Only by eating our son's flesh, can we cross the rest of this desert. Let not all three of us perish!'

"Then the husband and wife kill their son, prepare dried meat, and cross the rest of the desert. While they are eating their son's flesh, they beat their breasts and cry, 'Where are you, our only son? Where are you, our darling son?'

"What do you think? Would they eat that food for amusement, for enjoyment, or for the sake of physical beauty?"

"No, Venerable Sir. They would eat that food only for the sake of crossing the desert."

"That is how the nutriment edible food should be seen. When the nutriment edible food is fully understood, lust for the five aggregates is fully understood. When lust for the five aggregates is fully understood, there is no fetter bound by which a noble disciple will be reborn in this world.

"As for the nutriment contact, suppose there is a flayed cow. If she stands near a wall, she is attacked by the creatures in the wall. If she stands near a tree, she is attacked by the creatures in the tree. If she stands near water, she is attacked by the creatures in the water. If she stands in the open, she is attacked by the creatures in the air. Wherever that flayed cow stands, she is attacked by the creatures there.

"That is how the nutriment contact should be seen. When the nutriment contact is fully understood, the three kinds of feeling—pleasant, painful, and neutral—are fully understood. When the three kinds of feeling are fully understood, there is nothing further that a noble disciple needs to do.

"As for the nutriment mental volition, suppose there is a deep charcoal pit, filled with glowing coals. Along comes a man, wanting to live, not wanting to die, desiring happiness and averse to suffering. Then two strong men grab him by both arms and drag him toward the pit. The man's volition would be to get far away from the charcoal pit. He knows: 'I will fall into this charcoal pit and, because of that, I will meet deadly suffering or death.'

"That is how the nutriment mental volition should be seen. When the nutriment mental volition is fully understood, the three kinds of craving—for sense pleasures, for existence, and for non-existence—are fully understood. When the three kinds of craving are fully understood, there is nothing further that a noble disciple needs to do.

"As for the nutriment consciousness, suppose a bandit is arrested and brought before the king. His captors say, 'Sire, this man is a bandit. Impose on him whatever punishment you wish.' The king says to them, 'In the morning, pierce this man with one hundred spears.' The men do so. At noon, the king asks, 'How is that man?' 'Still alive, Sire,' reply the men. 'Pierce him with another one hundred spears,' orders the king. The men do so. In the evening, the king asks, 'How is that man?' 'Still alive, Sire,' reply the men. 'Pierce him with another one hundred spears,' orders the king. The men do so.

"What do you think. bhikkhus? Would that man, being pierced with three hundred spears, experience pain because of that?"

"Venerable Sir, even if he were pierced with one spear, he would experience pain, let alone three hundred spears."

"That is how the nutriment consciousness should be seen. When the nutriment consciousness is fully understood, name-and-form is fully understood. When name-and-form is fully understood, there is nothing further that a noble disciple needs to do."

—Samyutta Nikaya, 12, 63

Reflection

All Beings Will Die

All beings will die, for life ends in death; all beings will receive the fruit of their own merit and evil and will be born again accordingly. Evil doers will be born in hell, and merit doers will be born in a happy destination. Therefore, one should do what is good, an accumulation for a future life. Merits are the foundation for beings in the world beyond.

When life, vital heat, and consciousness abandon this body, then it will lie discarded, useless like a log.

As a cowherd drives the cattle to pasture with a stick, so old age and death drive away the life of living beings.

Day Twenty-five

Reading

The Advantages of Loving-kindness

Eleven advantages are to be expected from the liberation of the mind by cultivating loving-kindness, by regarding it as a vehicle of expression and as something to be treasured, by developing thoughts of loving-kindness, by constantly increasing those thoughts, by living in conformity with them, by putting them into practice, and by firmly establishing them. What are the eleven?

"One sleeps in comfort, awakes in comfort, and sees no evil dreams. One is dear to both human and non-human beings, protected by devas, and unharmed by fire, poison, or the sword. One gains concentration of the mind quickly and has a serene countenance. One dies without being confused in mind and, if failing to attain arahatship here and now, will be reborn in the Brahma-world.

—Anguttara Nikaya 9, 16

Reflection

The Fool

Victory breeds enmity,
The defeated one sleeps badly.
The peaceful one sleeps at ease,
Having abandoned both victory and defeat.

A man will go on plundering
So long as it serves his ends,
But, when others plunder him,
The plunderer is plundered.

The fool thinks fortune is on his side
So long as his evil does not ripen,
But, when the evil ripens,
The fool incurs suffering.

The killer brings forth a killer,
The conqueror, a conqueror.
The abuser, an abuser,
And the reviler, a reviler.
Thus, by the unfolding of kamma
The plunderer is plundered.

—Samyutta Nikaya 3, 14-15

Day Twenty-six

Reading

The Hen and Her Eggs

"Suppose that a hen has a clutch of eggs that she has not incubated properly. Even though she might wish, 'Oh, that each of my chicks might pierce its shell with its egg tooth and hatch safely!' the chicks would not be capable of doing so. Why not? Because that hen has not nurtured the eggs properly.

"In the same way, when one does not devote himself to development, even though he might wish, 'Oh, that my mind might be liberated from the taints by nonclinging!' his mind would not be liberated. Why not? Because he has not devoted himself to the development of the four foundations of mindfulness, the four kinds of effort,[1] the five spiritual faculties,[2] the seven factors of enlightenment,[3] and the Noble Eightfold Path.

"Suppose that a hen has a clutch of eggs that she has incubated properly. Even though she might not wish, 'Oh, that each of my chicks might pierce its shell with its egg tooth and hatch safely!' the chicks would be capable of doing so. Why? Because that hen has nurtured the eggs properly.

"In the same way, when one devotes himself to development, even though he might not wish, 'Oh, that my mind might be liberated from the taints by nonclinging!' his mind would be liberated. Why? Because he has devoted himself to the development of the four foundations of mindfulness, the four kinds of effort, the five spiritual faculties, the seven factors of enlightenment, and the Noble Eightfold Path."

—Samyutta Nikaya 22, 101

Notes

[1] to prevent unwholesome conditions from arising, to overcome unwholesome conditions already arisen, to bring about wholesome conditions not yet arisen, and to maintain wholesome conditions already arisen.

[2] confidence, energy, mindfulness, concentration, and wisdom.

[3] mindfulness, investigation of the dhamma, energy, joy, tranquillity, concentration, and equanimity.

Reflection

An Exhortation

Arise! Sit up!
Of what use are your dreams?
How can you, who are sick
And pierced with the arrow of grief,
Continue to sleep?
Arise! Sit up!
Train yourself to win peace.
Let not the king of death,
Knowing you to be lazy,
Trick you into his realm.
Cross over this attachment,
Tied to which both devas and men are trapped.
Do not let this chance slip by,
Because for those who do,
There is only hell.
Dusty is indolence.
Dust comes in its wake.
With knowledge and vigilance,
Draw out the arrow of suffering from yourself.

—Sutta Nipata 2,10

Day Twenty-seven

Reading

Kisa-Gotami

Kisa-Gotami came from a poor family in Savatthi, and she married into a prosperous family. She was not well-treated by her in-laws until she had a son. While her little boy was just a toddler, he suddenly died, and Kisa-Gotami was distraught from grief. Unable to accept that her son was dead, she carried his body on her hip, asking for medicine to restore him. Some people mocked her, but a kind man directed her to the Buddha. The Buddha instructed her to fetch mustard seed from a house where no one had yet died. In the course of her impossible quest, she became calm and understood the inevitability of death. Leaving her child's body in the charnel field, she returned to the Buddha and asked to become a bhikkhuni. In no long time, she attained arahatship.

One morning, Venerable Kisa-Gotami dressed, took her bowl and robe, and entered Savatthi for alms. After eating her meal, she went to the Blind Men's Grove and sat down at the foot of a tree for the day's abiding.

Mara, the Evil One, desiring to arouse fear, trepidation, and terror in her and desiring to make her fall away from concentration, approached Venerable Kisa-Gotami and said, "Why now, when your son is dead, do you sit alone with a tearful face? Having entered the woods all alone, are you on the lookout for a man?"

Venerable Kisa-Gotami wondered, "Who just spoke to me—a human being or a non-human being?" Realizing that it was Mara, she replied, "I've gotten past the death of sons. With this, the search for men has ended. I neither sorrow nor weep, nor do I fear you, Friend. Delight everywhere has been destroyed. The mass of darkness has been sundered. Having conquered the army of Death, I dwell without defiling taints."

Hearing this, Mara realized that Venerable Kisa-Gotami recognized him, and, disappointed, he disappeared.

—Samyutta Nikaya 1, 3

Reflection

No Village Law

No village law is this, no law of a town,
Nor the law of a single family;
This is the law of the entire world,
Inclusive of the devas, that is, impermanence.

No village law is this, no law of a town,
Nor the law of a single family;
This is the law of the entire world,
Inclusive of the devas, that is, suffering.

No village law is this, no law of a town,
Nor the law of a single family;
This is the law of the entire world,
Inclusive of the devas, that is, non-self.

—Therigatha, Kisa-Gotami

Day Twenty-eight

Reading

Insight Surpasses All

The Buddha said to Anathapindika: "In the past, a brahmin named Velama gave a great alms offering of eighty-four thousand golden bowls filled with silver, eighty-four thousand silver bowls filled with gold, eighty-four thousand bronze bowls filled with bullion, eighty-four thousand elephants, chariots, dairy cows, maidens, and couches, many millions of fine cloths, and indescribable amounts of food, drink, ointment, and bedding.

"As great as the alms offering that the brahmin Velama gave was, it would be even more fruitful if one were to feed a single person possessed of right view.

"As great as it would be to feed a hundred persons possessed of right view, it would be even more fruitful if one were to feed a single once-returner.

"As great as it would be to feed a hundred once-returners, it would be even more fruitful if one were to feed a single non-returner.

"As great as it would be to feed a hundred non-returners, it would be even more fruitful if one were to feed a single arahat.

"As great as it would be to feed a hundred arahats, it would be even more fruitful if one were to feed a single Pacceka Buddha.

"As great as it would be to feed a hundred Pacceka Buddhas, it would be even more fruitful if one were feed a single Perfectly Enlightened Buddha.

"As great as it would be to feed a hundred Perfectly Enlightened Buddhas, it would be even more fruitful if one were to feed the Sangha headed by the Buddha and to build a monastery dedicated to the worldwide Sangha.

"As great as it would be to feed the Sangha headed by the Buddha and to build a monastery dedicated to the worldwide Sangha, it would be even more fruitful if, with a trusting mind, one were to go for refuge to the Buddha, the Dhamma, and the Sangha, and to undertake the five precepts.

"As great as all this might be, with a trusting mind, to go for refuge to the Buddha, the Dhamma, and the Sangha, and to undertake the five precepts, it would be even more fruitful if one were to develop a mind of loving-kindness, even for the time it takes to pull a cow's udder.

"And, as great as that might be, it would be even more fruitful if one were to develop the perception of impermanence, just for the time it takes to snap one's fingers."

—Anguttara Nikaya 9, 20

Reflection

Recollection of Death

Seeing with wisdom the end of life in others and comparing this to a lamp kept in a windy place, one should meditate on death.

Just as in this world beings who once enjoyed great prosperity will die, even so one day will I die too. Death will indeed come to me.

Death comes along with birth. Therefore, like an executioner, death always seeks an opportunity to destroy.

Life, without halting for a moment, ever keen on moving, runs like the sun that rushes to set after its rise.

Life comes to an end like a streak of lightning, a bubble of water, a dew-drop on a leaf, or a line drawn on water, like an enemy intent on killing. Death can never be avoided.

If death can come in an instant to the Buddhas, endowed with great glory, merit, power and wisdom, what can be said of me?

Dying every instant, I will die within the blink of an eye, for lack of food, internal ailments or external injuries.

Day Twenty-nine

Reading

Five Ways of Subduing Anger

"Whenever anger arises," Venerable Sariputta said, "it must always be subdued, and there are five ways of doing so, depending on the type of person with whom one is angry.

"First, one might get angry with a person whose ways are impure in deed but pure in word. Suppose a bhikkhu, who wears only rag-robes, were to see a piece of cloth on the road. He would hold it down with his left foot, spread it out with his right, pick it up, make use of the best part of it, and go on his way. In the same way, with a person whose ways are impure in deed, but pure in word, one should ignore his impure deeds and concentrate on only his words which are pure. In this way, anger with that person should be subdued.

"Second, one might get angry with a person whose ways are impure in word but pure in deed. Suppose a person, tortured by heat, overcome by heat, weary, thirsty, and craving for water, were to come to a pond overgrown with mossy slime and water plants. He would plunge into that pond, scattering with both hands the moss and plants hither and thither, cup his hands, drink, and go on his way. In the same way, with a person whose ways are impure in word but pure in deed, one should ignore his impure words and concentrate on only his deeds which are pure. In this way, anger with that person should be subdued.

"Third, one might get angry with a person whose ways are impure in both deed and word but who, from time to time, achieves mental clarity and mental calm. Suppose a person, tortured by heat, overcome by heat, weary, thirsty, and craving for water, were to come upon a puddle in a cow's footprint. He might think, 'If I drink from this puddle by hand or cup, I will stir it up and make it unfit to drink.' Instead, he crouches on all fours, sips like a cow, and goes on his way. In the same way, with a person whose ways are impure in both deed and word but who, from time to time, obtains mental clarity and mental calm, one should ignore both his impure words and his impure deeds and concentrate on only the mental clarity and the mental calm, that he obtains from time to time. In this way, anger with that person should be subdued.

"Fourth, one might get angry with a person whose ways are impure in both deed and word and who never achieves mental clarity or mental calm. Suppose a person who was grievously ill were to go along the highway with no village anywhere nearby. If someone else were to see him, he might raise pity and compassion in that second person, who might say to himself, 'Alas! That poor man needs proper food, proper medicine, proper assistance, or a guide to lead him to a village, lest he suffer even more or die here.' In the same way, with a person whose ways are impure in both deed and word and who never obtains mental clarity or mental calm, pity and compassion should arise, so that one says to himself, 'Alas! He should give up his bad habits and develop good habits, so that, on the breaking up of the body after death, he is not reborn in a miserable realm.' In this way, anger with that person should be subdued.

"Finally, one might get angry with a person whose ways are pure in both deed and word and who often achieves mental clarity and mental calm. Suppose a person, tortured by heat, overcome by heat, weary, thirsty, and craving for water, were to come to a pool, clear, sweet, cool, and limpid, a lovely resting-place, shaded by all manner of trees. He might plunge into that pool, bathe, and drink. Then he would come out and sit or lie there in the shade of the trees. In the same way, with a person whose ways are pure in both deed and word and who often obtains mental clarity and mental calm, one should think about and remember his words which are pure, his deeds which are pure, and the mental calm and clarity which he often has. In this way, anger with that person should be subdued. When one becomes completely calm, the mind also becomes calm.

"These are the five ways of subduing anger, which should always be subdued."

—Anguttara Nikaya 5, 162

Reflection

Meditation on Death

Life in the world is unpredictable and uncertain. Life is difficult, short, and fraught with suffering.

Being born, one has to die; this is the nature of the world. With old age there is death; this is the way things are.

When fruit is ripe, it may drop early in the morning. In the same way, one who is born may die at any moment.

Just as all pots made by all potters end in being broken, so it is with the life of all who are born.

Neither young nor old, foolish nor wise, will escape the trap of death. All move toward death.

They are overcome by death. They pass on to another world. A father cannot save his son, nor a family, its members.

Look! With relatives watching, with tears and crying, people are carried off one by one, like cattle to the slaughter.

Death and aging are a natural part of the world. Thus, the wise grieve not, seeing the nature of the world.

—Sutta Nipata 3, 8

Day Thirty

Reading

The Goldsmith

There are gross impurities in gold—dirt, gravel, and grit. The dirt-washer places the gold in a pan and washes it again and again until he has washed away these impurities. There remain moderate impurities—coarse sand and fine grit. He washes the gold again and again until he has washed away these impurities. There remain fine impurities—fine sand and black dust. He washes the gold again and again until he has washed away these impurities.

Finally, the goldsmith places it in a crucible and heats it, liquefies it, and removes the dross. Until the gold has been washed, heated, and liquefied, and the dross removed, it is not malleable and glistening. It is brittle and cannot be worked. But there comes a time when the goldsmith has washed it sufficiently, heated and liquefied it, and has removed all the dross. At that point, the refined gold is malleable and glistening. Then the goldsmith can make from it whatever ornament he wishes—a belt, an earring, a necklace, or a chain. The gold will serve his purpose.

In the same way, there are gross defilements in one intent on attaining higher states of mind—misconduct in body, misconduct in speech, and misconduct in mind. With mindfulness, the meditator destroys and abandons these gross defilements.

There remain moderate defilements—thoughts of sensuality, thoughts of ill-will, and thoughts of harmfulness. With increased mindfulness, the meditator destroys and abandons these moderate defilements.

There remain the fine defilements—thoughts of his relatives, thoughts of his home, and thoughts of his reputation. With consummate mindfulness, the meditator destroys and abandons these fine defilements.

There remain only thoughts of the Dhamma, but his concentration is not yet refined. It has not yet attained serenity or unity. It can be maintained only by forceful restraint. There comes a time, however, when his mind settles down, becomes fully concentrated, and gains unity. At this point, his concentration is complete. He has attained serenity and unity, and forceful restraint is no longer needed to maintain concentration.

At this point, the meditator can realize any of the higher knowledges to which he turns his mind whenever the necessary conditions arise.

—Anguttara Nikaya 3,102

Reflection

A Time Will Come

A time will come when the ocean will dry up and be no more, but there will be no end of suffering for those who roam and wander, hindered by ignorance and fettered by craving.

A time will come when Mount Meru will burn up and be no more, but there will be no end of suffering for those who roam and wander, hindered by ignorance and fettered by craving.

A time will come when the earth will be devoured by fire and be no more, but there will be no end of suffering for those who roam and wander, hindered by ignorance and fettered by craving.

—Samyutta Nikaya, 22, 99

Day Thirty-one

Reading

Venerable Sunita, the Outcaste

Born into a low caste, I was poor and had little to eat. I eked out a living scavenging withered flowers left at shrines.

I was despised, abused, and so humbled that I was continually on my knees, paying deference to others.

How fortunate I was to see the Buddha with his train of bhikkhus entering Rajagaha!

I laid down my carrying-pole, approached, and paid obeisance to him, and he, the Blessed One, in compassion paused before me.

Lying there in prostration at his feet, I asked to be accepted into the Order.

"Come, Bhikkhu!" he said, and, thus, was I ordained.

Diligently following the Master's teaching, I stayed alone in the forest.

In the first watch of the night, I became conscious of my past births. In the middle watch I developed the divine eye.

In the last watch, just as the sun arose, I broke the gloom of ignorance.

Sakka and Brahma appeared and paid respect with folded hands. "All hail!" they declared. "You are the noblest and the highest of men, deserving of reverence, for you have eliminated all desires."

Seeing me revered by the devas, the Master smiled and said: "By discipline, virtue, and wisdom does one become a noble. This is holiness supreme!"

—Theragatha 2,2

Reflection

Metta Meditation

May I be free from harm and danger. May I be free from mental suffering. May I be free from physical suffering. May I be well, peaceful, and happy.

Likewise, may all those who are dear to me be free from harm and danger. May they be free from mental suffering. May they be free from physical suffering. May they be well, peaceful, and happy.

May all strangers, those unknown to me, be free from harm and danger. May they be free from mental suffering. May they be free from physical suffering. May they be well, peaceful, and happy.

May all enemies, those hostile to me, be free from harm and danger. May they be free from mental suffering. May they be free from physical suffering. May they be well, peaceful, and happy.

May all beings without exception, keep themselves happily. May none wish harm on another.

Day Thirty-two

Reading

On Sleeping Well in the Cold Forest

Prince Hatthaka of Alavi happened to see the Buddha sitting on a bed of leaves beside a cowpath in a simsapa forest. He paid his respects to the Buddha, sat down beside him, and said, "Venerable Sir, I hope the Blessed One has slept well."

"Yes, young man. I have slept very well and comfortably."

"But, Venerable Sir, the nights are cold, and this is the time of snow. The ground is hard and has been trampled by the hooves of cattle. There is but a thin layer of leaves, and the trees are almost bare. Your robes are thin, and the wind is cold. Still, the Blessed One says, 'Yes, young man. I have slept very well and comfortably.'"

"In that case, young man, let me ask you a question. Suppose a man has a house with a gabled roof, plastered inside and out, draft-free, with close-fitting doors and windows. In his room he has a luxurious bed, spread with comforters and woolen blankets, beautifully embroidered. Overhead is a lovely canopy, and on the floor is a magnificent carpet. The room is well-lit, and his wife is lovingly attending to him. Would that man sleep well?"

"Yes, Venerable Sir, he would sleep well."

"Is it possible, however, that that man would suffer from a bodily fever or a mental fever—his mind burning with passion—so that he would sleep badly?"

"Yes, Venerable Sir."

"As for those passion-born fevers which caused that man to sleep miserably, that passion has been abandoned by the Tathagata. Its root has been destroyed, and it will never again arise. Therefore, he sleeps well.

"Is it possible, also, that that man would suffer from a mental fever—his mind burning with aversion—so that he would sleep badly?"

"Yes, Venerable Sir."

"As for those aversion-born fevers which caused that man to sleep miserably, that aversion has been abandoned by the Tathagata. Its root has been destroyed, and it will never again arise. Therefore, he sleeps well.

"Is it possible, also, that that man would suffer from a mental fever—his mind burning with delusion—so that he would sleep badly?"

"Yes, Venerable Sir."

"As for those delusion-born fevers which caused that man to sleep badly, that delusion has been abandoned by the Tathagata. Its root has been destroyed, and it will never again arise. Therefore, he sleeps well."

—Anguttara Nikaya 3,34

Reflection

The Triple Gem

The supreme speaker in all mankind,
The Sakyan Sage, the Holy One, whose task is done.
Gone beyond this round of rebirths,
Possessed of power and energy.
To you, the Blessed One, I go for refuge!

Exempt from lust and craving, sorrow-free
Law unconditioned and delectable,
Sweet, potent, and profoundly analytical.
To this very Dhamma I go for refuge.

All generosity bears great fruit.
There are four pairs of persons—
Eight individuals who have realized the truth.
To this very Sangha I go for refuge.

Day Thirty-three

Reading

The Rarity of Human Birth

One day, the Buddha said to the bhikkhus, "Suppose that there were a yoke with a single hole in it, floating on the surface of the sea. The east wind carried it to the west, and the west wind carried it to the east; the north wind carried it to the south, and the south wind carried it to the north. Now suppose that there were in the sea a blind turtle which came to the surface only once every one hundred years. Would that blind turtle," the Buddha asked, "put his neck into the hole of that yoke?"

"Venerable Sir," the bhikkus answered, "sometime or other, at the end of a long period, he might put his neck into that hole, but it would be very unlikely."

"Bhikkhus," the Buddha said, "it would be more likely for that blind turtle to put his neck into that hole than for a fool who has fallen into hell to be reborn as a human because, for those in hell, it is impossible to practice the Dhamma. It is impossible for them to practice righteousness. It is impossible for them to make merit by performing wholesome deeds. Rare, indeed, is birth as a human.

—Samyutta Nikaya 129

Day Thirty-three

Reflection

The Eight Worldly Conditions

Gain and loss, fame and disgrace, praise and blame, and happiness and suffering:

Among human beings, these conditions are impermanent and constantly changing.

Knowing this, one who is wise mindfully regards them all.

He neither rejoices at the desirable conditions nor feels dismay at the undesirable.

For him, welcoming the good and rejecting the bad have ceased and no longer exist.

Having understood the nature of the world, he is unshaken and has reached the deathless shore.

—Anguttara Nikaya 8, 6

Day Thirty-four

Reading

The Discourse on Blessings

A deva once asked the Buddha "What brings happiness?" and the Buddha replied,

"Not to associate with fools, to have fellowship with the wise, and to honor those worthy of respect–this is the highest blessing.

"To live in a suitable place, to have performed meritorious deeds in the past, and to set oneself in the right direction–this is the highest blessing.

"A good education, training in a skill, respect for discipline, and pleasant speech–this is the highest blessing.

"To support one's parents, to cherish one's partner and children, and to have a peaceful occupation–this is the highest blessing.

"Generosity, morality, helpfulness, and blamelessness in deed–this is the highest blessing.

"To avoid evil, to abstain from alcohol, and to be diligent in righteousness–this is the highest blessing.

"Reverence, humility, contentment, gratitude, and hearing the Dhamma–this is the highest blessing.

"Patience, obedience, meeting the Sangha, and discussing the Dhamma–this is the highest blessing.

"Self-control, chastity, understanding the Noble Truths, and the attainment of Nibbana –this is the highest blessing.

"A mind untouched by worldly conditions, free from sorrow, stainless, and secure–this is the highest blessing.

"Those who have gained these qualities will be happy and victorious wherever they go. To them these are the highest blessings."

—Sutta Nipata 2, 4

Reflection

When Many Voices Shout at Once

When many voices shout at once,
None considers himself a fool;
Though the Sangha is being split,
None thinks himself to be at fault.

They have forgotten thoughtful speech,
They talk obsessed by words alone.
Uncurbed their mouths, they bawl at will;
None knows what leads him so to act.

'He abused me, he struck me,
He defeated me, he robbed me'—
In those who harbor thoughts like these
Hatred will never be allayed.

'He abused me, he struck me,
He defeated me, he robbed me'—
In those who do not harbor thoughts like these
Hatred will be allayed.

For, in this world, hatred is never
Allayed by further acts of hate.
It is allayed by non-hatred:
That is the fixed and ageless law.

Those others do not recognize
That here we should restrain ourselves.
But those wise ones who realize this
At once end all their enmity.

Breakers of bones and murderers,
Those who steal cattle, horses, wealth,
Those who pillage the entire realm —
When even these can act together,
Why can you not do so, too?

If one can find a worthy friend,
A virtuous, steadfast companion,
Then overcome all threats of danger
And walk with him content and mindful.

But, if one finds no worthy friend,
No virtuous, steadfast companion,
Then, as a king leaves his conquered realm,
Walk like a tusker in the woods alone.

Better it is to walk alone,
There is no companionship with fools.
Walk alone and do no evil,
At ease like a tusker in the woods."

—Majjhima Nikaya 128

Day Thirty-five

Reading

Few Are Those Beings

In Jambudîpa, delightful parks, groves, and lotus ponds are few, but steep hills, impassable rivers, and rugged mountains covered with brush and weeds are many. In the same way, those who are reborn as human beings are few, but those who are reborn in other realms are many.

Those who are endowed with the noble eye of wisdom are few, but those who are confused and mired in ignorance are many. Those who are able to see the Tathagata and to hear his Dhamma are few, but those who fail to gain this chance are many. Those who understand the Dhamma and practice it are few, but those who fail to do so are many. Those who are moved by Truth are few, but those who remain indifferent to it are many. Those who diligently strive are few, while those who put forth no effort are many. Those who gain the concentration leading to liberation are few, but those who fail to gain such concentration are many. Those who experience the taste of exquisite food are few, but those who subsist on scraps of stale food are many. Those who experience the taste of the goal, the taste of the Dhamma, and the taste of liberation are few, but those who never experience that taste are many.

Therefore, you should train yourselves thus: "We will experience the taste of the goal, the taste of the Dhamma, and the taste of liberation."

—Anguttara Nikaya 1, 19, 1

Reflection

The Unborn

The Buddha said, "There is, Bhikkhus, an unborn, unbecome, unmade, and unconditioned. If there were no unborn, unbecome, unmade, and unconditioned, there would be no escape. But, because there is an unborn, unbecome, unmade, and unconditioned, there is an escape from what is born, become, made, and conditioned."

—Udana 8, 3

Dedication of Merit

May all devas share this merit. Long may they protect the Buddha Sasana for the welfare of the world.

By this merit, never may I live with fools, but have fellowship with the wise until Nibbana is won.

May this merit bring about the extinction of defilements in me.

By this meritorious deed, may I attain Nibbana.

May this merit be passed to my departed relatives! May my relatives be happy!

By this practice, according with Truth, I revere the Buddha.

By this practice, according with Truth, I revere the Dhamma.

By this practice, according with Truth, I revere the Sangha.

By this practice, according with Truth, may I be liberated from the bondage of birth and death.

Well done! Well done!! Well done!!!

List of Original Sources

Vinaya Pitaka

The Book of the Discipline, translated by I.B. Horner, 6 volumes, Pali Text Society, Melksham, Wilts, U.K. 1938-1966.

Digha Nikaya

The Long Discourses of the Buddha, translated by Maurice Walshe, Wisdom Publications, Somerville, MA, 1987.

Dialogues of the Buddha, translated by T.W. Rhys Davids and Mrs C.A.F. Rhys Davids, 3 volumes, Pali Text Society, Melksham, Wilts, U.K., 1899-1921.

Majjhima Nikaya

The Middle Length Discourses of the Buddha, translated by Bhikkhu Nanamoli and Bhikkhu Bodhi, Wisdom Publications, Somerville, MA, 1995.

Middle Length Sayings, translated by I.B. Horner, 3 volumes, Pali Text Society, Melksham, Wilts, U.K., 1954-1959.

Samyutta Nikaya

The Connected Discourses of the Buddha, translated by Bhikkhu Bodhi, 2 volumes, Wisdom Publications, Somerville, MA, 2000.

The Book of the Kindred Sayings, translated by Mrs C.A.F. Rhys Davids and F.L. Woodward, 5 volumes, Pali Text Society, Melksham, Wilts, U.K., 1917 - 1930.

Samyutta Nikaya: An Anthology, Part I, translated by John D. Ireland, Buddhist Publication Society, Kandy, Sri Lanka, 1981,

(Wheels 107-109), available online at
<http://bps.lk/onlinelibrary_wheels.html#trans>.

Samyutta Nikaya: An Anthology, Part II, translated by Bhikkhu Ñananda, Buddhist Publication Society, Kandy, Sri Lanka, 1983, (Wheels 183-185), available online at
<http://bps.lk/onlinelibrary_wheels.html#trans>.

Anguttara Nikaya

Anguttara Nikaya Anthology: Numerical Discourses of the Buddha, translated by Nyanaponika Thera and Bhikkhu Bodhi, Buddhist Publication Society, Kandy, Sri Lanka, 1999.

The Book of the Gradual Sayings, translated by F.L. Woodward and E.M. Hare, 5 volumes, Pali Text Society, Melksham, Wilts, U.K., 1932-1936.

Numerical Discourses of the Buddha, translated by Bhikkhu Bodhi, Wisdom Publications, Somerville, MA, 2012.

Anguttara Nikaya: An Anthology, Part I-III, translated by Nyanaponika Thera, Buddhist Publication Society, Kandy, Sri Lanka, 1970-1976, (Wheels 155-158, 208-211, 238-240), available online at <http://bps.lk/onlinelibrary_wheels.html#trans> .

Dhammapada Commentary

Buddhist Legends, translated by E.W. Burlingame, 3 volumes, Pali Text Society, Melksham, Wilts, U.K., 1921; (Harvard Oriental Series Editon is available online at
<http://archive.org/search.php?query=Burlingame%2C%20Eugene%20Watson%20AND%20mediatype%3Atexts>.

Itivuttaka and Udana

The Udana, translated by Peter Masefield, Pali Text Society, Melksham, Wilts, U.K., 1994.

The Itivuttaka, translated by Peter Masefield, Pali Text Society, Melksham, Wilts, U.K., 2000.

The Udana & the Itivuttaka: Two Classics from the Pali Canon, translated by John D. Ireland, Buddhist Publication Society, Kandy, Sri Lanka, 1997.

Jataka

Jataka Tales of the Buddha: An Anthology, retold by Ken and Visakha Kawasaki, 3 volumes, Buddhist Publication Society, Kandy, Sri Lanka, 2009.

The Jataka or Stories of the Buddha's Former Births, translated by E.B. Cowell, R. Chalmers, W.H.D. Rouse, and H.T. Francis, edited by E.B. Cowell, 6 volumes, Pali Text Society, Melksham, Wilts, U.K., 1895-1907, available online at <http://www.sacred-texts.com/bud/index.htm>.

Theragatha and Therigatha

Elders' Verses,, translated by K.R. Norman, 2 volumes, Pali Text Society, Melksham, Wilts, U.K., 1969-1971, 2007.

Sutta Nipata

The Sutta Nipata, translated by H. Saddhatissa, Curzon Press, London, 1985.

Visuddhimagga

The Path of Purification: The Classic Manual of Buddhist Doctrine and Meditation, translated by Bhikkhu Ñanamoli, Buddhist Publication Society, Kandy, Sri Lanka, 2010, available online at <http://www.urbandharma.org/pdf/PathofPurification.pdf>.

Meditation readings and reflections

Buddha Vacana: Daily readings from the Sacred Literature of Buddhism, edited by S. Dhammika, The Buddha Dhamma Mandala Society, Singapore, 1989, available online at <http://www.buddhanet.net/pdf_file/words_of_buddha.pdf>; reprinted as *The Words of the Buddha: Daily Readings from the Buddhist Scriptures*, (2011).

Assorted

In the Buddha's Words: An Anthology of Discourses from the Pali Canon, translated and edited by Bhikkhu Bodhi, Wisdom Publications, Somerville, MA, 2005.

Buddhist Texts Through the Ages, translated from Pali, Sanskrit, Chinese, Tibetan, Japanese, and Apabhramsa, edited by Edward Conze, in collaboration with I.B. Horner, D. Snellgrove, and A. Waley, Harper & Row, New York, 1964.

Some of the readings in this collection, as well as many other texts from the Tipitaka, in various translations, are available at Access to Insight, <http://www.accesstoinsight.org/>.

The Life of Sariputta, compiled and translated from the Pali texts by Nyanaponka Thera, Buddhist Publication Society, Kandy, Sri Lanka, 1987 (Wheels 90-92), available online at <http://bps.lk/onlinelibrary_wheels.html#biogra>.

The Great Disciples of the Buddha: Their Lives, Their Works, Their Legacy, by Nyanaponika Thera and Hellmuth Hecker, Wisdom Publications, Somerville, MA, 2003.

Other Resources

Travel Guides

Middle Land, Middle Way: A Pilgrim's Guide to the Buddha's India, by Ven. S. Dhammika, Buddhist Publication Society, Kandy, Sri Lanka, 2008.

Rude Awakenings, Two Englishmen on Foot in Buddhism's Holy Land, by Ajahn Sucitto and Nick Scott,Wisdom Publications, Somerville, MA, 2005.

Reference

Dictionary of Pali Proper Names, G.P. Malalasekera, 2 volumes, Pali Text Society, Melksham, Wilts, U.K., 1937, available online at: <http://www.palikanon.com/english/pali_names/dic_idx.html>.

Notes

Notes

Notes